THE BOOK

of

DISCIPLINE

of the

CHRISTIAN METHODIST

EPISCOPAL CHURCH

Revised 1998

Published by
The C.M.E. Publishing House
REV. WILLIAM E. GEORGE
General Secretary
4466 Elvis Presley Blvd.
Memphis, Tennessee 38116

COMPILATION COMMITTEE
FOR THE
DISCIPLINE OF THE C.M.E. CHURCH

Revised 1998

Bishop Marshall Gilmore, Chair
Bishop L. L. Reddick III, Vice-Chair

First Episcopal District	Mrs. Vera Merriweather
Second Episcopal District	Mrs. Kimberly Harris
Third Episcopal District	Rev. Tony C. Henderson
Fourth Episcopal District	Mrs. Boyce Etta Blackmon
Fifth Episcopal District	Attorney Ouida Y. Brown
Sixth Episcopal District	Ms. Laveeta F. LaVant
Seventh Episcopal District	Rev. Roderick D. Lewis, Sr.
Eighth Episcopal District	Rev. Manuel Henderson
Ninth Episcopal District	Dr. Robert Peoples
Tenth Episcopal District	Dr. Godwin T. Umoette

Consultants
Bishop Othal H. Lakey
The Rev. John Marshall Gilmore
The Rev. William E. George
Bryan A. Lakey, Sr.

TABLE OF CONTENTS

The basic unit of reference in *The Book of Discipline, Revised, 1998*, is the **Paragraph [¶]**. Paragraphs are numbered consecutively within each chapter. However, in order to allow for future legislative enactments to fit the scheme of Parts, Chapters, and Paragraphs, some numbers are omitted between Parts and within Chapters. Where a page reference is used in the Table of Contents, it is so indicated.

TITLE PAGE
MEMBERS OF COMMITTEE ON COMPILATION
EPISCOPAL GREETINGS
HISTORICAL LISTING OF THE BISHOPS

PART I: BASIC PRINCIPLES

Chapter	Title	Paragraphs
1	Articles of Religion	¶101
2	The General Rules	¶126
3	The Church and General Welfare	
	The Social Creed	¶130
	Sexual Harassment Policy	¶131
4	The Constitution	(Pages 34 - 40)
	The Charter	(Page 41)

PART II: THE CONFERENCES

5	The General Conference	¶201
6	The Annual Conference	¶213
7	The District Conference	¶230
8	The Youth Conference	¶237
9	The Quarterly Conference	¶252
10	The Church Conference	¶257

11   The Official Board   ¶263

PART III: MEANS OF GRACE

12   Public Worship   ¶300
13   Order of Worship   ¶305
14   Prayer Meetings   ¶306
15   Class Meetings   ¶308
16   Love Feasts   ¶311
17   Children of the Church   ¶313

PART IV: THE MINISTRY

18   Exhorters   ¶401
19   The Call to Preach   ¶405
20   Local Preachers   ¶407
21   Admitting Preachers on Trial   ¶413
22   Traveling Deacons   ¶415
23   Traveling Elders   ¶417
24   Admitting Into Full Connection   ¶420
25   Receiving Ministers from Other Churches   ¶421
26   Preachers in Charge and Associate Ministers   ¶422
27   Chaplains   ¶423
28   Presiding Elders   ¶424
29   The Bishops of the Church   ¶426
30   College of Bishops   ¶437
31   Supernumerary Relations and
          Professional Care   ¶438
32   Retirement   ¶439
33   Support of Preachers in Charge   ¶441
34   Support of Presiding Elders   ¶443
35   Support of Bishops and Their Widows   ¶444
36   Support of Retired Ministers and Their Families   ¶445

PART V: THE LOCAL CHURCH

37	Definition of the Local Church	¶500
	Membership in the Church	¶505
	Types of Church Membership	¶508.2
	Membership Rolls	¶508.3
38	Church Officers, Boards and Auxiliaries	
	Spiritual Expectations	¶509
	Class Leaders	¶510
	Stewards	¶511
	Recording Steward	¶512
	Stewardesses	¶513
	Church Treasurer	¶514
	Trustees	¶515
	Board of Christian Education	¶516
	Director	¶516.3
	Sunday Church School	¶517
	Christian Youth Fellowship	¶518
	Young Adult Work	¶519
	Commission on Membership and Evangelism	¶520
	Women's Missionary Society	¶521
	Department of Lay Ministry	¶522
	Choirs and Personnel	¶523
	Boards of Ushers	¶524
39	Organizing a New Local Church	¶525

PART VI: CHURCH PROPERTY

40	Incorporation of Local Churches and Titles to Property	¶601
41	Episcopal Residences and District Parsonages	¶605
42	The Connectional Headquarters	¶606
43	Charitable Institutions	¶607
44	Committee on Deeds, Titles and Abstracts	¶608

PART VII: CONNECTIONAL DAYS, OBSERVANCES AND ORGANIZATIONS

45   Connectional Observances

       Connectional Days   ¶700 - ¶714

       Connectional Organizations   ¶720 - ¶720.8

PART VIII. JUDICIAL ADMINISTRATION

46   Judicial Administration

           Introduction   ¶801

           Practices Subject to Disciplinary Action   ¶802

           Judicial Process   ¶803

           Judicial Council   ¶804

PART IX: CLERGY CREDENTIALS

47   Certification of Ordination and Full Connection   ¶901

48   Deprivation of Credentials

           Traveling Preachers   ¶905

           Local Preachers   ¶906

PART X: THE GENERAL CONNECTIONAL BOARD

49   The General Connectional Board   ¶1000

       The Executive Secretary   ¶1001.7

       Editor, *The Christian Index*   ¶1001.8

PART XI: GENERAL CHURCH ADMINISTRATION: CONNECTIONAL OPERATIONS

50   The General Department of Finance   ¶1004

51   The General Department of Publications   ¶1018

52   *The Christian Index*   ¶1026

53   The General Board of Personnel Services   ¶1034

PART XII: GENERAL CHURCH ADMINISTRATION: CONNECTIONAL MINISTRIES

54	The General Department of Christian Education	¶1100
55	The Women's Missionary Council	¶1134
56	The General Department of Lay Ministry	¶1135
57	The General Department of Evangelism and Missions	¶1150

PART XIII: ANNUAL CONFERENCE BOUNDARIES

| 58 | Boundaries of the Annual Conferences | ¶1201 |

PART XIV: APPENDIX

59	Biography of Bishops Elected in 1998	¶1300
60	Episcopal Supervision 1998 - 2002	¶1301
61	Addresses of the Bishops	¶1302
62	Members of the Judicial Council	¶1303
63	Connectional Administration	¶1304
	General Officers	
	Members General Connectional Board	
	Members of Connectional Commissions	
64	Members of Committee on Episcopacy	¶1305
65	Commission on Pan-Methodist Cooperation	¶1306
66	The Bishops' Course of Study	¶1307
67	Rules and Procedures of the 1998 General Conference	¶1308

INDEX

EPISCOPAL GREETINGS

To the Members of the Christian Methodist Episcopal Church:

It is our responsibility and joy to present to you the *Book of Discipline, Revised 1998*. The *Discipline* is both the spiritual and legal guide for our denomination, the expression of our faith as the people of God, and the practice of our polity as members of the Christian Methodist Episcopal Church. We recommend its use to every member of our beloved community that you might grow in the knowledge of our beliefs as expressed in the *Articles of Religion,* the *General Rules*, the *Social Creed* and the Canons of the church. We trust that you will be governed by the spirit as well as the letter of the rules and regulations by which we conduct our affairs on every level of our structure. We believe that next to the Word of God, you ought to give yourselves unreservedly to the study and digestion of the truths and regulations contained herein. They constitute the sacred legacy passed down to us from our spiritual and ecclesiastical progenitors; and are the products of the prayerful, studious and laborious efforts of General Conferences from the Organizing Conference of 1870, the year of our founding, to the last session held in Birmingham, Alabama, in 1998.

The C.M.E. Church was organized December 16, 1870, in Jackson, Tennessee, by forty-one delegates from eight Colored Annual Conferences of the Methodist Episcopal Church, South. This conference to establish a new church had been authorized by the General Conference of the M.E. Church, South, meeting in New Orleans, Louisiana, in 1866 in response to the expressed desires and wishes of its African American constituents to have their own separate and independent organization. Having devoted the previous day to prayer, the delegates chose a name for their new church, and, together with the organizational structure and ordination requirements of American Methodism, adopted the *Articles of Religion*. With the election of two bishops, William H. Miles and Richard H. Vanderhorst, and the doctrines and polity of the new church firmly established, a new branch of Methodism was born among the followers of John Wesley and in the Church of Jesus Christ. Fully independent, yet amicable in ecumenical relations, the C.M.E. Church went forth to preach good news, teach divine truth and heal the brokenness of life by the power of God in our Risen Savior.

Through the years our church has shown a remarkable sensitivity to the spirit of changing times. Although founded and continued as a predominantly African American Church, it was at no time exclusively so. Membership in our church has always been open to any person "desiring to flee from the wrath to come." In 1954, a resolution was approved by the General Conference stating: "Aware of the inconsistency of having a racial designation in the name of our church . . . and without implying our disloyalty to, or disrespect for, the founding fathers . . . we recommend that, in harmony with Christian principles, in keeping with the times, and in accordance with the recommendations of the Bishops of the General Conference, proper steps be taken to change the name of our church from Colored Methodist Episcopal to Christian Methodist Episcopal Church or some other suitable name that retains the initials as a symbol of our founding and continuing witness." Ratification was reported by the College of Bishops in Detroit, Michigan, January 19, 1956.

The evangelistic fervor and missionary zeal of our early fathers and mothers and succeeding generations expanded the denomination from the Southeast to the Northwest, from the Atlantic to the Pacific, and from the Caribbean to West Africa. Education has ever been a strong denominational priority, extending from the efforts of our first generation pioneers to develop an educated clergy and meet the challenge of widespread illiteracy to the passionate desire of succeeding generations to provide opportunities for higher education for those for whom such opportunities were limited.

With departmentalized programmatic thrusts covering every phase of our mission and every part of our constituency, the denomination has sought to be true to our Lord from its founding and in every place where its influence could be felt. Understanding our mandate to include the salvation of sinners and the liberation of the oppressed from all forms of human bondage, we have sought to discern the work of Jesus Christ in human affairs and join Him in proclamation and deed for the fulfillment of that work that makes the kingdoms of this world the Kingdom of our Lord.

This revision of the *Discipline* will bridge the 20th and the 21st centuries. As we say good-bye, the Lord willing, to a century of great technological and scientific achievements and to a century of forms of religious revival, and as we are greeted, the Lord willing, by a century of great challenge and promise for the faithful people of God in Christ, we are hopeful that the sons and daughters of Miles and Vanderhorst will not be slaves of this book but that it will serve them as a guide into a more perfect unity, that as the body of Christ, His sense of peace may become more whole in them.

As we pursue these ends together, walking this faith walk, we remain your brothers in Christ and Chief Pastors:

Nathaniel L. Linsey	Charles L. Helton
Marshall Gilmore	Paul A. G. Stewart, Sr.
William H. Graves, Sr.	Lawrence L. Reddick III
Dotcy I. Isom, Jr.	Henry C. Bunton
Othal H. Lakey	C. D. Coleman
E. Lynn Brown	Oree Broomfield, Sr.
Thomas L. Hoyt, Jr.	Richard O. Bass, Sr.

HISTORICAL LISTING
OF THE
BISHOPS OF THE C.M.E CHURCH

Name	State of Birth	Place Elected	Year Elected
William H. Miles	Kentucky	Jackson, TN	1870
Richard H. Vanderhorst	S. Carolina	Jackson, TN	1870
Joseph A. Beebe	N. Carolina	Augusta, GA	1873
Lucius H. Holsey	Georgia	Augusta, GA	1873
Isaac Lane	Tennessee	Augusta, GA	1873
Robert S. Williams	Louisiana	Memphis, TN	1894
Elias Cottrell	Mississippi	Memphis, TN	1894
Charles Henry Phillips	Georgia	Nashville, TN	1902
M. F. Jamison	Georgia	Augusta, GA	1910
George W. Stewart	Virginia	Augusta, GA	1910
Randall A. Carter	Georgia	St. Louis, MO	1914
Nelson C. Cleaves	Tennessee	St. Louis, MO	1914
Robert T. Brown	Alabama	St. Louis, MO	1922
Joseph C. Martin	Tennessee	St. Louis, MO	1922
J. Arthur Hamlett	Tennessee	St. Louis, MO	1922
John W. McKinney	Texas	St. Louis, MO	1922
Henry P. Porter	Texas	St. Louis, MO	1934
James A. Bray	Georgia	St. Louis, MO	1934
John H. Moore	Alabama	St. Louis, MO	1934
William Yancey Bell	Tennessee	Hot Springs, AR	1938
Charles L. Russell	Alabama	Hot Springs, AR	1938
Luther C. Stewart	Alabama	St. Louis, MO	1946
Felix L. Lewis	Louisiana	St. Louis, MO	1946
Roy L. Young	Mississippi	St. Louis, MO	1946
Bertram W. Doyle	Alabama	Kansas City, MO	1950
Arthur W. Womack	Virginia	Kansas City, MO	1950
B. Julian Smith	Georgia	Memphis, TN	1954
J. Claude Allen	Alabama	Memphis, TN	1954

Name	State of Birth	Place Elected	Year Elected
Elisha P. Murchison	Texas	Detroit, MI	1958
P. Randolph Shy	Georgia	Detroit, MI	1958
Norris S. Curry	Texas	St. Louis, MO	1962
Walter H. Amos	Tennessee	St. Louis, MO	1962
Henry C. Bunton	Alabama	St. Louis, MO	1962
Joseph A. Johnson, Jr.	Louisiana	Miami, FL	1966
Chester A. Kirkendoll	Arkansas	Memphis, TN	1970
Caesar D. Coleman	Mississippi	Philadelphia, PA	1974
Joseph C. Coles, Jr.	Washington, DC	Philadelphia, PA	1974
J. Madison Exum	Tennessee	Philadelphia, PA	1974
Nathaniel L. Linsey	Georgia	Birmingham, AL	1978
James L. Cummings	Kentucky	Birmingham, AL	1978
Marshall Gilmore	N. Carolina	Memphis, TN	1982
William H. Graves	Tennessee	Memphis, TN	1982
Dotcy I. Isom, Jr.	Michigan	Memphis, TN	1982
Othal H. Lakey	Louisiana	Memphis, TN	1982
Oree Broomfield, Sr.	Mississippi	Memphis, TN	1982
Edward Lynn Brown	Tennessee	Birmingham, AL	1986
Richard Oliver Bass, Sr.	Tennessee	Birmingham, AL	1986
Thomas L. Hoyt, Jr.	Alabama	Memphis, TN	1994
Charles L. Helton	N. Carolina	Memphis. TN	1994
Paul A. G. Stewart, Sr.	Mississippi	Birmingham, AL	1998
Lawrence L. Reddick III	Alabama	Birmingham, AL	1998

PART 1
BASIC PRINCIPLES

1. Articles of Religion

2. The General Rules

3. The Church and General Welfare

The Social Creed
Sexual Harassment Policy

4. The Constitution

CHAPTER 1
ARTICLES OF RELIGION

Article 1. Of Faith in the Holy Trinity

¶ **101.** There is but one living and true God, everlasting, without body or parts; of infinite power, wisdom, and goodness; the maker and preserver of all things, both visible and invisible. And in unity of this God-head, there are three persons of one substance, power, and eternity— the Father, the Son, and the Holy Ghost.

Article 2. Of the Word or Son of God Who Was Made Very Man

¶ **102.** The Son, who is the Word of the Father, the very and eternal God, of one substance with the Father took man's nature in the womb of the blessed Virgin; so that two whole and perfect natures—that is to say the God-head and manhood— were joined together in one person never to be divided, whereof is one Christ very God and very man, who truly suffered, was crucified, dead and buried, to reconcile his Father to us and to be a sacrifice, not only for original guilt, but also for actual sins of men.

Article 3. Of the Resurrection of Christ

¶ **103.** Christ did truly rise again from the dead, and took again his body, with all things appertaining to the perfection of man's nature, wherewith he ascended into heaven, and there sitteth until he returns to judge all men at the last day.

Article 4. Of the Holy Ghost

¶ **104.** The Holy Ghost, proceeding from the Father and the Son, is of one substance, majesty, and glory, with the Father and the Son, very and eternal God.

Article 5. The Sufficiency of the Holy Scriptures for Salvation

¶ **105.** The Holy Scriptures containeth all things necessary to salvation; so that whatsoever is not read therein, nor may be proved thereby, is not to be required of any man, that it should be believed as an article of the faith, or be thought requisite or necessary to salvation. In the name of the Holy Scripture, we do understand those canonical books of the Old and New Testaments, of which authority was never any doubt in the church. The names of the canonical books are:

Genesis, Exodus, Leviticus, Numbers, Deuteronomy, Joshua, Judges, Ruth, the First Book of Samuel, the Second Book of Samuel, the First Book of Kings, the Second Book of Kings, the First Book of Chronicles, the Second Book of Chronicles, the Book of Ezra, the Book of Nehemiah, the Book of Esther, the Book of Job, the Psalms, the Proverbs, Ecclesiastes or the Preacher, Cantica or Songs of Solomon, Four Prophets the greater, Twelve Prophets the less. All the Books of the New Testament, as they are commonly received, we do receive and account canonical.

Article 6. Of the Old Testament

¶ **106.** The Old Testament is not contrary to the New; for both in the Old and New Testaments everlasting life is offered to mankind by Christ, who is the only Mediator between God and man, being both God and man. Wherefore, they are not to be heard who feign that the old fathers did look only for transitory promises. Although the law given from God to Moses, as touching ceremonies and rites, doth not bind Christians, nor ought the civil precepts thereof of necessity to be received in any Commonwealth; yet notwithstanding, no Christian whatsoever is free from the obedience of the commandments which are called moral.

Article 7. Of Original or Birth-Sin

¶ **107.** Original Sin standeth not in the following of Adam (as the Pelagians do vainly talk), but it is the corruption of the nature of every man, that naturally is engendered of the offspring of Adam, whereby man, is very far gone from original righteousness, and of his own nature inclined to do evil, and that continually.

Article 8. Of Free Will

¶ **108.** The condition of man after the fall of Adam is such that he cannot turn and prepare himself, by his own natural strength and works, to faith, and calling upon God; wherefore we have no power to do good works, pleasant and acceptable to God without the grace of God by Christ preventing us, that we may have a good will, and working with us, when we have that good will.

Article 9. Of the Justification of Man

¶ **109.** We are accounted righteous before God, only for the merit of our Lord and Savior Jesus Christ, by faith, and not for our own works or deservings; wherefore, that we are justified by faith only, is a most wholesome doctrine, and very full of comfort.

Article 10. Of Good Works

¶ **110.** Although good works, which are the fruits of faith, and follow after justification, cannot put away our sins, and endure the severity of God's judgment; yet are they pleasing and acceptable to God in Christ, and spring out of a true and lively faith, insomuch that by them a lively faith may be as evidently known, as a tree discerned by its fruit.

Article 11. Of Works of Supererogation

¶ **111.** Voluntary works, besides, over and above God's commandments, which are called works of supererogation, cannot be taught without arrogancy and impiety. For by them men do declare, that they do not only render unto God as much as they are bound to do, but that they do more for His sake than of bounden duty is required whereas Christ saith plainly, " When ye have done all that is commanded of you, say, We are unprofitable servants."

Article 12. Of Sin After Justification

¶ **112.** Not every sin, willingly committed after justification, is the sin against the Holy Ghost, and unpardonable. Wherefore, the grant of repentance is not denied to such as fall into sin after justification. After we have received the Holy Ghost, we may depart from grace given, and fall into sin, and, by the grace of God, rise again and amend our lives. And, therefore, they are to be condemned who say they can no more sin as long as they live here, or deny the place of forgiveness to such as truly repent.

Article 13. Of the Church

¶ **113.** The visible Church of Christ is a congregation of faithful men, in which the pure Word of God is preached, and the sacraments duly administered, according to Christ's ordinance, in all those things that of necessity are requisite to the same.

Article 14. Of Purgatory

¶ **114.** The Romish doctrine concerning purgatory, pardons, worshipping, and adoration as well of images as of relics, and also invocation of saints, is a fond thing, vainly invented, and grounded upon no warrant of Scripture but repugnant to the Word of God.

Article 15. Of Speaking in the Congregation in Such a Tongue as the People Understand

¶ **115.** It is a thing plainly repugnant to the Word of God, and the custom of the Primitive Church, to have public prayer in the church or to minister the sacraments in a tongue not understood by the people.

Article 16. Of the Sacraments

¶ **116.** Sacraments, ordained of Christ, are not only badges or tokens of Christian men's profession; but rather they are certain signs of grace, and God's good will toward us. He doth work invisibly in us and doth, not only quicken, but also strengthen and confirm our faith in Him. There are two sacraments ordained of Christ our Lord in the Gospel; that is to say, Baptism and the Supper of our Lord.

Those five commonly called sacraments—that is to say Confirmation, Penance, Orders, Matrimony, and Extreme Unction — are not to be counted for Sacraments of the Gospel, being such as have partly grown out of the corrupt following of the apostles and partly are states of life allowed in the Scriptures, but yet have not the like nature of Baptism and the Lord's Supper, because they have not any visible sign or ceremony ordained of God.

The sacraments were not ordained of Christ to be gazed upon, or to be carried about; but that we should duly use them. And in such only as worthily receive the same, they have a wholesome effect or operation; but they that receive them unworthily, purchase to themselves condemnation as Saint Paul saith, I Cor. xi. 29.

Article 17. Of Baptism

¶ **117.** Baptism is not only a sign of profession and mark of difference, whereby Christians are distinguished from others that are not baptized; but it is also a sign of regeneration, or the new birth. The baptism of young children is to be retained in the Church.

Article 18. Of the Lord's Supper

¶ **118.** The Supper of the Lord is not only a sign of the love that Christians ought to have among themselves one to another, but rather is a sacrament of our redemption by Christ's death; insomuch that, to such as rightly, worthily, and with faith receive the same, the bread which we break is a partaking of the body of Christ; and likewise the cup of blessing is a partaking of the blood of Christ.

Transubstantiation, or the change of the substance of bread and wine in the Supper of the Lord, cannot be proved by Holy Writ; but is repugnant to the plain words of Scripture, overthroweth the nature of a sacrament, and hath given occasion to many superstitions.

The body of Christ is given, taken, and eaten in the Supper only after a heavenly and spiritual manner. And the means whereby the body of Christ is received and eaten in the Supper, is faith.

The Sacrament of the Lord's Supper was not by Christ's ordinance reserved, carried about, lifted up, or worshipped.

Article 19. Of Both Kinds

¶ 119. The cup of the Lord is not to be denied to the lay people; for both parts of the Lord's Supper, by Christ's ordinance and commandment, ought to be administered to all Christians alike.

Article 20. Of the One Oblation of Christ Finished Upon the Cross

¶ 120. The offering of Christ once made is that perfect redemption, propitiation, and satisfaction for all the sins of the whole world, both original, and actual; and there is none other satisfaction for sin but that alone. Wherefore the sacrifice of masses, in which it is commonly said that the priest doth offer Christ for the quick and the dead, to have remission of pain or guilt, is a blasphemous fable and dangerous deceit.

Article 21. Of the Marriage of Ministers

¶ 121. The ministers of Christ are not commanded by God's law either to vow the estate of single life, or to abstain from marriage; therefore it is lawful for them, as for all other Christians to marry, at their own discretion as they shall judge the same to serve best to Godliness.

Article 22. Of the Rites and Ceremonies of Churches

¶ 122. It is not necessary that rites and ceremonies should in all places be the same, or exactly alike; for they have been always different, and may be changed according to the diversity of countries; times; and men's manners, so that nothing be ordained against God's Word. Whosoever, through his private judgment, willingly and purposely, doth openly break the rites and ceremonies of the Church to which he belongs, which are repugnant to the Word of God, and are ordained and approved by common authority, ought to be rebuked openly, that others may fear to do the like, as one that offendeth against the common order of the Church, and woundeth the conscience of weak brethren.

Every particular Church may ordain, change, or abolish rites and ceremonies, so that all things may be done to edification.

Article 23. Of the Rulers of the United States of America

¶ **123.** The President, the Congress and the general assemblies, the governors, and the councils of state, as the delegates of the people, are the rulers of the United States of America, according to the division of power made to them by the constitution of their respective states. And the said states are a sovereign and independent nation and ought not to be subject to any foreign jurisdiction.*

Article 24. Of Christian Men's Goods

¶ **124.** The riches and goods of Christians are not common, as touching the right, title, and possession of the same, as some do falsely boast. Notwithstanding every man ought, of such things as he possesseth, liberally to give alms to the poor according to his ability.

Article 25. Of a Christian Man's Oath

¶ **125.** As we confess that vain and rash swearing is forbidden Christian men by our Lord Jesus Christ and James, His apostle; so we judge that the Christian religion doth not prohibit, but that a man may swear when the magistrate requireth, in a cause of faith and charity, so it be done according to the prophet's teaching, in justice, judgment and truth.

---

*As far as it respects civil affairs we believe it the duty of Christians and especially all Christian ministers, to be subject to the supreme authority of the country where they reside, and to use all laudable means to enjoin obedience to the powers that be and therefore it is expected that all our preachers and people who may be under any foreign government, behave themselves as peaceable and orderly subjects.

CHAPTER 2
THE GENERAL RULES

¶ **126.** The General Rules of "The United Societies" organized by Mr. Wesley in 1739 are as follows:

There is only one condition previously required of those who desire admission into these societies, a "desire to flee from the wrath to come, and to be saved from their sins." But wherever this is really fixed in the soul, it will be shown by its fruits. It is, therefore, expected of all who continue therein that they shall continue to evidence their desire of salvation,

First, by doing no harm, by avoiding evil of every kind, especially that which is most generally practiced, such as:

The taking of the name of God in vain.

The profaning the day of the Lord, either by doing ordinary work therein, or by buying or selling.

Drunkenness, or drinking spirituous liquors unless in cases of necessity.

Fighting, quarrelling, brawling, brother going to law with brother, returning evil for evil, or railing for railing; the use of many words in buying or selling.

The buying or selling of goods that have not paid the duty.

The giving or taking things on usury, i.e. unlawful interest.

Uncharitable or unprofitable conversation, particularly, speaking evil of magistrates or of ministers.

Doing to others as we would not they should do unto us.

Doing what we know is not for the glory of God, such as:

The putting on of gold and costly apparel.

The taking such diversions as cannot be used in the Name of the Lord Jesus.

The singing those songs, or reading those books, which do not tend to the knowledge or love of God.

Softness or needless self-indulgence.

Laying up treasure upon earth.

Borrowing without a probability of paying, or taking up goods without a probability of paying for them.

¶ **127.** It is expected of all who continue in these societies, that they should continue to evidence their desire of salvation,

Secondly, by doing good, by being in every kind merciful after their power as they have opportunity, doing good of every possible sort, and as far as possible, to all men;

To their bodies, of the ability which God giveth by giving food to the hungry, by clothing the naked, by visiting or helping them that are sick or in prison.

To their souls, by instructing, reproving, or exhorting all that we have any intercourse with, trampling under foot that enthusiastic doctrine that "we are not to do good unless our hearts be free to do it."

By doing good, especially to them that are of the household of faith, or groaning so to be, employing them preferably to others, buying one of another, helping each other in business, and so much the more because the world will love its own, and them only.

By all possible diligence, and frugality, that the gospel be not blamed. By running with patience the race which is set before them, denying themselves, and taking up their cross daily; submitting to bear the reproach of Christ, to bear the filth and off scouring of the world; and looking that men should say all manner of evil of them for the Lord's sake.

¶ **128.** It is expected of all who desire to continue in these societies that they should continue to evidence their desire of salvation,

Thirdly, by attending upon all the ordinances of God, such as:
The Public Worship of God.
The Ministry of the Word, either read or expounded.
The Supper of the Lord.
Family and private prayer.
Searching the Scriptures, and
Fasting or abstinence.

¶ **129.** These are the General Rules of our societies; all of which we are taught of God to observe, even in His written Word, which is the only rule, and the sufficient rule, both of our faith and practice. And all these we know His Spirit writes on truly awakened hearts. If there be any among us who observe them not, who habitually break any of them, let it be known unto them who watch over that soul, as they who must give an account. We will admonish him of the error of his ways; we will bear with him for a season; but if then he repent not, he hath no more place among us; we have delivered our own souls.

CHAPTER 3
THE CHURCH AND GENERAL WELFARE

¶ 130. The Social Creed

¶ **130.1.** *Our Heritage.* The concern of the Christian Methodist Episcopal Church for the social well-being of humankind springs from the act of God in Jesus Christ as revealed in the Gospel, and from the life and witness of John Wesley and other fathers of Methodism who ministered to the physical, intellectual, and social needs of the people to whom they preached the gospel of personal redemption.

The interest and activity of the C.M.E. Church in the improvement of the human condition parallels the very history of our Church. In the opening editorial of the *Gospel Trumpet* published in 1897, Bishop Lucius H. Holsey stated that its purpose would be to "discuss without hesitation, any phase of the civic, social, and those economic and political questions that may affect the well-being of the Church and race." This policy of active participation in the solution of social problems has not been restricted to literary and journalistic endeavor. It can be seen in the individual contributions of some of the leaders of our church during its history— Lucius H. Holsey, Isaac Lane, C. H. Phillips, Randall A. Carter, J. A. Hamlett, J. A. Bray, J. A. Martin, and Channing H. Tobias. It can be seen in those official programs and practices on the local, regional and national levels that were designed to eradicate crime, disease, ignorance, poverty and racial injustice. It has been demonstrated by unknown thousands who are members of the Christian Methodist Episcopal Church as they have resisted oppression, and pursued liberty and justice for all humankind.

This is the historical tradition that undergirds and challenges our accomplishments in this day.

¶ **130.2.** *Theological Perspective.* We believe that the Christian Methodist Episcopal Church is a part of the body of Christ, and that it must express itself in the world in the light of the life and teachings of Jesus Christ. Jesus taught us many things both by word and example—to be concerned for the welfare and the well-being of others, to love our neighbors as ourselves, to be concerned for justice. For the Church to be silent in the face of need, injustice, and exploitation is to deny the Lord of the Church.

We believe "out of one blood God made all the nations who dwell on the face of the earth," that Jesus is most uniquely His Son, that all persons are brothers and sisters, and each person is of infinite worth, and a child of God. Thus, to exploit, to dehumanize any person through pride or arrogance is thoroughly unbiblical and un-christian.

We believe that all things come from God—the earth and its fullness, our own capacities and all we possess. We believe that all things should be held and used in joyous stewardship to Him to help God in His redemptive purpose in the world. The Church, then, must always be in the world actively obeying God's purpose for it. As a redeemed and redeeming fellowship, the Church must seek to serve and save society. This redemption is a continuing necessity.

We also test all institutions and practices by their effect upon persons. Since Jesus died for the redemption of all people, we believe that we should help save them from sin and from every evil influence which would harm or destroy them.

We believe that whatever is of interest and concern to the people— physical, intellectual, social, economic, and political—should also be of interest and concern to the Church. The purpose of our worship is to prepare the participants for their divinely ordained redemptive witness in every place and circumstance.

¶ **130.3.** *Economic Life.* With full acknowledgment of stewardship under God and accountability to Him, we stand for the acquisition of property by moral processes and the right to private ownership thereof. We are thus obligated to evaluate each aspect of every economic order by the commands of Christ and judge its practices by the Christian gospel.

We believe that it is not only our duty to bring Christ to the individual, but also to bring the increasingly technological society in which we live more nearly into conformity with the teachings of Christ.

(a) **Inflation.** The Christian community is concerned with maintaining economic stability. We affirm that there exists a fundamental ethical challenge in inflation itself. We believe that inflation is detrimental to equality and casts an uneven burden upon our citizens, the great burden often falling upon those who are weakest politically and economically.

(b) **Health Services.** We stand for the provision of adequate medical care for all people, with special attention being given the aging, the young, and low-income individuals and groups. We support our government, individuals, and foundations in required research in public health; and we support legislation to meet these needs. We believe that adequate support and appropriate accommodations must be made available for persons who are physically and/or mentally challenged.

(c) Wages and Working Conditions. Free collective bargaining has proved its values in our free society whenever the parties engaged in collective bargaining have acted in good faith to reach equitable and moral solutions of problems dealing with wages and working conditions. We do not support the opinion voiced in some quarrels that strikes should be made illegal. To declare strikes illegal would be to deprive workers of their right to collective action and, even more seriously, would place in the hands of government the power to force workers to remain on the job.

(d) Automation. Through automation a greater number of people face job displacement, economic loss, and jeopardy of their skills. We affirm that it is a Christian's duty to provide for all men opportunity to earn an adequate livelihood, to avoid unemployment and waste of personal and economic resources. We believe that workers who are displaced by automation should be given opportunity for retraining.

(e) Poverty and Unemployment. We believe that the economic development which makes possible material plenty for all imposes upon us great moral responsibility, in that physical, emotional and spiritual development of millions of people throughout the world is hindered by poverty. We, therefore, stand for the eradication of poverty everywhere.

(f) Urban Life. We believe the inner city to be a mission field crying out for bold, new creative ways of witness. Therefore, we call our urban congregations to a deeper involvement in neighborhood life.

(g) Christian Vocation. We believe that every employable person so far as possible should be engaged in some vocation to enhance the common good. Every such vocation should be viewed as a Christian calling for those who pursue it as well as by those who receive its benefits, and our daily work should be regarded as a sphere of service to God.

¶ **130.4.** *The Church and General Welfare.* We believe that in order for the Church to fulfill God's purpose in the world it must concern itself with persons in every phase of their historical and social existence by defining the meaning of that existence in terms of moral and social significance, by promoting those institutions and causes which strengthen the forces for good in society, and by using its influence to combat those forces in society detrimental to the fulfillment of life under God.

(a) Peace and World Order. We believe that it is God's will that peace and goodwill prevail among people and nations. Therefore, we consider all war as evil and oppose war as a means of reaching agreements between nations. Our Church must be on the side of every effort seeking to remove those conditions of heart and mind, of social, economic, and international injustice and of ideological conflict out of which wars arise. Further, our church must actively and constantly seek to promote understanding, reconciliation and goodwill to relieve suffering and raise living standards over the world.

1 – United Nations. We believe that the United Nations with its related agencies should be supported by all nations as a vital and necessary instrument for discussing international problems and seeking ways of resolving conflict.

2—Christian Military Service. Jesus Christ teaches us both love of country and love of all people. Thus, respect for properly constituted civil authority is a part of our tradition. When there is genuine conflict between one's conscience and one's duty to bear arms in defense of one's country, we believe that nations ought to exempt persons from such duties in the face of conscientious objections.

(b) The Liquor Problem. We condemn the use of alcoholic beverages, and feel it imperative to minister to those persons who are victims of alcohol. We condemn the sale and use of liquor as that which imperils the abundant life to which Christ calls us.

(c) Crime. We recognize individual, and personal responsibility to society. Yet we recognize that in many instances the growth of crime and delinquency is the result of family failure, and economic and social deprivation. When persons are found to be law-breakers, we feel that every effort should be made to rehabilitate them and return them to society. We are unalterably opposed to capital punishment.

(d) Gambling. Gambling is a menace to society, destructive of good government and deadly to the best interest of moral, social, and spiritual life. We stand for the achievement of community and personal standards which make unnecessary the resort to petty or commercial gambling as a recreation, escape, or producer of public or charitable revenue. As an act of faith and love, Christians should abstain from all acts of gambling and should participate in efforts to minister to those victimized by the practice, including compulsive gamblers.

(e) Human Rights. Since all persons are endowed by God with certain inalienable rights, we believe that no individual should be denied these rights because of race, creed, culture, national origin or social class. Further, we believe that persons should have freedom under law to petition for these rights.

(f) Sex and Christian Life. We believe that human sexuality as created by God is for the good of human life and is sacred, marriage is the context and the relation in which sexuality is to be expressed. Sexual relations between men and women united in holy wedlock is a means of personal and inter-personal communion, an expression of mutual love, and the means of procreation. Sexual relations outside of marriage are contrary to the will of God, and constitute a blasphemous disregard of God's purposes for men and women.

(g) Moral and Ethical Behavior. We believe that through the grace of Jesus Christ God calls all persons into covenant with God and one another. Sexual harassment and misconduct, and other like actions, disrupt the sacred covenant of God with us and are unacceptable in the church where God's grace in Jesus Christ is proclaimed and experienced. Therefore, all Christians are called to identify and prevent sexual harassment and misconduct whenever, however, and wherever it is encountered.

We recommend that this Social Creed be presented to our congregations orally or in printed form at least once each year and that frequent references be made to it. Every local Church shall encourage the study of the Social Creed and seek to apply its principles.

¶ 131. Sexual Harassment Policy of the C.M.E. Church

We believe that the Christian Methodist Episcopal Church is part of the body of Christ, and that it must express itself in the world in light of the life and teachings of Jesus Christ. Jesus taught us many things both by word and example to be concerned for the welfare and well-being of others, to love our neighbors as ourselves and to be concerned for justice. For the Church to be silent in the face of need, injustice, and exploitation is to deny the Lord of the Church.

In light of our theological perspective, it is the intent of this policy to provide for an experience of grace, justice, and reconciliation for both the aggrieved and the respondent when sexual harassment and/or sexual misconduct is alleged or proven. The minister and those in authority in the Church are in a position of sacred trust. Any such sexual harassment and sexual misconduct is a violation of that sacred trust.

Sexual harassment harms not only the spiritual life of the church, but it also violates the rights of human beings to be free of unwarranted sexual imposition. It refers to behavior that is not welcomed, which is personally offensive, which debilitates morale and interferes with the ministerial or employment relationship. In turning to the minister, persons become vulnerable to the minister and trust that their vulnerability will be respected and not abused. Sexual harassment and sexual misconduct as a matter of Christian principle, is totally unacceptable. Accordingly, sexual harassment and/or sexual misconduct by any person in the Christian Methodist Episcopal Church is a prohibited form of personal conduct. In light of the painfully traumatic and serious consequences that could result from an actionable offense, the C.M.E. Church shall not condone sexual harassment in any form. It is expected that all persons having supervisory or managerial responsibilities for the governance of the church, its ministry and ministries, shall be prudent in judgment and assure an environment that would eliminate adverse sexual harassment and/or sexual misconduct.

The Christian Methodist Episcopal Church, in recognition of biblical and moral principles, is committed to maintaining the highest ministerial and professional standards among all ordained and unordained ministers of C.M.E. Church, as well as all church officers, members, staff and anyone who holds an official capacity in the church. It is the intent of the Christian Methodist Episcopal Church that all persons uphold these standards and assure the integrity of our church ministry and administration. Any conduct that violates this trust may result in serious consequences.

CHAPTER 4
CONSTITUTION FOR THE
CHRISTIAN METHODIST EPISCOPAL CHURCH

PREAMBLE

Since the Church is of God, and will be preserved to the end of time, for the promotion of His worship and the due administration of His Word and Ordinances, the maintenance of Christian fellowship and discipline, the edification of believers, the conversion of the world and the transformation of social and economic structures so as to make possible the realization of peoplehood:

We, the members of the Christian Methodist Episcopal Church (C.M.E.) in order to advance the cause of the Church of Jesus Christ, safeguard the glorious heritage bequeathed to us by our forefathers, preserve our traditions as a Methodist people, and perfect our unity and structure, DO HEREBY ESTABLISH AND SET FORTH THIS CONSTITUTION.

DIVISION ONE—GENERAL

Article 1. Definition: This is a visible Church of Christ, consisting of faithful persons, in which the pure Word of God is preached and the Sacraments duly administered.

Article 2. Name: The name of this Church is the Christian Methodist Episcopal Church (C.M.E.), A Religious Corporation.

Article 3. Articles of Religion: The Articles of Religion shall be those historically held in common by churches of the Methodist tradition and shall be the standard and rule of doctrines of the Christian Methodist Episcopal Church (C.M.E.).

Article 4. The inclusiveness of the Church: The Christian Methodist Episcopal Church (C.M.E.) cherishes its place in the universal Church which is the body of Christ and is devoted to acceptance of the Apostolic faith. Therefore, all persons without regard to race, color, national origin, or economic condition shall be eligible to attend its worship services, to participate in its programs, and when they take the appropriate vows to be admitted into its membership in any local church in the Christian Methodist Episcopal (C.M.E.) Connection.

Article 5. The General Rules: The General Rules shall be those of the "United Societies" organized by John Wesley in 1739 and shall constitute the rules by which members of this Church shall strive to evidence their continual desire for salvation.

Article 6. Ecumenical Relations: The Christian Methodist Episcopal Church (C.M.E.) believes that the Lord of the Church is calling Christians everywhere to strive toward unity at all levels of Church life. The Church has maintained communication with other Churches and denominations in the growing movement to restore unity in the Christian Churches, as evidence of dedication to the Church as the body of Christ. Such activity is in keeping with the statement of John Wesley, the father of Methodism, "that the Methodists are one people in all the world," and as undergirded by his avowal that, "The World is my Parish." The Church is engaged in ecumenical movements. Directed in one instance, to reaching an accord in policy and polity among various Methodist bodies; and, in a second instance, with other denominations in seeking to repair, if not in some circumstances to obliterate divisions that impair our witness as true followers of Jesus Christ.

Article 7. Title of Properties: There shall be a Board of Trustees of the Christian Methodist Episcopal Church (C.M.E.) elected according to the *Discipline*, who shall hold title to all property, real, personal, or mixed, belonging to the Connection. No charter deed or conveyance or the receipt thereof for any house of worship; or any other property, shall contain any restriction or reservation prohibiting any minister and preacher belonging to the Christian Methodist Episcopal Church (C.M.E.), as shall from time to time be duly authorized by the General Conference of the Church or by the Annual Conference to preach and expound God's Holy Word, and to execute the Discipline of the Church, and to administer the Sacraments therein, according to the true meaning and purpose of the Church doctrine.

All written instruments of conveyance or receipt of property of any kind by which premises are held or hereafter acquired; shall be in accord with the rules and regulations of the Christian Methodist Episcopal Church (C.M.E.).

DIVISION TWO — ORGANIZATION
§1. Conferences and Boards

Article 1. There shall be a General Conference for the entire Church with such powers, duties, and privileges as are hereinafter set forth.

Article 2. There shall be annual conferences, the basic bodies of the Church with such powers and privileges as are hereinafter set forth.

Article 3. There shall be a General Connectional Board for the government of the Connectional affairs of the Church with powers, duties, and privileges as are hereinafter set forth.

Article 4. There shall be a Quarterly Conference for each charge with such powers, duties and privileges which are hereinafter set forth.

Article 5. There shall be a Church Conference for each charge with such powers, duties, and privileges which are hereinafter set forth.

Article 6. There shall be in every Local Church an Official Board which shall be the administrative body of the Church with such powers, duties, and authority which are hereinafter set forth.

§2. General Conference

Article 1. The General Conference shall be composed of delegates elected by the Annual Conferences, one half of whom shall be Ministers and one half lay members. The Bishops of the Christian Methodist Episcopal Church (C.M.E.) both active and honorably retired, shall be ex-officio members of the General Conference.

1. The College of Bishops, or majority of all of the Annual Conferences shall have authority to call a General Conference at any time.

2. When a General Conference is called, it shall be constituted of the delegates elected to the preceding General Conference, except when an Annual Conference shall prefer to have a new election.

3. At all times when the General Conference meets it shall take a majority of the representatives of all the Annual Conferences to make a quorum for transacting business.

4. One of the Bishops shall preside each day at the General Conference.

Article 2. The General Conference shall have full powers to make rules and regulations for the Church subject to the limitations of the restrictive rules and in the exercise of this power shall have authorities as follows:

1. To define and fix the conditions, privileges and duties of Church membership.

2. To define and fix the powers and duties of elders, deacons, probationers, supply preachers, local preachers and exhorters.

3. To define and fix the powers and duties of Annual Conferences, District Conferences, Quarterly Conferences, Church Conferences and Official Boards.

4. To provide for the organization, promotion and administration of the work of the Church outside of the United States of America.

5. To determine and provide for raising the funds necessary to carry

on the Connectional work of the church.

6. To define and fix the powers and duties of the Pastors in Charge and the Presiding Elders.

7. To define and fix the powers, duties, and privileges of the Episcopacy; to adopt a plan for the support of the Bishops; to provide for the discontinuance of a Bishop because of inefficiency or unacceptability.

8. To regulate all matters relating to the form and mode of worship, ritual, and religious services and ceremonies subject to the limitations of the First Restrictive rule.

9. To provide the judicial system and a method of judicial procedure for the Church.

10. To initiate and to direct all Connectional enterprises of the Church (such as publishing, evangelistic, missionary and benevolent) and to provide boards for their promotion and administration.

11. To enact such other legislation as may be necessary, subject to the limitations and restrictions of the Constitution of the Church.

§3. Restrictive Rules

1. The General Conference shall not revoke, alter or change our Articles of Religion; or establish any new standards or rules of doctrine contrary to our present existing and established standards of doctrine.

2. The General Conference shall not allow more than one representative for every fourteen (14) members of the Annual Conference; nor allow a less number than one for every thirty (30); provided, nevertheless, that when there shall be in any Annual Conference a fraction of two-thirds (2/3) the number which shall be fixed for the ratio of representation, such Annual Conference shall be entitled to an additional delegate for such fraction, and provided also, that no Conference shall be denied the privilege of two delegates.

3. The General Conference shall not change or alter any part or rule of our government; so as to do away with Episcopacy; or destroy the plan of our itinerant general superintendency.

4. The General Conference shall not revoke or change the General Rules of the United Societies.

5. The General Conference shall not do away with the privilege of our Ministers or Preachers of trial by a committee and of an appeal, neither shall they do away with

the privileges of our members of trial before the church or by a committee, and of an appeal.

6. The General Conference shall not appropriate the proceeds of the Publishing House to any purpose other than for the benefit of the retired Ministers, their widows and their orphans.

§4. Annual Conferences

Article 1. The Annual Conferences shall be composed of all Traveling Preachers in Full Connection with it, and a number of lay representatives determined by the General Conference.

Article 2. The Annual Conference is a basic body in the Christian Methodist Episcopal Church (C.M.E.) and reserves the right to vote on all constitutional amendments, on the election of delegates to the General Conferences, on all matters relating to the character, conference relations, and ordination of its ministerial members, and such other rights as have not been delegated to the General Conference, under the Constitution.

Article 3. The Annual Conference shall elect ministerial and lay delegates to the General Conference in the manner provided in this section. The ratio of representation in the General Conference shall be determined by the General Conference.

Article 4. The clergy representatives shall be elected by the clergy members of the Conference.

Article 5. The lay representatives shall be elected by the lay members of the Annual Conference.

Article 6. The Annual Conference, entitled under the Second Restrictive Rule to two ministerial delegates, shall also be entitled to two lay delegates.

§5. General Connectional Board

Article 1. There shall be a General Connectional Board for the government of the general affairs of the Christian Methodist Episcopal Church (C.M.E.) with such powers as may be fixed and determined by the General Conference.

§6. District Conferences

Article 1. There may be held annually, in each Presiding Elder's District, a District Conference, with such powers as may be fixed and determined by the General Conference.

§7. Quarterly Conference

Article 1. There shall be in each pastoral charge a Quarterly Conference composed of such persons and invested with such powers as the General Conference shall provide.

§8. Church Conference

Article 1. There shall be a Church Conference in each church with directions, powers and duties as the General Conference may prescribe.

§9. Official Board

Article 1. There shall be in every local Church an Official Board which shall be the administrative body of the church with such powers, duties, and authority as may be given by the General Conference.

DIVISION THREE—EPISCOPACY

Article 1. There shall be an Episcopacy with such powers, duties and privileges as shall be defined by the General Conference.

Article 2. The Bishops shall be elected by the General Conference and consecrated in the historic manner of Episcopal Methodism at such time and place as may be fixed by the General Conference.

Article 3. There shall be a College of Bishops composed of all the Bishops of the Church. The College shall meet at least once a year and plan for the general oversight and promotion of the temporal and spiritual interests of the entire church and for carrying into effect the rules, regulations, and responsibilities prescribed and enjoined by the General Conference.

Article 5. A Bishop presiding over an Annual Conference shall decide all questions of law and fact coming before him, provided that such questions be presented in writing, and with his decisions, be recorded on the journals of the conference.

DIVISION FOUR—JUDICIARY

Article 1. There shall be a Judicial Council. The General Conference shall determine the number and qualifications of its members, their terms of office, and the method of election and the filling of vacancies.

DIVISION FIVE—AMENDMENTS

Article 1. Amendments to the Constitution may originate in either the General or an Annual Conference.

Article 2. Amendments of the Constitution shall require reasonable notice and two-thirds (2/3) of the majority of the members of the General Conference; two-thirds (2/3) of the majority of all members of the Annual Conferences, excepting the First Restrictive Rule, it shall require three-fourths (3/4) majority of all the members of the General Conferences, and (3/4) majority of all the members of the Annual Conferences.

Article 3. The amendment voted upon shall become effective upon the announcement of the College of Bishops that the Amendment has received the required majority; and that no later than ten (10) days after said announcement the amendment shall become operative and effective. (As amendments to the Constitution are passed from time to time, they shall be placed in this section.)

CHARTER OF
CHRISTIAN METHODIST EPISCOPAL CHURCH

The CHRISTIAN METHODIST EPISCOPAL CHURCH has under the Tennessee Nonprofit Corporation Act adopted the following Charter:

1. The name of the corporation is

CHRISTIAN METHODIST EPISCOPAL CHURCH

2. The corporation is a public benefit corporation.

3. This corporation is a religious corporation.

4. (a) The complete address of the corporation's initial registered office in Tennessee is Suite 2000, FIRST TENNESSEE BANK BLDG., MEMPHIS, SHELBY COUNTY, TENNESSEE.

(b) The name of the initial registered agent is

JOHN MARSHALL GILMORE

5. The complete address of the corporation's principal office is:

4466 ELVIS PRESLEY BLVD., SUITE 222
MEMPHIS, TENNESSEE 38116.

6. This corporation is a non profit corporation.

7. This corporation will have members.

8. Upon the dissolution of the Corporation, the Board shall, after paying or making provision for the payment of all the liabilities of the Corporation, dispose of all the assets of the Corporation exclusively for the purposes of the Corporation in such manner or to such organization or organizations organized and operated exclusively for charitable, educational, religious or scientific purposes as is, at the time, qualified as an exempt organization under Section 501(c)(3) of the Internal Revenue Code of 1954, as amended.

THIS CHARTER WAS FILED BY
SECRETARY OF STATE FOR TENNESSEE
ON NOVEMBER 6, 1991 at 3:43 p.m. under
Reference No. 2306-0981.

Note: The Articles of Incorporation are located at the Board of Personnel Services of the Christian Methodist Episcopal Church.

PART II
THE CONFERENCES

5. The General Conference

6. The Annual Conference

7. The District Conference

8. The District Youth Conference

9. The Quarterly Conference

10. The Church Conference

11. The Official Board

CHAPTER 5
THE GENERAL CONFERENCE

¶ **201.** The General Conference shall be composed of delegates elected to it by the Annual Conferences, one-half of whom shall be ministers and one-half lay persons.

¶ **201.1.** The Bishops of the Christian Methodist Episcopal Church, both active and honorably retired, shall be ex-officio members of the General Conference without the privilege of debate or vote.

¶ **201.2.** The General Officers of the Christian Methodist Episcopal Church shall be ex-offcio members of the General Conference, without the privilege of the vote.

¶ **201.3.** The ratio of representation from the Annual Conferences to the General Conference shall be one clerical and one lay delegate for every twenty-one (21) members of the Annual Conference. Each Annual Conference shall be entitled to one additional clerical member and lay member for a two-thirds fraction of the number twenty-one. Any Annual Conference delegate or delegation not elected strictly in accordance herewith shall not be seated in the General Conference.

¶ **201.4.** The clerical delegates shall be elected by the clerical members of the Annual Conference. Clerical members of the Annual Conference shall not be eligible to vote in the election of clerical delegates to the General Conference unless they shall be at least eighteen years of age and a member of the C.M.E. Church and shall have traveled at least four years from the time they were received on trial, and are in Full Connection at the time of the holding of the Annual Conference.

¶ **201.5.** The lay delegates to the General Conference shall be elected by the lay delegates to the Annual Conference. Annual Conference lay delegates shall be at least eighteen (18) years of age in order to vote for General Conference lay delegates and shall have been members of the C.M.E. Church at least four years at the time of the holding of the Annual Conference. At least one young adult (18 - 35) shall be elected as one of the regular delegates from each Annual Conference.

¶ **201.6.** Elections, in all cases, shall be by ballot, and persons responsible for the conduct of the elections shall not interfere with the free expression of the voting rights of the delegation.

¶ **201.7.** Each Annual Conference may elect clerical and lay alternate delegates to the General Conference. Alternate delegates shall meet the same qualifications and be elected in the same manner as regular delegates. The alternate delegates shall replace regular delegates in their own Annual Conference as may be necessary, provided the replacements be made in the descending order in which they were elected.

¶ **201.8.** A special seating section shall be provided in the General Conference for alternate delegates. They shall also receive copies of all materials made available to regular delegates. Also, all registered visitors shall be provided the same on-site materials that are provided the delegates.

¶ **201.9.** The elected representatives from the Annual Conferences shall be furnished with credentials to be presented to the Committee on Credentials of the General Conference before the close of business on the first day of the General Conference.

¶ **201.10.** When more delegates from an Annual Conference to the General Conference are elected than that Annual Conference is entitled, the two delegates having received the lowest number of votes shall share equally in time of voting and any General Conference funds allocated.

¶ **201.11.** An Annual Conference entitled under the Second Restrictive Rule to two clerical delegates shall not be denied the privilege of two lay delegates also.

¶ **201.12.** The clerical and lay delegates shall deliberate in one body, but upon a call of one-fifth of the members of the Conference, the lay and clerical members shall vote separately, and no measure shall be passed without the concurrence of a majority of both classes of representatives

¶ **201.13.** Beginning with the year 2002 the Christian Methodist Episcopal Church will use voting machines in the election process at the General Conference.

¶ **202.** The General Conference shall meet in quadrennial session for nine days between June 15 and July 15 commencing on a Saturday. The Call announcing the time and place of the session shall be published in *The Christian Index* at least two (2) years before and not less than eighteen (18) months by the Senior Bishop before the scheduled opening of the General Conference.

¶ **203.** The Bishops, or a majority of all the Annual Conferences, shall have authority to call a General Conference at any time.

¶ **204.** When a General Conference is called, it shall be constituted of the delegates elected to the preceding General Conference, except when an Annual Conference shall prefer to have a new election. The place of holding a called session of the General Conference shall be that fixed by the preceding General Conference or by the College of Bishops.

¶ **205.** The authority and responsibility for selecting the location for the General Conference shall rest with the College of Bishops.

¶ **206.** There shall be a Committee on Resolutions appointed by the College of Bishops. Each Bishop shall appoint one member to the Resolutions Committee by September 1 of the year preceding the General Conference. The Presiding Bishop of the District shall publish the name of the committee member throughout the District.

¶ **206.1.** All resolutions, memorials, and other materials contemplated for presentation to the General Conference shall be sent to the appropriate Episcopal District Resolutions Committee member on or before January 31 of the year of the General Conference.

¶ **206.2.** Resolutions mailed, sent or given to the Episcopal District representative shall be examined by him or her to ascertain if they meet the requirements for proposed legislation (cf. ¶1308.7, §20, 1998 *Discipline*). In addition to the requirements referenced, resolutions shall not contain more than three preamble paragraphs. If the resolutions do not meet the requirements, they shall be returned for corrections.

¶ **206.3.** The Chairman of the Committee on Resolutions appointed by the College of Bishops shall requisition funds from the General Secretary of the Department of Finance for expenses accrued in preparation of the manuscript for the Resolutions Book. Said funds shall be in addition to the funds that shall be made available for the costs of the Committee on Resolutions to meet. All funds used shall be charged against the line item in the Connectional Budget designated, "General Conference Expense".

¶ **206.4.** The manuscript for the Resolutions Book shall be forwarded to the Publications Department in sufficient time to be printed and mailed to the delegates, alternate delegates, and other officials on or before May 15 of the year of the General Conference.

¶ **207.** At all times when the General Conference is meeting, it shall take a majority of the representatives of all the Annual Conferences to make a quorum for transacting business.

¶ **208.** If, by a majority vote, the delegates present and voting under the quorum requirement deem it necessary to delegate, for future consideration or action, unfinished business to an agency, agencies, agent, or agents, the nature of the business shall be explicitly stated and the limits of actions to be taken shall be clearly defined. The chairperson shall be named and the committee shall be funded.

¶ **209.** One of the Bishops shall preside each day the General Conference is in session, beginning with the Senior Bishop, and proceeding in the order of their seniority until all have presided. Beginning with the Senior Bishop, this order shall be followed until the close of the General Conference.

¶ **210.** The General Conference shall elect General Officers.

¶ **211.** The General Conference shall have full powers to make rules and regulations for our Church under the following limitations and restrictions, viz.:
§1. The General Conference shall not revoke, alter, or change our Articles of Religion, or establish any new standards or rule of doctrine contrary to our present existing and established standards of doctrine.

§2. They shall not allow more than one representative for every fourteen members of the Annual Conference, nor allow a less number than one for every thirty; provided, nevertheless, that when there shall be in any Annual Conference a fraction of two-thirds, the number which shall be fixed for the ratio of representation, such Annual Conference shall be entitled to an additional delegate for such fraction: and provided also that no Annual Conference shall be denied the privilege of two delegates.

§3. They shall not change or alter any part or rule of our government, so as to do away with the Episcopacy, or destroy the plan of itinerant general superintendency.

§4. They shall not revoke or change the General Rules of the United Societies.

§5. They shall not do away with the privilege of our Ministers or Preachers of trial by a committee and of an appeal; neither shall they do away with the privileges of our members of trial before the Church or by a committee, and of an appeal.

§6. They shall not appropriate the proceeds of the Publishing House to any purpose other than for the benefit of superannuated, and retired Preachers, widow(er)s, and children.

¶ 212. Provided, nevertheless, that upon the concurrent recommendation of three-fourths of all the members of the several Annual Conferences, who shall be present and vote on such recommendation, then a majority of two-thirds of the General Conference succeeding shall suffice to alter any of the above restrictions, excepting the first article; and also, whenever such alterations shall have been first recommended by two-thirds of the General Conference, so soon as three-fourths of the members of all the Annual Conferences shall have concurred as aforesaid, such alteration or alterations shall take effect.

CHAPTER 6
THE ANNUAL CONFERENCE

¶213. Meaning and Membership

§1. The Annual Conference is a basic unit with such powers as those not granted to the General Conference (cf. Constitution, Div. II, §4).

§2. The Annual Conference is a defined geographical area which consists of the pastoral charges within the area.

§3. The Annual Conference is a yearly meeting of its ministerial members as defined by the General Conference, together with lay representatives elected to it by the several pastoral charges that constitute the particular Annual Conference.

(a) Ministerial members of the Annual Conference shall consist of all who have been received into Full Connection with it, both active and retired; and probationary ministers or those ministers who are on trial.

(b) Ministerial members of the Annual Conference shall be voted into Full Connection by the ministers who are in full connection, which status effectively removes the membership of a minister from the Local Church to the Annual Conference. Probationers shall be voted admission on trial by ministers in Full Connection, subject to future actions by the voting ministerial members.

(c) Lay members (persons unordained) of the Annual Conference shall be elected to its sessions by the Church Conference to which they are members. Delegates elected by the Church Conference shall be certified by the Quarterly Conference. The process shall be:

1. The Secretary of the Church Conference shall read into the records of the next Quarterly Conference a written list of elected delegates, to which with the Pastor they shall attest to the authenticity of the names.

2. A signed copy of the list shall be presented at the time to the Presiding Elder.

3. The Presiding Elder shall present the lists of delegates elected from each charge to the Annual Conference.

(d) Each pastoral charge shall have the right to elect two (2) lay members to the next session of the Annual Conference. Further, each pastoral charge shall have the right to elect one (1) additional delegate to the next session of the Annual Conference for every three hundred (300) reported members; and one for a major fraction of three hundred (151).

(e) Lay members who are full members shall be eligible for election as delegates by the charge where they hold full membership provided they are in good standing, which means, any member who upholds the church by his/her prayers, presence, gifts and service, and who has no judicial proceedings completed adversely against him/her at the time of the election; and are at least eighteen (18) years of age, or have been emancipated by marriage, at the time of the convening of the Annual Conference.

(f) Associate or affiliate members are eligible for election as lay delegates to the Annual Conference by their home church only.

(g) "Voting Delegates" to the Connectional Lay Institute held quadrennially, shall be read into the Annual Conference record by the same process as lay members elected to the Annual Conference.

¶ 214. Voting

§1. Ministerial members in Full Connection, active and retired, shall have the right to vote on all matters coming before the Annual Conference except where the right has been limited by action of the General Conference. (Exceptions now by the General Conference actions are the election of lay delegates to the General Conference. (cf.¶ 201.5)

§2. Ministerial members in Full Connection shall have sole authority and voting privilege on all matters related to ministerial conference relations, including admission on trial, discontinuance, readmission, Full Connection, character, and orders.

§3. Probationary members, preachers on trial, shall not have the right of either voice or vote. Permission to speak but not debate, may be granted by the chair upon request by a probationer.

§4. Lay delegates shall have the right of participation in all matters coming before the Annual Conference, except where prohibited by action of the General Conference. (Exclusions at present include voting on the election of ministerial delegates to the General Conference; ministerial conference relations, membership, orders, and character (cf. ¶ 214, §2).

¶ 215. Attendance at the session of the Annual Conference is required of all ministers in Full Connection, probationers, candidates to be recommended for admission on trial, and lay delegates. If providentially hindered from attending part or all of a session a minister in Full Connection, active or retired, and a probationer shall notify the Presiding Elder of his/her district of the reason for being unable to attend or for being absent for any part of the session. In the case of a Presiding Elder, she/he shall notify the Bishop who is to preside over the session of the inability to attend the Conference. Arrangements shall be made with the Bishop for all reports, both of pastoral charges and of conference funds collected with all written receipts, to be collected by the Chair and the Secretary of the Joint Board of Finance and brought to the seat of the Conference. They shall issue written receipts for all items collected. Lay delegates who are providentially hindered from attending the Annual Conference shall notify his or her pastor. In every case a person leaving the seat of the Conference shall request permission from the Chair to be absent and in every case the Annual Conference shall make the final decision.

¶ 216. Meeting Time and Place

§1. The Annual Conference shall meet once yearly for a time appointed by the Presiding Bishop. The Conference shall be allowed to sit as long as necessary to complete its business in an orderly manner.

§2. The voting members of the Annual Conference shall decide by vote the place for the annual meeting.

§3. The Presiding Bishop with the concurrence of the Presiding Elders may change the place for holding the next session when it serves the best interest of the Annual Conference.

¶ 217. The Bishop assigned by the General Conference to superintend the Annual Conference shall preside over its sessions. In the absence of the Presiding Bishop from the seat of the Conference, he or she shall appoint a presiding officer from among the traveling elders who are full members of that conference. Once appointed, the Presiding Officer shall discharge all the duties of a Bishop related to the work of the conference in session, except ordination.

¶ 218. The duties and responsibilities of the Annual Conference are:

§1. To elect personnel, including Secretary, Treasurer, Statistician.

§2. To decide all matters related to ministerial conference relations according to the *Discipline*; such as admission on trial; readmission; election to orders; questions of character and full connection.

§3. To try, suspend, locate, expel, retire and supernumerate ministers according to the *Discipline*.

§4. To elect delegates to the General Conference.

§5. To adopt an operating budget for the ensuing year. The budget shall be presented to the Annual Conference prior to the reading of the appointments.

§6. To approve the establishing of schools provided no member of the C.M.E. Church, clergy or lay, shall establish a school in the name of the Church, without the prior consent and approval of the Quarterly Conference or the Annual Conference having immediate jurisdiction.

§7. To inquire as to whether the deeds for all church property are drawn so as to bind it to the Connection.

§8. To secure a fidelity bond for the Conference Treasurer and Presiding Elders.

§9. To select with the approval of the Presiding Bishop a bank(s) in which all monies collected or received or raised by the authority or in the name of the Annual Conference shall be deposited. Any bank used to rent lock box(es) used for holding documents, contracts and deeds of the Annual Conference shall be chosen in the same manner. The Presiding Bishop shall have the right of refusal to sign off on lock or safe deposit boxes at his discretion.

§10. To vote on all constitutional amendments and all other rights that have not been delegated to the General Conference under the Constitution.

§11. To execute and revise as shall be appropriate from time to time the course of study for ministers and lay persons prepared by the General Department of Christian Education.

§12. Each Annual Conference shall allow 30 days for a pastor to move out of a parsonage, except under special circumstances, after a move from the charge to which the parsonage belongs.

¶ 219. The Annual Conference has the further responsibility:

§1. To organize with the Presiding Bishop the Annual Conference Board of Evangelism and Missions according to the By-laws of its General Department.

§2. To organize with the Presiding Bishop the Annual Conference Board of Christian Education according to the By-laws of its General Department.

§3. To organize with the Presiding Bishop a Board of Personnel Services in accordance with the By-laws of its General Board.

¶ 220. Boundaries and Numbers. The number of Annual Conferences and the geographic boundaries of each shall be determined by the General Conference. The General Conference shall make a complete study of the layout of the several Annual

Conferences. The structure shall be rearranged from time to time to eliminate small Annual Conferences, except in the far western and far eastern areas of the United States.

¶ 221. Creating New Conferences. In the interval of the General Conference, an Annual Conference or Annual Conferences shall have the right to create other Annual Conferences. The General Conference shall determine in the next General Conference whether the new Annual Conference shall or shall not be allowed.

§1. Two or more Annual Conferences that wish to consolidate thereby forming one Annual Conference may appoint a Commission on Consolidation consisting of five lay and clergy members from each participating Annual Conference, with a Presiding Bishop as the Chair.

§2. The Commission on Consolidation shall choose a name and it shall report to the ensuing session of the Annual Conferences involved for ratification or rejection. Final determination of the action taken by the Annual Conferences shall be made by the General Conference in the next session of the General Conference.

¶ 221.1. Dissolution of Conferences. Any dissolution, alterations, and reconstructions of Districts and/or Annual Conferences must include the following appropriate actions, and except they are carried out, no Annual Conference shall be allowed to split or be reconstituted.

§1. A proper prior accounting must be made of all monies and properties and a prior and proper allocation made of the same to each of the respective entities involved, Districts or Annual Conferences.

§2 . In the event an Annual Conference Board of Trustees or Joint Board of Finance holds property or funds for a local church or charge or where such have been earmarked for a local church or charge, the funds or property so held shall be allocated and/or given either to the church or charge or to the Annual Conference to which the church or charge will become a part.

§3. All records relating and pertaining to the monies and/ or properties shall be given to the proper officials of the newly constituted Districts or Annual Conferences.

§4. All of the said records related to the monies and properties of the Districts and/or Annual Conferences shall be prepared at least one year prior to the proposed dissolution, alteration and/or reconstitution of Districts and/or Annual Conferences.

¶ 222. The personnel of the Annual Conference shall be chosen and shall fulfill their respective duties according to the following procedures:

¶ 222.1. **Secretary.** The Secretary shall be recommended by the Cabinet, subject to confirmation by the Annual Conference. The election shall be held annually. The Secretary shall perform the following duties:

§1. Take down the full proceedings of the session and keep a written record of them. The record kept in a Journal shall be signed by the President and the Secretary of the Annual Conference after each session. When filled it shall be deposited with the Presiding Bishop who shall store it in the Episcopal Office for safe keeping.

§2 . Keep in the Journal a current personnel record of each preacher showing the name, status and disposition, including:

  (a) Year admitted on trial

  (b) Year ordained deacon and elder

  (c) Year admitted in full connection

  (d) Year transferred

  (e) Year withdrawn

  (f) Year supernumerated

  (g) Year expelled or suspended

  (h) Year retired

  (i) Year and date of death.

§3. Send certified lists to the General Conference Secretary of the delegates elected to the next session of the General Conference. The delegates, regular and alternate, clergy and lay, shall be listed in the order in which they were elected. The lists of delegates, one for the clergy and one for the lay, shall include the name and full address of each delegate. The same information shall be provided to the Presiding Bishop.

§4. Send certified lists to the General Secretary of Lay Ministry and the President of the Connectional Lay Council of voting delegates elected to the next session of the Connectional Lay Institute. This list of delegates shall include the name and full address of each delegate, if available. The same information shall be provided to the Presiding Bishop.

§5. Provide the Presiding Bishop with information necessary for the operations of the Episcopal Office, such as, lists of the current names and addresses of retired preachers and widows of deceased preachers; names of recently deceased preachers and widows; lists of the names of members of all boards and committees appointed and/or elected; list of all persons ordained and/or admitted into Full Connection;

names and addresses of presidents and program or age group directors of Annual Conference organizations.

¶ **222.2. Treasurer.** The Treasurer shall be recommended annually by the Joint Board of Finance subject to confirmation by the Annual Conference. The duties of the Treasurer shall be:

§1. To receive, verify, record, and deposit all funds in the bank(s) approved by the Bishop and the Annual Conference.

§2. To issue receipts from the properly approved Annual Conference receipt book to the remitter for all funds or monies received, with an itemized listing of the purpose for receiving the money.

§3. To disburse funds during the session of the Annual Conference upon the orders of the Presiding Bishop and the Joint Board of Finance.

§4. To disburse funds for budgeted operations during the interim of the Annual Conference upon order of the Presiding Bishop and in emergencies upon written order of the cabinet with the Presiding Bishop's verbal consent.

§5. To submit annually a written report to the Annual Conference in session. The report shall show all revenues received, including loans, balances brought forward, expenditures, savings, and certificates of deposit.

§6. To cause to be printed the Treasurer's Report in numbers sufficient to provide every minister and lay delegate with a copy.

§7. To have an audit made by a Certified Public Accountant of the records of the Treasurer.

§8. To send to the Presiding Bishop monthly or however frequent it is received, copies of all bank statements and copies of deposit slips. And to notify the Bishop when bad checks have been received or other impediments to the cash flow have developed.

§9. To bring all receipts and records of financial transactions to the seat of the Annual Conference and to other meetings normally held involving the collection and disbursement of money.

¶ **222.3. Statistician.** The Statistician shall be nominated by the Cabinet and elected annually by the Annual Conference. The duties of the Statistician are:

§1. To collect and compile all relevant data pertaining to reported membership, lay and clergy; finances assessed, and reported; the amount of literature purchased; the number of C.M.E. organizations organized; the value of church properties; and the amount of insurance carried on the properties, with special note on the properties enrolled in the C.M.E. Church Group Fire and Casualty Program;

§2. To provide the Annual Conference President and Secretary with individual copies of the statistics.

¶ **222.4. Records Clerk.** The Presiding Bishop shall appoint a Records Clerk for Pensions and Insurance. The duties of the Records Clerk shall be those related to providing business information and statistical data to the General Board of Personnel Services, which shall include:

§1. To maintain a current listing of the names, addresses and other pertinent data such as year of retirement, date of death, etc. of participants in the Retirement Plan and the Gift Fund Program.

§2. To distribute enrollment forms for the Retirement Plan.

§3. To maintain a current listing of the churches enrolled in the Fire and Casualty Insurance Program, inclusive of name, type(s) of property insured, and expiration date of coverage.

§4. To compile the necessary information and provide a copy to the Presiding Bishop, the Annual Conference Secretary, and the General Secretary of Personnel Services at the close of each session of the Annual Conference.

¶ **223.** The Annual Conference shall establish the following Boards to carry out the duties prescribed in the *Discipline*.

¶ **223.1. Board of Evangelism.**

§1. To promote the program of evangelism as outlined by the General Department of Evangelism and Missions (cf.¶ 1150 and ¶ 1152.1).

§2. To work in cooperation with the General, Episcopal and District Boards. (cf. ¶ 1154 to ¶ 1154.2).

¶ **223.2. Board of Christian Education.**

§1.To promote the program of Christian Education throughout the Annual Conference in harmony with the program of the General Department of Christian Education (cf.¶ 1112).

§2. To be constituted, organized, and operated in accordance with ¶1111.1 to ¶ 1113.2 of the *Discipline*.

¶ 223.3. Board of Personnel Services.

§1. To be constituted and function in accordance with ¶ 1036 and ¶ 1036.1 of the *Discipline*.

§2. To work with the Records Clerk in compiling a classified list of its claimants, inclusive of the name, address, zip code, annual salary, and the amount of twelve percent paid on the annual salary of each; and forward a report to the General Secretary of Personnel Services within ten days after the close of the Annual Conference (cf. ¶ 222.4).

¶ 223.4. The Joint Board of Finance

§1. The members of the Joint Board of Finance, consisting of one clerical and one lay person from each Presiding Elder's District, shall be appointed by the President of the Annual Conference at the close of the annual session of the Conference. The members shall hold their appointment until the close of the next annual session of the conference.

§2. The organization of the Joint Board of Finance shall consist of a chairperson and a secretary elected by the members.

§3. Vacancies on the Board shall be filled by the Presiding Bishop. However, the clergy-lay balance must be maintained.

§4. Duties of the Joint Board of Finance shall be to:

(a) Prepare with Presiding Bishop a line-item budget indicating General Funds and Conference Funds, a copy of which shall be sent to each local church.

(b) By way of its Chairperson forward within thirty (30) days of the close of the Annual Conference, or within thirty days of such revisions as the Annual Conference may direct,the adopted budget to the General Secretary of Finance.

(c) Apportion to all of the charges of the Annual Conference the General Funds assessed to the Annual Conference for the quadrennium by the General Conference and make a full report to the Annual Conference of all its proceedings giving the conference the opportunity to study, amend or recommit prior to final approval.

(d) Apportion to all of the charges the assessments necessary to balance the budget adopted by the Annual Conference.

(e) Estimate the compensation and traveling expenses of each Presiding Elder and apportion the same to the charges within the respective district of each Presiding Elder (cf. ¶424, §5).

(f) The Joint Board of Finance has sole authority for levying assessments, askings, allocations, requests upon local churches. No department of the church, nor church organization, General Officer, Presiding Elder or his or her district has the inherent right to ask local churches for funds in the name of the CME Church. All such requests must have prior approval of the Annual Conference Joint Board of Finance.

(g) Announce the amount of General Funds and Conference Claims the local charges in each Presiding Elder's District are expected to raise and report the ensuing Conference year. The announcement shall be made at the close of the Annual Conference session and before the reading of the appointments of the Preachers.

(h) Receive and turn over to the Treasurer of the Annual Conference all funds raised under the direction of the Annual Conference.

(i) Issue orders upon the Treasurer for disbursement of funds when the Conference is in session according to the *Discipline* and remit General Funds to the General Secretary of Finance as provided in the *Discipline*.

(j) Allocate and pay in equal monthly increments the compensation of each Presiding Elder.

(k) Decide all issues regarding salary that may arise between stewards and Presiding Elders, or between stewards and pastors. The decision of the Joint Board of Finance shall be final. (After a pastor has been moved from a charge, in no case shall that pastor hold claim against that charge for unpaid salary.)

(l) Consider and report to the Annual Conference all financial matters referred to it.

(m) Make a full report to the Annual Conference of all its proceedings. The Conference shall have the power to amend, approve, or re-commit.

¶ 223.5. Committee on Ministerial Examination

§1. The Committee shall be appointed by the Bishop. It shall consist of no less than three (3) nor more than eleven of the most competent ministerial members of the conference. One member shall be appointed Chair of the Committee.

§2 . The Committee shall serve for four years if the members are appointed at the first session of the Annual Conference following the General Conference.

§3. The Bishop, in the interest of improving the efficiency and the quality of the Committee at work, may appoint one or more of the Committee as often as it becomes necessary.

§4. The work of the Committee shall be focused upon the Bishops' Course of Study. It shall meet one day in advance of the opening of the Annual Conference, and at the same place, to hold examinations for all candidates for the traveling ministry.

§5. To facilitate the work, each Presiding Elder in accordance with the *Discipline* and in cooperation with the Committee on Examination, shall set up classes during the District Conference (or at another time) for all preachers on trial in the Presiding Elder's District and for those who have been recommended for admission by the Quarterly Conference (cf. ¶1107.7).

§6. The examinations for each year of study as far as practical shall be conducted in writing and shall consist of at least ten (10) questions for each year. The standard of examination shall be one hundred (100) but in no case shall an applicant be promoted or ordained who falls below seventy (70) on the examination, provided, nevertheless, the provisions for ordaining Missionaries be not changed.

§7. The report of the Committee to the Annual Conference shall be in writing. It shall show the full name, address, telephone number, local church name and location, local church pastor and the age, marital status, children, and education of each candidate recommended for admission on trial. Supporting documents for education and any other claim shall be furnished by the candidate. Further, ordination status, year on trial, and the recommendation and/or the action of the committee for each candidate shall be a part of the written report, a copy of which shall be filed with the Secretary of the Annual Conference.

§8. To prepare an examination to be administered in each Quarterly Conference by the Presiding Elder before a candidate for Local Preacher's License is granted a license by the Quarterly Conference.

¶ 223.6 Board of Trustees

§1. Each Annual Conference shall have a Board of Trustees, which shall be incorporated unless the Conference is incorporated in its own name. The Board shall consist of either five, seven or nine persons, who must be at least twenty-one years of age, and of whom half shall be Ministers in effective relation in the Conference and approximately half shall be lay members in good standing of Local Churches within the bounds of the Conference in accordance with the *Discipline* of the Christian Methodist Episcopal Church and the Annual Conference that elects them.

§2. Subject to the direction and approval of the Annual Conference and the Presiding Bishop, the said Corporation shall receive, collect, and hold in trust for the benefit of the Annual Conference any and all donations, bequests and devises of any kind or character, real or personal, that may be given, devised, bequested or conveyed to the said Board for the Annual Conference as such for any benevolent, charitable or religious purpose, and shall administer the same and the income therefrom in accordance with the directions of the donor, trustor, or testator, and the interest of the church, society, institution, or agency contemplated by such donor, trustor or testator.

§3 As directed and approved by the Annual Conference and the Presiding Bishop, the Board shall have the power to invest, reinvest, buy, sell, transfer and convey any and all funds and properties which it may hold in trust, subject always to the terms of the legacy, devise or donation; provided, however, that the foregoing shall not apply to churches, colleges, campuses, conference grounds, orphanages or incorporated boards. When the use to be made of any such donations, bequest or devise is not otherwise designated the same shall be added to and become a part of a "Permanent Fund" of the Annual Conference.

§4. The Board shall make to each session of the Annual Conference a full, true and faithful report of its doings, of all funds, monies, securities, and property held in trust by it, and its receipts and disbursements during the Conference year.

¶ 223.7. Stewardess Board

§1. The Stewardesses shall elect their own officers consisting of President, Vice-President, Secretary, Treasurer, and Chaplain.

§2. The duties of the Board shall be to:

(a) Facilitate the work of the District Boards and provide workshops/training experiences.

(b) Prepare for the celebration of the Holy Communion, Love Feast, etc., as directed by the Presiding Bishop.

(c) Perform such duties that are customary during worship services.

(d) Perform any other duties as ascribed by the Presiding Bishop.

¶ 223.8. Collecting and Submitting General Funds-Conference Claims

§1. The Presiding Elder shall collect the General Funds and the Conference Claims from the local charges and shall receipt the charges for all funds collected and shall forward to the Annual Conference Treasurer who shall receipt the Presiding Elder. The receipts from the Treasurer shall be held by the Presiding Elder and turned over to the Joint Board of Finance of the Annual Conference.

§2. The Presiding Bishop shall be fully responsible for the reporting and delivery of General Funds collected during a session of the Annual Conference, Winter Council, Spring Convocation or any other reporting meeting. The General Funds shall be reported within thirty (30) days of receipt to the General Department of Finance of the Christian Methodist Episcopal Church.

§3. The Presiding Bishop having notified the General Secretary of Finance of the dates of the above meetings, shall report the funds by check, certified mail, return receipt requested, within the thirty (30) day time frame.

§4. The General Secretary of Finance shall notify by certified letter any Presiding Bishop where the funds are not received within thirty (30) days.

§5. If the funds owed are not received by the General Secretary of Finance within ten (10) days after the letter has been sent, the Secretary is directed to send a notice of warning to the Bishop stating that said Bishop is in violation of the laws of the Christian Methodist Episcopal Church, and that continued withholding of funds shall give cause for an investigation for malfeasance, if such funds are not received within ten (10) days. After such notice to the Bishop, notification of such violation shall be sent to the Committee on Finance of the General Connectional Board. Notification shall be to the Chairman and Secretary of the Committee who shall in turn notify the members of the Committee. The Committee shall then give warning and notice to the non-complying Bishop that all appropriate action will be taken against him/her to recover said funds if:

(a) Funds are not reported and received within ten (10) days of notice; and

(b) If another reporting period occurs again. In the event the Presiding Bishop fails to comply with the request to report funds from an Annual Conference that should properly be forwarded to the Department of Finance for Connectional purposes, the Committee on Finance shall have authority to hold a hearing to determine if that Bishop, or Joint Board of Finance is guilty of withholding or delaying such funds, and report results of the hearing to the Connectional Board and the College of Bishops which shall pursue the matter according to the procedure outlined in the *Book of Discipline*, ¶ 803.

¶ 224. The Bishop and Annual Conference Matters

The Presiding Bishop shall see that: the Treasurer's report is audited annually; the moving expenses of Preachers are paid; the Annual Conference Journal is forwarded to the General Conference; and a copy of the report of the Certified Public Accountant accompanies the Journal to the General Conference.

¶ 225. Ministerial Character

§1. *Passing Character*. When the preachers are being examined on their life and official administration, only members of the Annual Conference and others who may be present for business with the Conference, shall be present, except the Conference may vote that it be otherwise.

§2. *Procedure.* The name of every preacher shall be called. The Presiding Elder or another ministerial member of the Conference shall state whether or not there be any complaint against each preacher. If there is no complaint, the character of the preacher may be passed without a vote.

§3. *Complaint.* When the name of a Preacher has been called while character is being passed and it is stated by the Presiding Elder or the member who is acting in an official capacity that there is a complaint, and the Preacher has been advised of it, the complaint shall be stated to the Annual Conference. The accused shall have the privilege of replying. The Preacher shall then leave the room and the Conference shall determine by vote whether the character of the Preacher shall pass.

§4. *Tribunal.* If it is determined that a formal hearing to determined whether a charge against a preacher is necessary(a Tribunal), it shall be conducted according to the provision of the *Discipline* governing Tribunals (cf. ¶803.4).

¶ **226.** The following questions shall be asked at the Annual Conference:

A. Conference Relations

§1. Who are admitted on trial? List each individually. Record full name, full address, local church with address, birth date, marital status, education.

§2. Who remain on trial? (The Minutes shall list names and the year each was admitted).

§3. What preachers have had their conference membership discontinued, terminated or withdrawn as:

(a) Probationers?

(b) Preachers in Full Connection? (The reason(s) for the discontinuance must be recorded).

(c) Withdrawn?

(d) Terminated by Conference action?

§4. Who are admitted into Full Connection?

§5. Who are readmitted as:

(a) Probationers?

(b) Preachers in Full Connection?

§6. Who are the preachers in full connection that are received by transfer from other Annual Conferences in the C.M.E. Church?

§7. What preachers in Full Connection are transferred this year?

§8. What preachers in good standing in other Christian denominations are received as:

(a) Local Preachers?

(b) Preachers in Full Connnection?

§9. Who are the preachers Located this year:

(a) Voluntarily?

(b) Involuntarily?

§10. Who are the preachers granted Supernumerary Relations this year?

§11. What preachers are retiring at this session of the Annual Conference:

(a) Due to mandatory age requirement?

(b) By request?

(c) By determination of the Annual Conference?

§12. Who are the Retired Preachers and families of deceased preachers? (Include name, address and zip code of each person listed.)

§13. Are all the preachers blameless in their lives and official administration?

§14. What preachers, who are members of the Conference, have died during the year?

§15. Who are the deacons of one year?

§16. What traveling preachers are elected deacons?

§17. What traveling preachers are ordained deacons?

§18. What local preachers are elected deacons?

§19. What local preachers are ordained deacons?

§20. What traveling preachers are elected elders?

§21. What traveling preachers are ordained elders?

§22. What local preachers are elected elders?

§23. What local preachers are ordained elders?

B. Statistics

§24. What is the number of charges in this conference? Number of churches?

§25. What is the number of Traveling Preachers in this Conference in Full Connection: (a) Active? (b) Retired? (c) Supernumerary?

§26. What is the number of local preachers in this conference as reported by the local churches?

§27. What is the number of probationers on trial this conference? Licentiates?

Deacons? Elders?

§28. What was the number of lay members in this Conference reported to the last Annual Conference by the local churches as:

    (a) Preparatory?

    (b) Full membership?

    (c) Associate or affiliate?

§29. What is the number of members added this year as:

    Converts?

    Otherwise?

§30. What is the number of members lost:

    (a) By death?

    (b) Moved away?

    (c) Transferred membership?

    (d) Lost otherwise?

§31. What is the number of lay members in this conference reported to the Annual Conference by local churches as:

    (a) Preparatory?

    (b) Full membership?

    (c) Associate or affiliate?

§32. How many infants have been baptized this conference year?

§33. How many persons have been baptized this conference year:

    (a) Children?

    (b) Youth?

    (c) Adults?

    (d) Total?

§34. What is the number of Sunday Church Schools in this Annual Conference?

§35. What is the number of Sunday Church School officers?

§36. What is the number of Sunday Church School classes?

§37. What is the number of Sunday Church School teachers?

§38. What is the number of Sunday Church School students?

§39. What is the number of Christian Youth Fellowship Chapters? Counselors? Officers? Members?

§40. What is the number of Young Adult Fellowship organizations? Officers? Members?

§41. What is the number of local church training classes conducted such as: New member classes? Seminars? Workshops? Institutes? Teachers? Church Officers?

§42. What is the number of persons enrolled in local church training classes?

§43. What is the total number of pieces of literature purchased for Sunday Church School? Christian Youth Fellowship?

§44. What is the number of:

(a) Local boards of Christian Education?

(b) Commissions on Membership and Evangelism?

(c) Social Concerns Commissions?

(d) Boards of Missions?

§45. What is the number of schools conducted such as:

Weekday Church Schools? Vacation Bible Schools?

§46. What is the number of:

(a) Women's Missionary Societies?

(b) Members of Women's Missionary Societies?

(c) Lay Activities Councils?

(d) Members of Lay Activities?

C. Finance

§47. What amount was apportioned this conference for General Funds?

§48. What amount has been raised this year by this conference for General Funds?

§49. What amount has been received by Gift Fund Recipients in this conference?

§50. What amount has been paid by the churches in this conference for the retirement of pastors and presiding elders?

§51. What amount has been contributed by this conference for educational institutions? Other charitable causes?

§52. What amount was raised by this conference for education on Children's Day?

§53. What amount was raised by this conference for Christian Education activities and how has it been applied?

D. Insurance

§54. Regarding insurance on property:

(a) What is the number of churches covered by the C.M.E. Group Fire and Casualty Insurance Plan?

(b) Are all premiums current?

(c) What is the number of church parsonages covered by the C.M.E. Church Group Fire and Casualty Insurance Plan?

E. Miscellaneous

§55. Who are the officers of the Annual Conference:

    (a)   Board of Evangelism?

    (b)   Board of Personnel Services?

    (c)   Women s Missionary Society?

    (d)   Lay Activities Council?

    (e)   Board of Social Concerns?

    (f)   Board of Christian Education?

    (g)   Christian Youth Fellowship?

    (h)   Young Adult Fellowship?

    (i)   Board of Missions?

    (j)   Board of Publishing Interests?

    (k)   Board of Trustees?

§56. Where shall the next session of the Annual Conference be held?

§57. Where are the preachers stationed for the ensuing Conference year?

CHAPTER 7
DISTRICT CONFERENCE

¶ **230.** There may be held annually, in each Presiding Elder's District, a District Conference. The time shall be fixed by the Presiding Elder and the place by the Conference.

¶ **231.** The District Conference shall be composed of all Preachers in the District, both traveling and local, including retired preachers, exhorters, the Missionary President, Director of Christian Education, Director of Children's Ministry, Director of Adult Ministry, Lay President, Stewardess Board, Director of Youth Ministry, Trustees, Steward Board, Choirs, Board of Evangelism, Treasurer and Secretary. There shall be at least one delegate elected from each charge, and each charge also may elect one additional delegate for every two hundred members above the first 300. All delegates shall be elected by the Church Conference and confirmed by the Quarterly Conference.

¶ **232.** The Presiding Elder shall preside. In his or her absence, the Conference shall elect a president.

¶ **233.** The Conference shall elect a secretary, who shall keep a record of all its proceedings.

¶ **234.** It shall be the duty of the Conference to examine Quarterly Conference Journals, and to inquire particularly into the condition of the several charges in the District as to:

1. Their spiritual state;

2. Missions within the District, where new ones should be established, or what missions should be raised to enlarged charges or charges.

3. Ministry of religious education:

(a) The condition of the Sunday Church School, enrollment, increase of membership, improvements made, and pieces of literature taken.

(b) The Christian Youth Fellowship, enrollments, increase in membership, description of activities: report of progress and improvement.

(c) Leadership training classes; number of classes conducted; number of persons enrolled; indications of value received from classes.

(d) Plans or report of Vacation Church Schools; Weekday Church Schools; adult fellowship meetings; organizations and work of local Boards of Christian Education.

(e) As to the Christian Youth Fellowship Chapters and manners of conducting them.

4. As to the financial system, the contribution to church purposes, and the condition of houses of worship and parsonages.

5. As to the Mission work and Church Extension; the amount raised for each.

¶ **235.** The District Conference may also hear reports from special committees and hear and discuss papers presented to it.

¶ **236.** At these Conferences prominence shall be given to religious exercises, such as preaching, praying, love feast, and the administration of the Sacraments.

CHAPTER 8
YOUTH CONFERENCE

¶ **237.** There shall be held annually in each Presiding Elder's District a Sunday Church School and Christian Youth Fellowship Convention or Youth Conference. The time shall be fixed by the Presiding Elder and the place by the convention.

¶ **238.** The Sunday Church School and Christian Youth Fellowship Convention shall be composed of persons under 18 years of age elected from the Sunday Church School, Christian Youth Fellowship and youth of the local churches in the District, Preachers, Sunday Church School general and departmental superintendents, presidents of Christian Youth Fellowship and youth organizations, District Director of Christian Education, and other officers of local Sunday Church Schools and Christian Youth Fellowships in the district.

¶ **239.** The Convention shall, from year to year, elect a Program Committee consisting of the Presiding Elder, District Sunday Church School Superintendent, Christian Youth Fellowship presidents, one Pastor, Director of Christian Education and ten members who are elected by the Convention.

¶ **240.** The Presiding Elder shall be ex-officio chairperson. The Convention shall elect annually by ballot a person under18 years of age to preside at the Convention sessions. The Convention shall be under the supervision of the Presiding Elder and the District Director of Christian Education.

¶ **241.** It shall be the duty of the Convention or Youth Conference to:
(a) Receive reports from the Sunday Church Schools and Christian Youth Fellowship.
(b) Provide a program of worship, fellowship, and evangelism, missions, training, service, and recreation for the young people in harmony with the Disciplinary provisions and with the standards established by the General Board of Christian Education.
(c) Sponsor debates, discussions, contests, pageants, etc., for young people.
(d) Plan and help promote a program of religious education in every Local Church.
(e) To see that reports are made to the General Board of Christian Education on forms supplied by the Board for that purpose.

CHAPTER 9
THE QUARTERLY CONFERENCE

¶ **252.** There shall be in each local charge a council of leaders of the local congregation, to be known as the Quarterly Conference, which shall have authority to supervise the official operation and oversee the ministry and membership of the local church as well as monitor the interests and claims of the Christian Methodist Episcopal Church in the local church.

¶ **252.1.** The presiding officer of the Quarterly Conference, without the privilege of vote, shall be the Presiding Elder. In the absence of the Presiding Elder, the Pastor shall preside, provided that, in the event there is no pastor, the Presiding Elder shall designate someone else to preside.

¶ **252.2.** The Quarterly Conference shall be composed of the Pastor-in-Charge, Local Preachers, Exhorters, Stewards, Stewardesses, Treasurer, Trustees of church property, and all other organizations authorized by the Church Conference.

¶ **252.3.** Sessions of the Quarterly Conference shall be held at least twice per year at such time as set by the Presiding Elder. Special or call sessions of the Quarterly Conference may be called by the Presiding Elder as occasion requires, provided that due notice of such sessions shall be given, that is, not less than ten (10) days, consisting of announcements from the pulpit on two (2) consecutive Sundays during worship services.

¶ **253.** The Quarterly Conference shall have authority as follows:

§1. To confirm the officers of the local church as required by the *Discipline*.

§2. To elect the Stewards, Stewardesses, the Recording Steward, Trustees of church property, Sunday Church School Superintendents, and members of the Board of Christian Education as specified by the *Discipline*.

§3. To confirm the President of the Women's Missionary Society.

§4. To authorize and approve all matters related to the purchase, sale, or the building and/or remodeling of or conveyance or leasing church properties.

§5. To approve any mortgages or other indebtedness of the local church and to empower with a resolution the persons who are to execute them.

§6. To license persons to exhort and to preach after examining them, and to renew such licenses annually.

§7. To recommend persons to the Annual Conference for Admission on Trial or Full Connection, where applicable.

§8. To recommend local preachers for ordination as local deacons and local elders.

§9. To hear complaints that have been registered according to the provisions of the *Discipline.*

§10. To hear and try appeals from rulings and interpretations of the laws of the church in accordance with the *Discipline.*

§11. To direct its secretary to send letters to the Presiding Bishop and the Presiding Elder detailing actions that have been taken for which the *Discipline* requires them to give written consent for the implementation of the actions or decisions.

§12. To certify the 'voting delegates' elected by the local Lay Council to the Connectional Lay Institute, the same to be submitted to the Annual Conference by the Presiding Elder.

§13. To certify the delegates elected from the local church to the Annual Conferences.

§14. To make inquiry into the spiritual, temporal, physical, and financial condition of the local church.

¶ **254.** The Quarterly Conference shall be the conference of record for the interests and claims of the Christian Methodist Episcopal Church in the local church and shall seek answers to the following questions:

1. What is the estimated salary, housing, pension, and other benefits provided for the pastor and the assistant pastor?

2. What were the Annual Conference Apportionments and the final settlement of the same, assessed the local church by the Joint Board of Finance of the Annual Conference for the previous conference year?

3. What were the Askings for the support of the District and Annual Conferences?

4. What real, personal, and mixed properties are held by the local church? How are such properties titled? Where are the deeds? Has the property been exempted from state and local taxes in accordance with the provisions of the state law?

5. What is the nature and amount of insurance being carried on the properties of the church? With what company is the insurance carried? What are the annual premiums? Are the premiums up-to-date? What is the expiration date?

6. Have the programs and ministries of the Annual Conference and the Christian Methodist Episcopal Church been promoted and supported?

7. What are the statistical data of the local congregation that are required by the Annual Conference and/or the *Discipline*?

¶ **255.** The order of business for the Quarterly Conference shall be as follows:

1. Devotional services.

2. Roll call.

3. Report from the pastor on the number and state of the Church, converts added, infants baptized, members added otherwise; deaths, expelled, withdrawn, lost otherwise; number of members at present and the spiritual state of officers.

4. Report from the Director of Christian Education on:

(a) Total program of religious education.

(b) Training classes.

(c) Other educational work.

5. Report from the General Superintendent of the Sunday Church School on the number and state of the Sunday Church School:

(a) Number of officers and teachers.

(b) Number of classes.

(c) Number of students on roll.

(d) Record of attendance for each Sunday.

(e) Number of pieces of literature used.

(f) Publishing House and/or other establishments whence literature, educational materials, audiovisual equipment, and supplies were purchased.

§6. Report from the following boards:

(a) Stewards.

(b) Stewardesses.

(c) Trustees of church property.

§7. Reports from auxiliaries of the church:

(a) Women 's Missionary Societies.

(b) Christian Youth Fellowship and Young Adult Council.

(c) Choirs.

(d) Ushers.

(e) Lay Activities Council.

(f) Commission on Membership and Evangelism.

§8. Stewardship Reports:

(a) What amount has been paid on bonded indebtedness?

    1. Amount of debt?

    2. Rate of interest?

    3. When incurred?

    4. Paid on principal?

    5. Paid on interest?

(b) What amount has been estimated by the Board of Stewards and Board of Stewardesses for the support of the pastor and his/her assistant for the current Annual Conference year?

(c) What were the apportionments from the Annual Conference on this charge for the preceding Annual Conference year and what was the final settlement of the same?

(d) What amount has been apportioned this charge by the Annual Conference Joint Board of Finance for the current Annual Conference year for:

    1. Salary and travel expense for the Presiding Elder?

    2. General Funds?

    3. Special Askings?

(e) What amount has been raised by this charge for the following Connectional interests:

    1. Education on Children s Day?

    2. Missions Beyond U.S.A. Sunday?

    3. Christian Education?

    4. General Board of Personnel Services?

    5. Connectional Hospital?

    6. Christian Youth Fellowship Day?

    7. Subscriptions to *The Christian Index*?

    8. Christian Ministry Sunday?

(f) What were the Askings for the support of the District and Annual Conferences?

§9. Insurance:

(a) What is the total amount and extent of coverage of insurance on the Church of this charge?

(b) What is the total amount and extent of coverage of insurance on the parsonage?

(c) What is the total amount and extent of coverage of other church properties?

(d) When do the current policies expire?

(e) When are the premiums due? Have they been paid?

(f) Is the church enrolled in the C.M.E. Church Group Fire and Casualty Insurance Plan?

¶ 256. Other Business:

    1. Are there any applications

        (a) For license to exhort?

        (b) For license to preach?

    2. Who are nominated to fill vacancies in the Board of Trustees?

    3. Have the General Rules been read?

    4. Is there a Church Register, and a Record of Church Conferences for each Church on the charge, and have they been faithfully kept?

    5. Are there any appeals from decisions made on interpretations of our laws?

    6. Are there any written complaints that have been properly registered?

    7. Have the exhorters and local preachers passed an examination of character, and have their licenses been renewed?

    8. Are there any applicants to be recommended to the Annual Conference for Admission on Trial into the Traveling Connection? Or for re-admittance?

    9. What local preachers are recommended to the Annual Conference for:

        (a) Local Deacons Orders?

        (b) Local Elders Orders?

    10. Who are nominated Stewards for the ensuing Conference year?

    11. Who is nominated Recording Steward?

    12. Who are nominated Stewardesses for the ensuing Conference year?

    13. Who is elected Church Treasurer?

    14. Who are nominated members of the Board of Christian Education?

    15. Who is appointed Director of Christian Education?

    16. Who is elected General Superintendent of the Sunday Church School ?

    17. Who are nominated Departmental Superintendents?

    18. Who is elected President of the Christian Youth Fellowship?

    19. Who is elected President of the Young Adult Council?

    20. Who is elected Chairperson of the Commission on Membership and Evangelism?

    21. Who is elected President of the Women's Missionary Society?

    22. Who is elected Lay Leader?

23. Who are elected president (s) of the church choir (s)?

24. Who is to be confirmed Chorister?

25. Who are the members of the Commission on Membership and Evangelism?

26. What are the statistics to be reported to the Annual Conference?

27. Who are the Gift Fund recipients in this charge? (Answers should include retired preachers, widows of the deceased ministers, who were in Full Connection before 1986, and their children under 18 years of age).

28. Is there any other business?

29. Where shall the next Quarterly Conference be held?

CHAPTER 10
CHURCH CONFERENCE

¶ **257.** All the members of the church shall come together once a month to hold a Church Conference. The Preacher in Charge shall preside. It may be held at any time most convenient for assembling the greatest number of members; but if on Sunday, it should not interfere with the morning public worship. (cf. *Articles of Incorporation* for age requirements for voting in official meetings).

¶ **258.** Annually, at the first meeting after the close of the Annual Conference, a secretary shall be elected to perform the following duties:

1. Keep a record of all proceedings.

2. Provide to the Quarterly Conference those statistics that are to be reported to the Annual Conference.

3. Be a member of the Quarterly Conference and shall attend its session.

¶ **259.** The roll of members shall be called at every meeting, unless otherwise ordered, and the Conference may strike off the names of any who, on account of removal or other causes, have been lost sight of for twelve months; provided, however, that if such member appears and claims membership, he or she may be restored by a vote of the meeting.

¶ **260.** The following is suggested as the general order of business for the Church Conference:

1. Receive reports from these leaders and organizations:

    (a) Preachers of their labors since the last meeting.

    (b) Class leaders.

    (c) Director of Christian Education.

    (d) Sunday Church School.

    (e) Christian Youth Fellowship.

    (f) Stewards.

    (g) Stewardesses.

    (h) Laymen's Activities Council.

    (i) Commission on Membership and Evangelism.

    (j) Young Adult Fellowship.

(k) Women's Missionary Society.

(l) From the Commission on Social Concerns.

2. Inquire into its expanded ministry and mission as follows:

(a) What is the number of the poor of the church?

(b) Have they been provided for?

(c) Is the church doing its duty for the cause of Mission and other church enterprises, and for the collections ordered by the Annual Conference?

(d) Is religious literature recommended by the CME Church circulated and read?

(e) Can the church extend its work by establishing additional prayer meetings, schools or in any other way?

(f) Can anything more be done to strengthen, and build up the church in the community, and to advance the cause of Christ?

3. Elect delegates to the District and Annual Conferences.

¶ 261. If the observance of this order of business is likely to protract the session beyond a reasonable limit, the president may, from time to time, select the most important matters and bring them forward.

¶ 262. Let the Church Conference be opened and closed with religious service, and conducted in a devout and prayerful spirit.

CHAPTER 11
THE OFFICAL BOARD

¶ **263.** There shall be in each charge an official body known as the Official Board.

¶ **263.1** The Official Board may be held weekly based on the demand of its duties and responsibilities, but shall be held monthly to carry on the business of the charge. The Pastor or his/her appointee shall preside.

¶ **264.** The membership of the Official Board shall be the Preacher-in-Charge; all Trustees; Stewards; Stewardesses; Church Treasurer; Secretary of the Church Conference; Class Leaders; the Presidents of the Women's Missionary Society, the Lay Council, the Choir(s), Usher Boards, Board of Christian Education, Young Adult Fellowship, Christian Youth Fellowship, and Presidents of other auxiliaries approved by the Quarterly Conference, Chairpersons of the Commission on Membership Evangelism, Director of Christian Education, Superintendents of the Sunday School, Exhorters and Local Preachers of that Charge.

¶ **265.** The following shall be the general order of business after the devotions and approval of minutes:
1. Are there any sick?
2. Any who require financial assistance?
3. Any members or families that need our special attention?
4. Any who walk disorderly and will not be reproved?
5. Any deliquent members who are not being visited regularly?
6. Any to be recommended for license to Exhort? Or for Local Preachers License?
7. Review of Ministries
    (a) Attendance in connection with the means of grace: Worship Services, Sunday Church School, Bible Study, and Prayer Meeting.
    (b) Attendance at Annual Programs, Organizational Meetings, District Conference, Annual Conference and Connectional Meetings.
    (c) Outreach Ministries such as food and clothing, shelter for homeless, AIDS programs, One Church-One School, etc.
    (d) Children, Youth, and Young Adult Ministries.
8. The Official Board may serve as a planning committee and a monitoring committee for ministries and mission.

PART III
MEANS OF GRACE

12. Public Worship

13. Order of Worship

14. Prayer Meetings

15. Class Meetings

16. Love Feasts

17. Children of the Church

CHAPTER 12
PUBLIC WORSHIP

¶ **300. Sunday Morning Worship.**The primary service of Public Worship in CME Churches, usually held on Sunday Morning, shall be conducted according to the prescribed Order of Worship (cf. ¶ 306) in the following manner:

§1. Let all services begin promptly at the hour appointed. The Ministers should give the example of punctuality in this matter.

§2. Let every person claiming to be a believer in God kneel or bow in silent prayer upon entering the pews.

§3. At the services during which the Sacraments are administered, any of the items of the Order of Public Worship may be omitted except singing, prayer, and the Apostolic Benediction.

§4. It is urged that the Minister earnestly request all of the people to join in the Public Worship of God; first by singing; second by prayer, in the scriptural attitude of kneeling, and by all repeating the Lord's Prayer in unison audibly.

§5. More effective singing shall be attempted by the following means:

(a) Choosing hymns that are properly suited for the occasion.

(b) Limiting the number of stanzas sung at one time.

(c) Suiting the tune to the words.

(d) Encouraging the members to learn to sing.

(e) Using the The CME Hymnal.

(f) Exhorting the congregation to participate in the singing.

§6. In order that there may be uniformity in the manner of conducting services in all CME Churches, so that any CME Minister visiting churches in any part of the Connection may know just what he/she is to do when conducting the services, it is especially urged that the prescribed services of worship be used. *The Book of Ritual and Aids to Worship* contains such services that are to be followed.

¶ **301. The Lord's Supper.** The Lord's Supper (cf. ¶118, *Articles of Religion*) shall be administered monthly, in every congregation where it is practical; where it is not, the Lord's Supper shall be administered every quarterly meeting. Let the service preceding the administration be so proportioned as to admit due time for this solemn ordinance.

¶ **302. The Lord's Prayer.** Let the *Lord's Prayer* be used on all occasions of public worship, at the conclusion of the first morning prayer or the pastoral prayer, either chanted or with the congregation repeating after the Minister.

¶ **303. The Benediction.** In dismissing the congregation, the *Apostolic Benediction* found in II Corinthians 13:14 is to be used. The benediction shall be pronounced with the congregation seated.

¶ **304. Occasional Services.** For the occasional and various special services and ceremonies of the church, e. g., Dedications, Ground Breaking, Mortgage Burnings, etc, appropriate rituals are in *The Book of Ritual and Aids to Worship,* the official book of ritual for the CME Church, which shall be used invariably in all of the offices for which it is prescribed.

CHAPTER 13
ORDER OF WORSHIP

¶ **305.** The order for public worship in the Christian Methodist Episcopal Church shall be as follows:

Prelude

Processional (with hymn)

Call to worship

Hymn of Praise

Affirmation of Faith (The Apostles' Creed)

Minister: Let us unite in this historic confession of the Christian faith:

Minister and People: *I believe in God the Father Almighty, Maker of heaven and earth; And in Jesus Christ His only Son, Our Lord, who was conceived by the Holy Spirit, born of the Virgin Mary, suffered under Pontius Pilate, was crucified, dead, and buried; the third day He rose from the dead, He ascended into heaven, and sitteth at the right hand of God the Father Almighty; from thence He shall come to judge the quick and the dead.*

I believe in the Holy Spirit, the holy catholic Church, the communion of saints, the forgiveness of sins, the resurrection of the body, and life everlasting. Amen.

Invocation

Anthem, Hymn, or Song

Scripture Readings

    Old Testament (or a Responsive Reading)

        Gloria Patri

    New Testament

Benevolent Offering

Announcements

Song

Pastoral Prayer

Lord's Prayer

Song

Announcements

Recognition of Visitors

Offering (with Offertory)

Hymn of Preparation

Sermon

Hymn of Invitation and Altar Prayer

Doxology

Benediction

CHAPTER 14
PRAYER MEETINGS

¶ **306.** Let the pastor hold prayer meeting, weekly, in every church where it is practical; and when the Pastor cannot attend, let Local Preachers, Exhorters, Class Leaders, and others be engaged by the Pastor to hold prayer meetings.

¶ **307.** Let the prayer meetings be held also at other places where there is a probability of enhancing the spiritual life of the church.

CHAPTER 15
CLASS MEETINGS

¶ **308.** Let the membership of every church, wherever it is practical, be divided into smaller companies called classes, according to their respective places of abode; and let the members be exhorted to attend the meetings of the same.

¶ **308.1.** Two or more classes may meet at the same time and place, at their own option and their leaders may alternate in conducting the exercises.

¶ **309.** The pastor shall visit every class once a quarter, and report its condition to the Quarterly Conference.

¶ **309.1.** General Class meeting shall be held as often as it is deemed expedient by the Pastor.

¶ **310.** In an effort to make Class Meetings more meaningful and effective the following is recommended for use:

(a) Change Class Leaders who are not functioning.

(b) Encourage the Leaders to meet each other's classes.

(c) Choose the more effective Leaders to visit and counsel with the classes that may be less effective.

CHAPTER 16
LOVE FEASTS

¶ **311.** Love Feasts shall be held quarterly or at such other times as the Preacher in Charge may consider expedient, with closed doors, to which none besides church members are to be admitted. Other serious persons may be admitted by the Pastor.

An Order of Service for Love Feast

1. Short devotional services.

2. A brief explanation of Love Feast, its purpose and objectives.

3. Short sermon by Pastor or someone designated by him/her.

4. After the message, the stewardesses come to the altar to pass the water in communion glasses which have been filled before the service and properly covered. The Pastor drinks the water first and then serves any other Minister present. Then the water is passed to everyone. They drink it; the glasses are then gathered and returned to the table.

5. Plain loaf bread which the Pastor breaks up into reasonably small pieces is then passed to each one. They take a reasonable amount into their left hand, then under direction of the Pastor the members pass and shake hands with their fellow members. Before they shake hands each person takes a small part of the bread out of the left hand with the right hand and puts this morsel in the left hand of a brother or sister. As they shake hands, some such salutation as, "May God bless you," "Peace be unto you," "I greet you in the name of Jesus," "Let us rejoice in the God of our salvation," etc., may be used.

6. After breaking of bread and the following of handshaking, each one returns to his place. Then follows short testimonies and singing of hymns.

7. This should be followed by a financial report from class leaders or the reports of any other money that may have been brought to the meeting.

8. Closing remarks. Doxology.

9. Benediction: And now may the blessings of God Almighty, Father, Son and Holy Spirit, be among you and abide with you now and ever more. Amen.

¶ **312.** Strangers are to be admitted with the utmost caution; and the same person no more than twice or thrice.

CHAPTER 17
CHILDREN OF THE CHURCH

¶ **313.** Let the minister diligently instruct and make clear to all parents to dedicate their children to the Lord in baptism as early as convenient.

¶ **313.1.** In pastoral visitations let the pastor pay special attention to the children; speak to them personally and kindly on practical Godliness, according to their capacity to learn, pray earnestly for them, and cause them to be faithfully instructed in the nature, design, privileges and obligations of their baptism.

¶ **313.2.** As soon as they understand the responsibilities involved in a public profession of faith in Christ, and give evidence of a sincere and earnest determination to discharge the same, let the pastor see that they be duly recognized as members of the church in accordance to the provisions of the *Discipline*.

¶ **313.3**. Let our Catechisms be used as extensively as possible, both in our Sunday Church Schools and families; and let the preachers faithfully urge upon parents and Sunday Church School teachers the great importance of instructing the children in the doctrine and duties of our holy religion.

¶ **313.4.** It shall be the duty of the pastors to form Bible Classes, wherever they can, for the instruction of older children and youth; and if necessary, appoint suitable leaders for this purpose.

PART IV
THE MINISTRY

18. Exhorters
19. The Call to Preach
20. Local Preachers
21. Admitting Preachers on Trial
22. Traveling Deacons
23. Traveling Elders
24. Admitting Into Full Connection
25. Receiving Ministers from
    Other Churches
26. Preachers in Charge
27. Chaplains
28. Presiding Elders
29. Bishops
30. The College of Bishops
31. Supernumerary Relations and
    Professional Care
32. Retired Preachers
33. Support of Preachers in Charge
34. Support of Presiding Elders
35. Support of Bishops and Widows
    of Bishops
36. Support of Retired Ministers and
    their Families

CHAPTER 18
EXHORTERS

¶ **401.** Directions concerning the licensing of persons to exhort are:

§1 The Quarterly Conference shall have authority to license proper persons to exhort, and to renew their license annually, when in its judgment, their gifts, grace and usefulness will warrant it.

§2. No persons shall be licensed to exhort without the recommendation of the church of which he or she is a member or of the Leaders Meeting or Official Board of the charge to which he or she belongs; nor shall any license be valid unless signed by the President of the Conference.

¶ **402.** It shall be the duties of Exhorters to:

§1. Hold meetings for prayer and exhortation whenever opportunity is afforded, subject to the direction of the Preacher in Charge.

§2. Exercise the functions of the office, without assuming those of a Preacher.

¶ **403.** Every Exhorter, by virtue of the office, shall be a member of the Quarterly Conference of the charge to which he or she belongs; but in all other respects the Exhorter shall be dealt with as a regular member of the church.

¶ **404.** When an Exhorter moves from one charge or enlarged charge to another, the Exhorter shall not be recognized as such unless he or she obtains a certificate of official character from the Presiding Elder of the District, or the Preacher to whose charge he or she belongs at the time of moving.

CHAPTER 19
THE CALL TO PREACH

¶ **405.** The following questions shall be asked of those who profess to be moved by the Holy Ghost to preach:

§1. Do they know God as a pardoning God? Have they the love of God abiding in them? Do they desire nothing but God? And are they holy in all manner of conversation?

§2. Have they gifts (as well as grace) for the work? Have they (in some tolerable degree) a clear, sound understanding, a right judgment in the things of God, a just conception of salvation by faith? Do they speak justly, readily, clearly?

§3. Have they fruit? Are they truly convinced of sin and converted to God by their preaching?

§4. As long as these three marks concur in any one, we believe such person is called of God to preach. These we receive as sufficient proof that said person is moved by the Holy Ghost.

§5. Women in the C.M.E. Church have "Full Clergy Rights" in accordance with all the rights and privileges afforded under the laws of our *Discipline*.

¶ **406.** The General Board of Christian Education, the C.M.E. Colleges, Phillips School of Theology and the Bishops of the Church, in conjunction with the Local Churches of the Connection, shall develop and implement more meaningful and effective enlistment, recruitment and training programs designed to create more incentive for young men and women to hear the voice of God calling them to Christian service and ministries. The responsibility of initiating and implementing the program shall be that of the General Board of Christian Education.

CHAPTER 20
LOCAL PREACHERS

Licentiate

¶ **407.** The following procedures and regulations shall govern the licensing of a person as a Local Preacher.

§1. A Local Preacher is a person who has a license to preach the Gospel issued by the Presiding Elder by authority of the Quarterly Conference of which charge the person is a member and in which charge the license is to be used under the supervision of the Pastor in charge.

§2. A Local Preacher maintains a lay member status in the local church and in that status is eligible to hold local church offices and represent the local church as a delegate to District and Annual Conferences in keeping with the lay status.

§3. The authority to license proper persons to preach the Gospel is with the Quarterly Conference. A *proper* person is one who is a member in good standing, that is, a member who has proved obedient to the *Discipline* of the Christian Methodist Episcopal Church, and is faithful in upholding the promise and vow of church membership by his or her prayers, presence, gifts, and service in the worship and work of Christ.

§4. The procedure for issuing a Local Preacher's license is as follows: The candidate must have been a member in good standing for at least one year of the church authorizing the license at the time the vote is taken by the Quarterly Conference; the candidate must be recommended to the Quarterly Conference through the Preacher in Charge; the candidate shall have been given an opportunity by the Preacher in Charge to publicly read the Word of God and to publicly expound on the Word of God from in front of the pulpit; the Quarterly Conference under the supervision of the Presiding Elder shall examine a candidate on the history, polity, doctrine and discipline of the C.M.E. Church; if the Quarterly Conference is satisfied that the candidate is a proper person to receive a license as a Local Preacher, it will show the same by its vote; after an affirmative majority vote by ballot, the Presiding Elder shall issue a local Preacher's license to the preacher which shall be signed by the Presiding Elder and the Secretary of the Quarterly Conference.

§5. The license of a Local Preacher shall be valid for a maximum of one year, at the end of which the license must be renewed; provided the Quarterly Conference in its judgment holds that the gifts, grace and usefulness of a Local Preacher warrant the renewal of his or her license. Without renewal, the license is invalid immediately.

¶ **408.** The following shall be the duties of a Local Preacher.

§1. To assist, upon request, the Preacher in Charge of the pastoral appointment in which the Local Preacher holds membership.

§2. To attend services of corporate worship, Love Feast and Prayer Meeting.

§3. To subscribe annually to *The Christian Index.*

§4. To attend sessions of the Official Board, Church, Quarterly and District Conferences.

§5. To serve on Committees of Investigation involving other Local Preachers.

§6. To form new congregations when authorized by his or her Pastor. In doing so, the names of persons who are candidates for church membership shall be recorded and if expedient such persons may be received into the church as probationary members. However, a congregation formed in this manner along with candidates for church membership and probationary members shall be reported to the Preacher in Charge as soon as possible in order that these persons may be placed immediately under his or her pastoral care.

Local Deacon

¶ **409.** The provisions governing the meaning, procedures and requirements for Local Deacon:

§1. A Local Deacon is a Local Preacher who upon the recommendation of his or her Quarterly Conference was elected to orders by the Annual Conference and was ordained as a helper of the Elder by a Bishop in an Annual Conference. The Deacon is ordained for service in the local charge of his or her membership under the supervision of the Preacher in Charge.

§2. A Local Preacher shall be eligible for the office of a Deacon after he or she has received a regular license and has preached for two years.

§3. A Local Preacher shall not be ordained a Local Deacon by a Bishop in an Annual Conference in session without the Local Preacher having received a written recommendation from the Quarterly Conference. The recommendation shall be signed by the Secretary and the President of the Quarterly Conference.

§4. Only after a Local Preacher has been ordained a Local Deacon shall he or she wear a clerical shirt and collar or other such vestments.

Local Elder

¶ **410.** The provisions governing the meaning, procedures, and requirements for Local Elder.

§ 1. A Local Elder is a Local Preacher who has met the requirements for the order of Elder in the Church of Christ and has received authority to preach the Word and administer the sacraments in the congregation by the Laying on of Hands of a Bishop and other Elders in an Annual Conference.

§2. A Local Deacon shall be eligible for the office of Local Elder after he or she has preached two years from the time of being ordained Deacon.

§3. A Local Deacon before being ordained Local Elder must get a recommendation for election to the office of Local Elder from the Quarterly Conference to the Annual Conference. It must be signed by the President and Secretary of the Quarterly Conference.

§4. The recommendation of the Quarterly Conference shall be the consequence of the Local Deacon having taken and passed a written examination on Methodist doctrine, and the *Discipline* of the C.M.E Church and a verbal examination on the understanding of the meaning of ministry, the Local Deacon's goals and objectives and talents for the ordained ministry in the Local Church.

§5. The Local Deacon who has been recommended to the Annual Conference for the office of Local Elder must present also a note certifying his or her belief in and submission to the Doctrines and *Discipline* of the C.M.E. Church.

§6. **Exception to the two-year time requirement:** In the case of Missionaries and Supply Pastors, the two-year eligibility requirement (§2) may be waived at the discretion of the Presiding Bishop.

¶ **411.** The provisions governing the membership of the Licentiate, the Local Deacon, and the Local Elder; and the location of a Traveling Preacher.

§1. The name of each Licentiate, Local Deacon, and Local Elder shall be recorded in the Quarterly Conference Journal with appropriate dates showing when the Local License was issued and renewed, and the dates and places when orders were received. The Licentiate, Local Deacon, and Local Elder are members of the Quarterly Conference of the charge to which they belong as church members.

§2. A Licentiate, Local Deacon, or Local Elder may move or transfer local church membership from one local church to another. However, in order for a church member of any one of the three groups to transfer as a Licentiate, Local

Deacon or Local Elder from one C.M.E. Church to another C.M.E. Church, the person moving must get certification of his or her standing in the church from the Presiding Elder of the District or from the Preacher in charge of the congregation in which his or her membership is held. Without a letter of certification showing good standing, a Licentiate, Local Deacon or Local Elder shall not be received as such by another C.M.E. Church nor shall he or she function as a Local Preacher, Deacon, or Elder in the church to which membership has been moved until the matter of standing has been cleared and validated in writing.

§3. A Traveling Preacher may be located voluntarily or involuntarily by the Annual Conference. To be located means that the status of a Traveling Preacher has been changed to Local Preacher. A located Preacher is amenable to the Quarterly Conference of the charge he or she last filled until that Preacher presents the Certificate of Location to another Quarterly Conference.

Supply Pastor and Conference Evangelist

¶ **412.** The provisions governing the meaning and the amenability of Supply Pastors and Conference Evangelists.

§1. A Supply Pastor is a Preacher who has been assigned to a pastoral charge under the signature of a Bishop but serves without Annual Conference relations which require accepting an appointment.

§2. A Preacher used by a Bishop as a Supply Pastor whether a Local Preacher, ordained or unordained, Probationer, Superannuate, Supernumerate or a Preacher on loan from another Annual Conference, shall be amenable to the Annual Conference in which he or she works for the passing of character.

§3. A Conference Evangelist is a Preacher appointed by a Bishop in Annual Conference to the ministry of evangelism, whereby the Preacher travels about in the Annual Conference preaching the Gospel, teaching and planting new churches.

§4. A Conference Evangelist is amenable to the Annual Conference in which he or she serves for the passing of character.

CHAPTER 21
ADMITTING PREACHERS ON TRIAL

¶ **413.** The following regulations apply in Admitting Preachers on Trial:

§1. Being admitted on trial is preparatory to a Preacher being admitted into full connection. The trial aspect is in the fact that a Preacher may be admitted into full connection or rejected without doing the Preacher any harm. The trial is in experiencing being sent and in serving where a Preacher as a Probationer has been sent and in the annual evaluation of a preacher's fitness for the Traveling Connection or Ministry. A Preacher may discontinue the trial at his or her discretion.

§2. There shall be an Annual Conference Committee On Ministerial Examination of five to thirteen ministerial members in full connection appointed by the Presiding Bishop. The Committee appointed in the first session of the Annual Conference following the General Conference shall serve for four years except where the President of the Annual Conference regards a change as strengthening the Committee. It shall examine all ministers coming before it according to the *Discipline.*

§3. Preachers shall be admitted on trial by the vote of the ministers in full connection with the Annual Conference.

§4. A candidate for admission on trial shall meet the following requirements in order to be eligible for consideration for admission by the Annual Conference: (a) Have a recommendation for admission on trial from the Quarterly Conference; (b) Have documented evidence of having graduated from an accredited high school or have certified evidence of having passed the GED; (c) have passed an approved examination given by the Committee On Ministerial Examination on the Bishops' Course of Study; (d) have a birth certificate or other proof of age acceptable to the Committee On Examination; and (e) have held a valid license as Local Preacher in the C.M.E. for not less than one year.

¶ **414.** *Remaining On Trial:* A Preacher on Trial is required by *Discipline* to meet the Annual Conference yearly in order (a) to meet the Committee On Ministerial Examination; (b) to develop the appreciation and responsibility for attending the yearly meeting of the Annual Conference; and (c) to stay eligible for remaining on trial, except where an excuse for being absent is received and accepted by the Annual Conference.

CHAPTER 22
TRAVELING DEACONS

¶ **415.** A Traveling Deacon is a preacher who, having been Admitted on Trial or into Full Connection with an Annual Conference, has received the first ordination given by the CME Church, the order which consists of helping the Elder. The requirements and procedure for ordination to the Order of Traveling Deacon are as follows:

§1. Conference relations, either as a Preacher on Trial or a Preacher in Full Connection.

§2. One year in the regular itinerant work; except the Presiding Bishop may select a Preacher for missionary work and if the Annual Conference judges it expedient to do so, it may elect said Preacher to the Order with less than one year of regular itinerant work.

§3. Pass an approved examination on the Bishops' Course of Study.

§2. Recommendation to the Annual Conference for election to the Order by the Committee on Ministerial Examination.

§5. Election to the Order by a majority vote of the clergy members in the Annual Conference.

§6. Ordained by the laying on of the hands of the Presiding Bishop.

§7. After proper ordination as a Traveling Deacon, a Preacher on Trial in the Traveling Connection may wear appropriate clergy vestments.

¶ **416.** The dutes of a Traveling Deacon are to:

§1. Preach the Gospel and assist in the leadership of worship.

§2. Administer holy Baptism in the absence of an Elder.

§3. Assist the Elder in the administration of the Lord's Supper.

§4. Perform the rite of holy matrimony in the absence of an Elder.

§5. Bury the dead in the absence of an Elder.

§6. Execute the office of Deacon in the Church of God.

CHAPTER 23
TRAVELING ELDERS

¶ **417.** The Traveling Elder is a Preacher who is either on Trial in an Annual Conference or is in Full Connection as a member of an Annual Conference and has received ordination to the order of Elder with the laying on of hands by a Bishop and other Traveling Elders in an Annual Conference. The procedure and requirements for election and ordination are as follows:

§1. The time in office before a Traveling Deacon shall be eligible for election to the order of Elder is two years. Except in the case of missionaries, the Annual Conference may elect them to the order of Elder sooner than two years.

§2. The candidate for the order of Elder must (a) pass an approved examination upon the Course of Study prescribed by the Bishops and (b) be recommended by the Committee on Ministerial Examination before a vote to elect to orders by the Annual Conference is taken.

§3.The Traveling Elder shall be constituted by the election to Elder by a majority of the clergy in Full Connection of the Annual Conference and by the laying on of the hands of a Bishop and some of the Traveling Elders present in the conference.

¶ **418.** The two-year time requirement for a traveling Deacon to be eligible for the order of Elder begins to be met on the date of election to the order of Deacon. If a Deacon-elect is not ordained because of the absence of a Bishop, eligibility for election to the Order of Elder shall run from the time of his/her election to the order of Deacon.

¶ **419.** A Traveling Elder shall have authority to:

§1. Preach the Word of God.

§2. Conduct all parts of Divine Worship.

§3. Administer the Holy Sacraments of Baptism and the Lord's Supper.

§4. Perform the rite of Holy Matrimony.

§5. Bury the dead.

§6. Do all of the duties of a Traveling Preacher.

CHAPTER 24
ADMITTING INTO FULL CONNECTION

¶ **420.** Full Connection is the historic term for the itinerancy of the Christian Methodist Episcopal Church, a particular community of persons joined together by their mutual call to preach the Gospel of Jesus Christ and their common vow to be subject to the authority and Discipline of the Christian Methodist Episcopal Church.

¶ **420.1.** Admission into Full Connection is a privilege granted a preacher by an Annual Conference, and does not give a new preacher entering into Full Connection the right or guarantee to a pastoral appointment, nor places any obligation on the Annual Conference, Presiding Bishop, or the Christian Methodist Episcopal Church to provide any pastoral appointment for any preacher thusly admitted; except, those preachers in Full Connection, who are currently serving pastoral appointments, and any preacher who will have served ten (10) years or more, will be offered pastoral appointments anywhere in the Christian Methodist Episcopal Church (cf. ¶ 213, §3(b), ¶ 901).

¶ **420.2.** The requirements for a Preacher being admitted to full membership in the Traveling Connection is as follows:

§1. A Preacher must have been employed two consecutive years as a Traveling Preacher on appointment by a Bishop.

§2. Proof, documented by credentials or by letter from an accepted college, showing that at least two years of college work has been completed. In lieu of two years of college work an equivalent may be established provided it involves actual classroom experience acceptable to our church in doctrine and polity.

§3. A passing score must have been made on an approved examination upon the Bishops' Course of Study.

§4. The Committee on Ministerial Examination must recommend a candidate before a vote can be taken by the Annual Conference.

§6. A missionary, employed on a foreign mission field, may be admitted into Full Connection, if recommended by the superintendent of the mission where he or she labors, without being present at the Annual Conference.

¶ **420.3.** The method to be used in admitting Preachers into Full Connection at the Conference is as follows:

§1. After solemn fasting and prayer, every person proposed shall then be asked, in the presence of the Conference, the following questions (with any others that may be thought necessary).

(a) Have you faith in Christ?

(b) Are you going on to perfection? Are you groaning after it?

(c) Are you resolving to devote yourself wholly to God's work?

(d) Are you willing to conform to the *Discipline* of the church?

(e) Will you diligently instruct the children in every place?

(f) Will you visit from house to house?

(g) Will you recommend fasting or abstinence, both by precept and example?

(h) Will you especially observe the following directions?

1. Be diligent. Never be unemployed. Never trifle away time; neither spend any more time at any place than is strictly necessary.

2. Be punctual. Do everything exactly on time. And do not mend our rules, but keep them; not for wrath, but for conscience sake.

3. Act in all things not according to your own will but as a son or daughter of the Gospel. It is, therefore, your duty to employ your time in the manner which we direct:

a) In preaching.

b) In meeting the classes.

c) In visiting from house to house and, especially, the sick.

d) In reading, meditation and prayer.

§2. If the candidates give satisfactory answers to these questions, the Conference, by a majority vote, may admit them into Full Connection.

¶ **420.4** When a clergy person with membership in the Christian Methodist Episcopal Church either establishes a congregation or a denomination outside of the Christian Methodist Episcopal Church, except in cases where associate membership is officially recognized by *The Book of Discipline* or by General Conference action, the clergy person shall be considered to have withdrawn from the Christian Methodist Episcopal Church. The name of the person who so acts shall be removed from the roll of the conference(s) of which he or she is a member. The individuals shall be required to surrender clergy credentials or the church shall act to retrieve them.

CHAPTER 25
RECEIVING MINISTERS FROM OTHER CHURCHES

¶ **421.** Ministers coming to the Christian Methodist Episcopal Church from other Christian churches may be received into the ordained ministry of the traveling connection, provided they are in good standing in their church; they present suitable credentials to the Committee on Ministerial Examination; give assurance of their faith; give evidence of their Christian experience; give evidence by written and oral examination of their agreement with C.M.E. Church *Discipline*, doctrine, and polity; and give suitable evidence of meeting the education requirement for admission into Full Connection.

The procedure for receiving preachers from other Christian churches into the ordained ministry of the Christian Methodist Episcopal Church is as follows:

§1. The Quarterly Conference may receive them as Local Preachers provided they have completed an accredited high school or have passed the General Education Development (GED) test and meet the above stated requirements. However, they shall not exercise the authority of their orders, neither Deacon nor Elder, until their orders have been recognized by the Annual Conference.

§2. Ordained ministers, Deacons and Elders, who have been received by a Quarterly Conference as Local Preachers may have their orders recognized as Local Deacon or as Local Elder. To do so, the Quarterly Conference must vote to request recognition from the Annual Conference. On recommendation of the Committee on Ministerial Examination, the Annual Conference, by vote of its ministerial members in Full Connection may recognize their ordination. The level of recognition of a Local Ordinand whether as a Deacon or as an Elder, shall be governed by the same rules that govern a Traveling Preacher from other churches. The Bishop may recognize such orders *ad interim*.

§3. Ministers seeking admission into an Annual Conference or credentials must first become a member of a Quarterly Conference. An examination and check of the credentials shall be performed by the Pastor in Charge and the findings reported in writing to the Quarterly Conference with the Presiding Elder present. If a minister's credentials are valid and the minister meets the requirements after an examination by the Quarterly Conference for Admission on Trial or for Full Connection, the Quarterly Conference may recommend to the Annual Conference that the minister be Admitted on Trial or be admitted into Full Connection.

§4. The Committee on Ministerial Examination after its examination of a candidate shall make its recommendation to the Annual Conference. The Committee may recommend that a minister be Admitted on Trial or it may recommend Full Connection for a minister based upon education and experience, gifts and grace, and the meeting of the one year membership in a Quarterly Conference of the C.M.E. Church. The Committee shall be governed in its recommendation relative to a minister's order being accepted in the C.M.E. Church by the following rules:

(a) The order must have been issued by an orthodox religious denomination of an historical Protestant tradition which theology is Trinitarian.

(b) The order must be original, and bear a signature and a seal.

(c) The authorizing body and the issuing officer must bear a name and a title commonly recognized in religious circles.

(d) The recognition of the order on face value whether Deacon or Elder shall be based upon the number of orders that the issuing denomination requires for its ministers to be fully in orders. Where Deacon and Elder are required and a minister is a Deacon he or she may be received as a Deacon. If the minister is an Elder, he or she may be recognized as an Elder without the reimposition of hands.

(e) Where one order is given to ministers by a denomination the minister may be received as an Elder by vote of the ministerial members of an Annual Conference provided the Committee on Ministerial Examination recommends it. Further, Full Connection may be voted for a Deacon or Elder after an examination of the candidate on doctrine, the *Discipline*, polity and an examination of his or her credentials if the Committee so recommends.

§5. When a minister from another Church has been received and Ministerial orders recognized, the Bishop presiding in the Annual Conference shall issue to the minister a signed and sealed certificate in the following words, viz. This is to certify that *(name of preacher)* has been admitted into *(name of Confereance)* Conference as a Traveling Preacher (or has been received as a Local Preacher in the *(name of local church)* C.M.E. Church), he/she having been ordained to the office of a Deacon (or Elder, as the case may be), according to the usages of the *(name of denomination)* Church, of which he/she has been a member and minister; and he/she is hereby authorized to exercise the functions pertaining to this office in the Christian Methodist Episcopal Church so long as his/her life and conversation are such as become the Gospel of Christ. Given under my hand and seal, at this _____ day of _____ in the year of our Lord _____.

CHAPTER 26
PREACHERS IN CHARGE
AND ASSOCIATE MINISTERS

¶ **422.** The Preacher-in-Charge and Associate Minister(s) serve by appointment. The following are the duties of a Preacher who has been appointed pastor of a charge or an enlarged charge:

§1. To preach the gospel, administer the Holy Communion, to administer Baptism, to solemnize the rite of matrimony, to visit the sick, and bury the dead. In no case shall the Preacher in Charge administer Baptism or the Communion or perform the Marriage ceremony without proper ordination.

§2. To serve as Chief Administrator of the Local Church.

§3. To serve as the president of the corporation, as allowed by state law, when the local church to which he or she is appointed is incorporated (cf. ¶ 601-¶ 601.5).

§4. To be a counter-signatory on all bank accounts held in the name of the local church as he/she deems necessary.

§5. To direct the appointment of all the services in the charge assigned in the absence of the Bishop or Presiding Elder.

§6. To nominate members to the Quarterly Conference for positions in keeping with the *Discipline* and to provide for the training classes in keeping with positions for which they will be nominated. The training classes must be held and attended before persons are nominated (cf. ¶ 509.2; ¶ 509.3).

§7. To receive, try and expel members according to the provisions of the *Discipline*.

§8. To subscribe for *The Christian Index*.

§9. To hold Quarterly Conferences in the absence of the Presiding Elder.

§10. To hold a meeting of the class leaders and stewards of the charge once a week, if practical, to receive their reports.

§11. To report at each Quarterly Conference the names of all who have been received into the Church, and of all who have died, been removed, withdrawn, or been excluded from it during the preceding quarter and give a statement of the general condition of the charge or enlarged charge, and to give an account of the charge every quarter to the Presiding Elder.

§12. To see that reports are made at each session of the Quarterly Conference of the number and state of the Sunday Church School, Christian Youth Fellowship, and Women's Missionary Society, Lay Organizations, and that the report of the ministry for the year in the above named departments be sent to the fourth Quarterly Conference and Annual Conference.

§13. To keep or see that a roll be kept in which the residence of all the members shall be noted, wherever it may be necessary to facilitate pastoral visitation.

§14. To see that a register be kept in which shall be noted the names and addresses with the time and manner of the reception and disposal of every person belonging to the Church in his/her charge or enlarged charge, distinguishing between Local Elders, Deacons, Local Preachers, and lay members; and to report to the Annual Conference the number of each that may be under his or her charge at the time of its session.

§15. To see that a permanent record is kept of all baptisms and marriages within the bounds of the charge.

§16. To encourage all members in the charge to purchase, read and study the books, periodicals and other materials recommended by the CME Church.

§17. To leave his or her successor a particular account of the charge including an account of the subscribers for our periodicals.

§18. To promote all the interests of the Sunday Church Schools, Christian Youth Fellowship, Commission on Membership and Evangelism, Board of Social Concerns, Board of Missions, Board of Personnel Services, and the American Bible Society as the *Discipline* and Annual Conference may direct, and to report to the Annual Conference the amount raised in the charge during the year for these several claims.

§19. To see that a local Board of Christian Education is organized in each church, and that its duties are performed according to the *Discipline*.

§20. To furnish every one moving from the charge with a certificate in the following form:

CERTIFICATE OF TRANSFER

The bearer hereof, _____, is a member in good standing of the Christian Methodist Episcopal Church located in the _____ Annual Conference and hereby prayerfully commended to the _____ CME Church located _____.

---

§21. To attend all sessions of the Annual Conference unless providentially hindered and to report or to provide a report to be made on the charge or work assigned.

§22. To attend all sessions of the District Conference.

§23. To collect the General Funds quarterly with the assistance of the Official Board.

§24. To see that funds raised during Missions Beyond the U. S. A. Sunday are sent to the Presiding Bishop of the Tenth Episcopal District.

§25. To provide for the spiritual nurture and spiritual formation of all officers listed in ¶ 509.1, ¶509.2, and ¶509.3 of the *Discipline,* examine quarterly for progress, remove officers who refuse spiritual nurture and formation, and report the same to the Quarterly Conference when it meets.

§26. To obtain a designated number of Continuing Education (CE) units per conference year from an approved institution or course of study as determined by the Department of Christian Education in conjunction with the College of Bishops in order to maintain credentials for eligibility for pastoral appointments. Proof of attendance and completion of such units shall be a certificate and/or an affidavit from the attended institution/course.

¶ 422.1 Associate Ministers

§1. Associate Ministers may be assigned when a Quarterly Conference petitions the Annual Conference for the assignment of an Associate Minister.

§2. Associate Ministers assigned from the Annual Conference to a local charge shall be under the direct supervision of the Pastor-in-Charge.

§3. Associate Ministers may be deacons or elders and may be either probationers (Preachers on Trial) or have been admitted into Full Connection of an Annual Conference.

CHAPTER 27
CHAPLAINS

¶ 423. Chaplains Board

§1. The Chaplains Board shall be composed of at least one (1) active duty military chaplain; one (1) Veterans Administration chaplain; one (1) retired military chaplain; one (1) reserve chaplain; one (1) civilian pastor; and one (1) prison chaplain.

§2. The Chaplains Board shall assist the endorsing agent in informing chaplains of all official meetings and of their responsibilities to the C.M.E. Church.

§3. The endorsing agent shall convene the Chaplains Board annually.

¶ 423.1. Military chaplains shall:

§1. Submit quarterly reports to the Endorsing Agent and to the Coordinator of Chaplain Services.

§2. Attend and report to their respective Annual Conference, except when excused by the President of the Conference.

CHAPTER 28
PRESIDING ELDERS

¶ **424.** Duties of a Presiding Elder:

§1. Presiding Elders are Traveling Elders who have been appointed by the Presiding Bishop to supervise one of the Districts of the Annual Conference.

§2. It shall be the primary responsibility of the Presiding Elder to supervise:

(a) The preachers appointed pastors-in-charge of local congregations within the Annual Conference District to which he/she has been assigned.

(b) The local congregations within the District.

(c) The local preachers and local pastors within the District.

(d) Probationers who are candidates for the ministry in the Annual Conference, especially in directing and guiding them in the prescribed Courses of Study and encouraging them in the pursuit both of formal theological study and in Continuing Education.

§3. The Presiding Elder shall serve as the official liaison between the Annual Conference and the local congregations within the District, and as such shall have authority to:

(a) Preside over the Quarterly Conferences of local congregations.

(b) License persons to preach and renew local preachers license in accordance with the *Discipline.*

(c) Decide, in accordance with the *Discipline*, all questions of law and disciplinary procedure which may arise in the Quarterly Conference.

(d) Advise, approve, and, where required by law and Discipline, represent the interest of the C.M.E. Church in transactions related to the purchase, sale, and encumbrances of the property of local congregation.

(e) Confirm the elected officers of local congregations and delegates elected to the Annual Conference as required by the *Discipline.*

(f) Receive, receipt, and forward to the Annual Conference treasurer all Connectional funds, Annual Conference Claims and any other funds that may be reported by pastors, local congregations, and other agencies or persons within the District as directed by the Presiding Bishop and/or the Annual Conference Joint Board of Finance.

(g) Receive, verify, and report statistical data from local congregations as may be required by the *Discipline* and/or the Presiding Bishop.

§4. It shall be the duty of the Presiding Elder to promote within the District all Connectional and Annual Conference ministries and programs as required by the *Discipline* and directed by the Presiding Bishop, in the fulfillment of these duties the Presiding Elder may:

(a) Call together the pastors, local preachers, lay members and youth of the District in conferences, conventions, or convocations for worship, preaching, training, and fellowship.

(b) In accordance with the departments of the Annual Conference, promote workshops, retreats, special training sessions, seminars, etc. in specific areas and different zones within the District to enhance the ministries of Christian Education, Evangelism, Social Concerns, and Missions.

§5. The salary, housing, and travel expenses of the Presiding Elder shall be estimated by the Joint Board of Finance of the Annual Conference and paid from the funds of the Annual Conference. Funds generated from programs within and in the name of the District that may from time to time be received by the Presiding Elder shall be monitored by and subject to the authority of the Annual Conference Joint Board of Finance and may be taken into account when the expenses of the Presiding Elder are estimated.

§6. The Presiding Elder shall be subject to the *Discipline* of the C.M.E. Church and responsible directly to the Presiding Bishop.

§7. Upon being appointed, Presiding Elders are to receive initially at least two weeks specialty training. Time for In-Service training for all Presiding Elders is to be allocated at the C.M.E. Annual Convocation. The In-Service training during the Convocation shall be at the discretion and under the direction of the College of Bishops.

¶ 425. The Presiding Elder shall not have the power to employ a Preacher rejected by any Annual Conference's previous session unless liberty to do so under certain conditions has been granted.

¶ 425.1. The Presiding Elders' Conference shall have as its advisor and sponsor the Senior Bishop of the Church. It shall be part of the C.M.E. Convocation.

CHAPTER 29
THE BISHOPS OF THE CHURCH

¶ **426.** The following is the method for constituting a Bishop:

§1. A Bishop in the Christian Methodist Episcopal Church shall be constituted by the election of the General Conference and the laying on of hands of three Bishops or at least one Bishop and two Elders.

§2. The Bishop-Elect shall be required to furnish a birth certificate or satisfactory proof of age, before consecration to the Episcopacy.

¶ **427.** Should death and/or expulsion or other events result where there is no Bishop remaining in the Christian Methodist Episcopal Church, the General Conference shall elect a Bishop and the Elders or any three of them, who shall be appointed by the General Conference for that purpose, shall consecrate said Bishop-Elect according to the prescribed form of consecration.

¶ **428.** The following shall be the duties of a Bishop:

§1. To preside in the General and Annual Conferences.

§2. To fix the appointments of the Preachers in the Annual Conferences in accordance with these procedures:

(a) No preacher is to remain at the same charge or enlarged charge more than eight years successively, except where the Presiding Bishop thinks a longer term of service will promote the welfare of the charge.

(b) Any Preacher in the active itinerancy serving a pastoral charge, enlarged charge, or as Presiding Elder, shall, whenever practicable, be notified by the Presiding Elder or Presiding Bishop at least thirty days prior to the convening of the Annual Conference if a change in said pastoral assignment is contemplated; however, such notification may be less than thirty days if no change in the residence of the preacher will be required in order to serve the new assignment, or, if in the judgment of the Cabinet, such notification may prove harmful to the welfare of the church from which the preacher is being moved.

(c) Any Preacher who is to be transferred from the Annual Conference of which he/she is a member to an Annual Conference within the Episcopal District in which his/her Annual Conference is situated shall be consulted by the Presiding Bishop no less than sixty days prior to the convening of the Annual Conference from which the

Preacher is being transferred, provided that the sixty day notice may be waived if the preacher consents to the transfer.

(d) A Bishop shall not have authority to transfer a Preacher to an Annual Conference in another Episcopal District without the written consent of the Preacher and the written consent of the Presiding Bishop of the Annual Conference to which the transfer is to be made, provided, that the Bishop to whom the transfer is being made shall have communicated a request for the transfer of said Preacher at least sixty days prior to the convening of that Preacher's Annual Conference.

§3. To appoint Associate Ministers when petitioned to do so by a Quarterly Conference (cf. ¶ 422.1).

§4. To appoint a Preacher for a term of years to any seminary or institution of learning not under our supervision, when requested by an Annual Conference.

§5. To see that the Annual Conference Board of Christian Education is organized in each Conference and see that the duties of the Annual Conference Board of Christian Education are performed. To see that a Conference Director of Christian Education is elected according to the By-laws of the General Board of Christian Education.

§6. To have authority to appoint an agent or agents who shall travel and work in the interest of our literary institutions, when requested by an Annual Conference.

§7. To choose the Presiding Elders, fix their stations, and to change them when the Bishop judges it necessary, provided, however, that no Elder shall preside longer than eight years consecutively, except where the Presiding Bishop thinks a longer term will be necessary for the welfare of the District; nor shall the person be reappointed to a District until he or she has served at least two years in the pastorate or otherwise. (Mission fields excepted.)

§8. To change, receive, and suspend Preachers in the interval of the Conferences, as necessity may require, and as the *Discipline* directs.

§9. To consecrate Bishops, ordain Elders and Deacons; to see that the names of persons ordained be entered on the Journals of the Conference.

§10. To decide all questions of law arising in the regular business of an Annual Conference; provided, such questions be presented in writing, and the decisions are recorded on the Journals of the Conference. When the Bishop shall have decided a question of law, the Conference shall have the right to determine how far the law thus decided or interpreted is applicable to the case pending. An Annual Conference shall have the right to appeal from such a decision to the Judicial Council, which decision in such cases shall be final. And no Episcopal decision shall be authoritative except in the case pending, nor shall any such be published until it shall have been affirmed by the Judicial Council at the next meeting to be held by them. Such decisions, when affirmed by the Council, shall be recorded in a permanent form, and published in such manner as the General Conference shall determine; and when so affirmed, recorded, and published, they shall be authoritative interpretations or constructions of the law.

§11. To hear and decide appeals of the Quarterly Conference on questions of law, when presiding in any Annual Conference; and the question contained in the appeal, together with the Bishop's decision, shall be recorded on the Journal of the Annual Conference.

§12 . To see that the Presiding Elders' Districts be formed; provided that each District shall contain twelve (12) self-supporting charges, except Districts in mission sections of Annual Conferences and Mission Conferences. A Mission is a charge having less than fifty members. The Districts shall be arranged according to this law at the first session of each Annual Conference following the General Conference.

§13. To unite two or more charges or enlarged charges together, for Quarterly Conference purposes, allowing the financial interests and pastoral duties of each to remain separate and independent; and to divide an enlarged charge into two or more when it is deemed necessary.

§14. To spend at least six months annually, from charge to charge, in traveling throughout the Episcopal District, in order to preach, and to oversee the spiritual and temporal affairs of the Church.

§15. To organize Annual Conferences in the interval of the General Conference when, in his judgment, it seems wise to do so, and to see that delegates are elected from such Conferences to the General Conference according to the provision of the Second Restrictive Rule.

§16. To see to it that all the Journals in their Episcopal Districts are properly signed after each session of the Annual Conference and that said Journals and a copy of the audit made by the Certified Public Accountant be forwarded to the seat of the General Conference. To see to it that all statistics are properly entered into the Journals before they affix their signatures.

§17. In conjunction with the Annual Conference Treasurer and the Joint Board of Finance to forward the General Funds collected to the General Secretary of Finance within thirty (30) days after receiving them.

§18. To make a written quadrennial report to the General Conference depicting a full account of the work accomplished in each of the respective Annual Conferences over which the Bishop has been assigned, said report shall be in accordance with ¶ 435.

¶ **429.** They shall appoint one of their number to preach the Quadrennial Sermon before the General Conference on the day of its opening.

¶ **430.** The Bishops in joint consultation with the Committee on Episcopacy shall divide the entire Church into permanent Episcopal Districts.

¶ **431.** The Bishops shall see to it that a policy on moral and ethical behavior for the Christian Methodist Episcopal Church be developed and implemented in accordance with the directives of the General Conference.

¶ **432.** The Committee on Episcopacy shall recommend the assignment of Bishops to their respective Districts after conferring with the College of Bishops for final action by the General Conference; provided, that no Bishop shall be recommended to the same District for more than eight years consecutively.

¶ **432.1.** However, when a Bishop has served a District exceptionally well, that Bishop may be returned for a longer period.

¶ **432.2.** The Committee on Episcopacy shall recommend how many Bishops shall be elected at any given General Conference.

¶ **432.3.** The Committee on Episcopacy shall, in joint consultation with the College of Bishops, determine over which Episcopal Districts the several Bishops shall preside. The General Conference shall have the final action.

¶ **432.4.** The Committee on Episcopacy shall, in joint consultation with the College of Bishops, determine the tenure of a Bishop in any Episcopal District.

¶ **432.5.** The Committee on Episcopacy shall receive, study, and approve the reports and referrals from Committees and Commissions of the several Bishops.

¶ **432.6.** Bishops shall be automatically retired, after the approval of their respective Quadrennial Reports, at the General Conference nearest their seventy-fourth birthday. Provided that any Bishop who has been in the itinerant services for ten (10) years or more, upon reaching the age of sixty-five (65) and upon expressing the desire to do so, may have the right of retirement.

¶ 432.7. The Committee on Episcopacy shall determine whether the characters of the several Bishops shall or shall not pass. If, however, the character of any one Bishop is questioned, the Christian Methodist Episcopal Church process shall be taken. Final action shall be taken by the General Conference.

¶ 432.8. Upon notification of the death of a Presiding Bishop, or certification by legal and/or medical officials of incapacitation, either physical or mental of an assigned Bishop, the Senior Bishop shall be in charge, immediately, of the Episcopal District thereby affected. If the death/incapacitation is of the Senior Bishop, the next bishop in line of seniority shall take charge immediately. The bishop shall freeze all accounts immediately and shall handle all business necessary until the Committee on Episcopacy shall have met to make an assignment.

¶ 433. No Bishop shall be treasurer or custodian of any Educational, General Church or Annual Conference monies.

¶ 433.1. A Bishop shall not raise or cause to be raised, collect or cause to be collected, or receive for personal use any public donation from any Annual Conference or Conferences in the Christian Methodist Episcopal Church.

¶ 433.2. No Bishop shall receive additional remuneration, honorarium, travel expense from an Annual Conference, a Church, Church related institution, Pastor, District, Presiding Elder or any official of the Conference or Church for visits, sermons or any service in the performance of Official duties in that Bishop's Episcopal District; nor may any member of the Bishop's family receive honoraria from any Annual Conference, District Conference, Church, Church-related institution, Minister or Church Official.

¶ 433.3. Bishops shall not be prohibited from receiving nor denied the privilege to receive unsolicited donations given by individual groups or local congregations.

¶ **434.** A Bishop shall be a member of the Board of Trustees of all C.M.E. schools and colleges located in the Episcopal District over which that Bishop presides.

¶ **435. Quadrennial Reports of Bishops.** In accordance with their responsibilities stated in ¶428, § 18, Bishops shall include the following in their quadrennial reports to the General Conference:

Section 1: The Numbering of God's People:

The number of local congregations in each Annual Conference.

The number of new local congregations started in each Annual Conference during the quadrennium.

The number of any congregations lost during the quadrennium by way of merger, atrophy or otherwise.

The total number of lay members in each Annual Conference during each year of the quadrennium.

The total number of members added to each Annual Conference by way of baptism, conversion, and otherwise for each year of the quadrennium.

The total number of members enrolled in Sunday Schools of each Annual Conference.

The total number of members of the Women's Missionary Societies and Lay Activity Councils for each year of the quadrennium.

Section II: The Ministry of God's Church

The number of active traveling preachers in each Annual Conference.

The number of preachers admitted into Full Connection in each Annual Conference during the quadrennium.

The number of preachers lost in each Annual Conference during the quadrennium by way of death, transfer or otherwise.

The level of academic attainment of the preachers in each Annual Conference.

Section III: Special Ministries, Programs and Projects

A narrative description of those ministries that exemplify plausible solutions to the problems plaguing the church.

Section IV: Stewardship and Fiscal Condition

Total amount of General Funds assessed and paid during each year of the quadrennium.

Total amount of General Funds paid during the current year of the General Conference. The fiscal condition of all Episcopal District properties including valuations and indebtness.

A current Auditor's Statement from each Annual Conference in the Episcopal District with recommendations.

The total amount raised in the Annual Conferences for each year of the quadrennium.

Section V: The State of Academic Institutions

A narrative reflecting the condition of the institution and a description of any liabilities that involve the Episcopal District.

Section VI: Challenges and Concerns

A narrative stating such from the Episcopal leader.

Retired and Retiring Bishops

¶ **436.** Bishops shall be automatically retired, after the approval of their respective Quadrennial Reports, at the General Conference nearest their seventy-fourth birthday. Provided that any Bishop who has been in the itinerant services for ten (10) years or more, upon reaching the age of sixty five (65) and upon expressing the desire to do so, may have the right of retirement.

¶ **436.1.** The seniority of said retiring Bishops shall be immediately passed on to the next Bishop in accordance with the ranks of their election.

§1. When Bishops are retired they shall be relieved of the responsibility of presiding over the daily sessions of the General Conference, except at intervals, when they may be requested by the Presiding Bishop at that day, or by the College of Bishops or the General Conference itself.

§2.During the sessions of the General Conference the newly retired Bishop(s) may, where necessary, perform the routine duties attendant to the administration of the delegation from the Annual Conference of the Episcopal District over which said retired Bishop(s) was presiding immediately prior to retirement.

CHAPTER 30
COLLEGE OF BISHOPS

¶ **437.** There shall be a College of Bishops composed of all the Bishops of the Christian Methodist Episcopal Church: provided, however, that bishops who are retired shall have full voice in all deliberations but without the privilege of vote.

¶ **437.1.** The College of Bishops shall meet in formal session at least twice per year to give general oversight and supervision to the spiritual and temporal work of the Christian Methodist Episcopal Church, and shall meet in such other sessions as deemed necessary to fulfill the duties and responsibilities assigned by the General Conference and/or the General Connectional Board or to address emergencies or other extenuating circumstances.

¶ **437.2.** The College of Bishops shall be the Executive Body of the Christian Methodist Episcopal Church with authority to speak and act for the Christian Methodist Church in the interim of the General Conference and the General Connectional Board.

¶ **437.3.** Unless otherwise specified by the General Conference or the General Connectional Board, the College of Bishops shall appoint all Connectional Commissions and Committees, and shall name persons to represent the C.M.E. Church where such representation is desirable, feasible, or required.

¶ **437.4.** The College of Bishops shall be responsible for keeping the Charter and The Articles of Incorporation of the C.M.E. Church, housed with the Board of Personnel Services, current.

¶ **437.5.** Unless otherwise directed by the General Conference the College of Bishops shall, upon advice of the Legal Counsel, make the legal decisions and take the steps necessary to preserve and protect the interests of the Christian Methodist Episcopal Church.

¶ **437.6.** The College of Bishops shall appoint one of the bishops to prepare and deliver, on their behalf, an Episcopal Address to each General Conference of the

Christian Methodist Episcopal Church. Said Address shall be given no later than the second day of the General Conference and before the report of the Committee on Credentials.

¶ 437.7. The College of Bishops shall appoint one of their number to deliver the Quadrennial Sermon before the General Conference on the day of its opening.

¶ 437.8. The College of Bishops shall be organized in such fashion as the bishops may desire.

¶ 437.9. The College of Bishops shall see to it that the financial reports are made of all Connectional meetings, that is, General Conference, the CME Convocation,Connectional Youth and Young Adult Conferences, and the Connectional Lay Council Institute. The College of Bishops shall cause the report to be made to the General Connectional Board Meeting immediately following the General Conference.

CHAPTER 31
SUPERNUMERARY RELATIONS AND PROFESSIONAL CARE

¶ **438.** The following are the regulations concerning Supernumerary Preachers:

§1. A Supernumerary Preacher is one who is so disabled by affliction as to be unable to preach constantly, but is willing to do any work in the ministry which the Bishop may direct, and he may be able to perform.

§2. A Supernumerary Preacher who refuses to attend to the work assigned him or her, unless in case of sickness or other unavoidable cause or causes, shall not be allowed to exercise the functions of his or her office, nor even to preach among us; nevertheless, the final determination of the case shall be with the Annual Conference of which the Preacher is a member, which shall have power to acquit, suspend, locate, or expel as the case may be.

¶ 438.1 Professional Health Services

§1. Any minister who is forced to resign from his/her position in the church as a result of serious personal and/or social problems shall be asked to accept professional help provided by a professional and/or agency that deals with that particular problem. Such minister shall not be reassigned until such time as the professional recommends.

§2. Each Annual Conference shall be encouraged to secure appropriate insurance coverage and/or other avenues needed to provide such services.

§3.Each Episcopal leader is urged to provide the organizational structure required to implement said services.

CHAPTER 32
RETIREMENT

¶ **439.** The following regulations shall govern persons retired and retiring:

§1. A Retired Preacher is one who has been retired from itinerant services in keeping with the law of the Christian Methodist Episcopal Church which governs retirement.

§2. Members of the Judicial Council, General Officers, Presiding Elders, Pastors and all other of the clergy rank shall be automatically retired at the Conference nearest their seventy-fourth (74) birthday; provided, that any Minister who has been in the itinerant service for ten (10) years or more, upon reaching the age of sixty-five (65) and upon expressing a desire to do so may have the right of retirement.

§3. No Ministers are otherwise eligible for retirement (superannuated), under this provision except in cases where the Annual Conference determines mental or physical disability which impairs him or her for further service in the itinerancy.

§4. When retirement occurs, either mandatory or elective, any and all offices held by the retiring individual, clergy or lay, are automatically affected, effectively vacated and subject to immediate or subsequent replacement.

¶ **439.1.** An honorably Retired Minister may be continued in service if it is considered to be in the best interest of the church; failure to accept responsibility beyond retirement (superannuation) shall in no wise be charged against the Minister.

¶ **439.2.** Retired Preachers, living out of the bounds of the Conference of which they are members, shall be held responsible to the Annual Conference within whose bounds they reside. Said Conference shall have the power to try and acquit, suspend or expel the respective Retired Preachers in the same manner as if they were members of said Conference; provided said Preachers may have the privilege of being officially transferred to the Conference in whose bounds they reside, if they desire and request the same.

¶ **440.** The preacher who refuses to attend an assigned work shall be dealt with as follows:

§1. No Deacon or Elder who ceases to travel without the consent of the Annual Conference, certified under the hand of the President of the Conference, except in case of sickness, disability, or other unavoidable circumstances shall, on any account, exercise the peculiar functions of his office, or even be allowed to preach among us; but the final determination in all such cases is with the Annual Conference.

§2. Nevertheless, in all the above mentioned cases of trial and conviction, an appeal to the Judicial Council shall be allowed, if the condemned person signifies to the President, or the Secretary of the Conference, his or her intention to appeal at the time of his condemnation; or at any time within two months thereafter.

CHAPTER 33
SUPPORT OF PREACHERS IN CHARGE

¶ **441.** Every Minister who by the rules and usages of the church is a claimant on its funds, shall as far as practicable, have such a claim estimated by those who are to pay it, or by an agent authorized to act for them.

¶ **441.1.** The compensation and traveling expenses of Pastors-in-Charge of charges or enlarged charges shall be estimated by their respective Stewards and Stewardesses in joint deliberations, with the Minister sitting in for consultation without a vote. Said estimated compensation and traveling expenses shall then be presented to the Local Church Conference of respective charge or enlarged charge for final approval. In cases of the compensation and traveling expenses of Preachers-in-Charge of congregations, the Bishops and Presiding Elders are urged to encourage the increased support of the ministry as much as possible.

¶ **441.2.** The *recommended minimum* salary for a full-time Pastor is Sixteen Thousand Dollars ($16,000). In addition, churches that are financially able are asked to give a cost of living increase annually.

¶ **441.3.** The moving expenses of a pastor, moving from one Charge to another, shall be shared by the local church and the Annual Conference when the need demands. The decision of need must be determined by representatives of the local church, the pastor, the presiding elder of the respective district, and the Presiding Bishop of the respective annual conference.

¶ **442.** The Stewards of an enlarged charge shall report to each church meeting the whole amount to be raised, and that part of it which each congregation is expected to pay. The Church Conference shall adopt its own method of raising the money.

¶ **442.1.** All pastors who meet the requirements to be considered full-time shall be allowed at least ten (10) days, exclusive of Saturday and Sunday, to pursue Continuing Education that will enhance their ministry. Pastors are encouraged to take advantage of the period for study and to enroll in an accredited program (cf. ¶ 1107.7)

The Board(s) of Stewards and the Board(s) of Stewardesses are to present a proposal for adequate financial provisions for the study time to the Church Conference for final action after joint deliberation with the Pastor.

CHAPTER 34
SUPPORT OF PRESIDING ELDERS

¶ **443.** The salary and traveling expenses of Presiding Elders shall be estimated by the Joint Board of Finance.

¶ **443.1.** The recommended minimum salary for Presiding Elders is Twenty-Two thousand dollars ($22,000), if an Annual Conference is able. The Joint Board of Finance will provide an annual cost of living increase.

§1. Each Annual Conference shall raise and report 12% of the Presiding Elder's salary to the CME Retirement Plan. The same to be reported to the Annual Conference Joint Board of Finance. The said 12% contributed shall be reported within 60 days to the General Board of Personnel Services to be credited to that person's Christian Methodist Episcopal Church Retirement Account, giving and receiving a receipt.

¶ **443.2.** The Presiding Elder's compensation shall be paid monthly by the Treasurer of the Annual Conference as allocated by the Joint Board of Finance.

¶ **443.3.** The Joint Board of Finance shall apportion the amount allowed the different pastoral charges of the District, whose Board(s) of Stewards shall add the sum, thus apportioned, to the amounts agreed upon to be raised for their Preachers, and its collection shall be provided for in the same way.

CHAPTER 35
SUPPORT OF BISHOPS AND THEIR WIDOWS

¶ **444.** A Bishop's salary and traveling expenses shall be estimated by the General Conference Committee on Finance and submitted to the General Conference for its approval. The approved sum shall be paid out of the General Funds by the Financial Secretary.

¶ **444.1.** The Financial Secretary shall pay each Bishop one-twelfth of the sum allowed per annum, monthly, according to the provision in the Connectional Budget.

¶ **444.2.** Those Bishops who are unable to do full work shall be paid the same amount and in the same way as those who are effective and actively engaged in the work.

¶ **444.3.** Those Bishops participating in the Retirement Plan, upon retirement, shall receive one-half the annual salary of an active Bishop to be paid in the following manner:

(a) The company shall pay according to the amount of retirement benefits purchased to the credit of the participant.

(b) The Financial Secretary of the C.M.E. Church shall pay the difference between the amount paid by the company and the one-half salary of an active Bishop.

¶ **444.4.** In case of the death of a Retired Bishop, the remainder of the salary for that year shall be paid to the widow.

¶ **444.5.** The Financial Secretary shall pay to the widow of a deceased Bishop in accordance with the budget of the General Conference per annum to be paid monthly as long as she remains a widow in good standing in the C.M.E. Church. If she should die leaving children under eighteen years old, they shall receive the allowance until they become of age.

CHAPTER 36
SUPPORT OF RETIRED MINISTERS
AND THEIR FAMILIES

¶ **445.** The distribution for the claimants shall accrue from the amount allocated in the Connectional Budget and from the net income of the operation of the Publishing Department; and interest accruing from Endowment (cf. ¶ 1035.3, "Gift Plan" and § 1039.1, "C.M.E. Retirement Plan").

PART V
DEFINITION AND ORGANIZATION OF THE LOCAL CHURCH

37. The Local Church
38. Church Officers, Boards, and Auxiliaries

Spiritual Expectations
Class Leaders
Stewards
Recording Steward
Stewardesses
Church Treasurer
Trustees
Board of Christian Education
Director
Sunday Church School
Christian Youth Fellowship
Young Adult Work
Commission on Membership
    and Evangelism
Women's Missionary Society
Department of Lay Ministry
Choirs and Personnel
Board of Ushers

39. Organizing a New Local Church

CHAPTER 37
THE LOCAL CHURCH

¶ 500. Definition. A Local Church is a congregation of faithful believers under the Lordship of Jesus the Christ. It is the redemptive fellowship in which God's Word is preached by those whom He has called, and where the Sacraments are duly administered, according to Christ's own appointment.

¶ 501. The Church exists under the authority and discipline of the Holy Spirit for the maintenance of Christian worship, fellowship and discipline, the nurture and building up in the faith of believers, the conversion of sinners and the world, and for witnessing so that societal structures may become just in order that the personhood of all peoples may be more fully realized according to the image of God in human beings. The Church exists in and for the world. At the Local Church level believers move from formal worship of God into the world where worship is witnessing through service to human beings.

¶ 502. The Local Church is a Connectional society of persons who have professed faith in Jesus the Christ as Savior and Lord, have been baptized, have assumed vows of membership in the Christian Methodist Episcopal Church, pledging to support the church by their prayers, presence, gifts, and service. It is an assembly of believers who meet for worship in response to the Word of God and go out into the world to witness to God and His Christ from the unit where there is primary encounter with the world.

¶503. A Pastoral Charge may consist of one church, or it may be an Enlarged Charge consisting of two or more autonomous churches placed under the same pastor. Each church of an Enlarged Charge shall elects its officers, have its Quarterly Conference, have the right to elect its delegates to the District and Annual Conferences.

¶ 504. The Inclusiveness of the Church. The Christian Methodist Episcopal Church (C.M.E.) cherishes its place in the universal Church which is the body of Christ and is devoted to acceptance of the Apostolic faith. Therefore, all persons without regard to race, color, national origin, or economic condition shall be eligible to attend its worship services, to participate in its programs, and when they take the appropriate vows to be admitted into its membership in any local church in the Christian Methodist Episcopal (C.M.E.) Connection (cf. *Constitution of the CME Church*, Article 4).

¶505. Membership. The membership of a local Christian Methodist Episcopal Church shall include all baptized persons who have come into full membership by confession of faith, or transfer of membership, and whose names have not been removed from the membership rolls by reason of death, transfer, withdrawal or removal for cause.

¶ 506. All persons seeking to be saved from their sins and sincerely desiring to be Christian in faith and practice are proper candidates for membership in the Christian Methodist Episcopal Church.

¶ 507. When such persons offer themselves for membership, it shall be the duty of the pastor, or a person appointed by the pastor:

§1. To lead them to commit themselves to Jesus Christ as Lord and Savior.

§2. To explain the meaning of the vows of baptism and church membership;of dedication and service.

§3. To instruct candidates in the meaning of the Christian faith, and the history, organization and teachings of the C.M.E. Church.

§4. To use the official training manual *"A Catechism For Members of the C.M.E. Church"* by Bishop Marshall Gilmore for instruction.

§5. To select lay persons to assist in instructing new members and encourage such persons to register for new member instructional courses that shall be offered by the Annual C.M.E. Convocation.

§6. The Department of Evangelism and Missions shall provide a course of study for enriching the lives of those who are seeking a greater spirituality as they become part of the new structure.

§7. The course of study will be jointly administered by the Departments of Evangelism, Missions and Christian Education.

¶ 508. A member in good standing of any local Christian Methodist Episcopal Church is a member of the total C.M.E. Connection.

¶ 508.1. If a member should show a lack of commitment and become slack in fulfilling the sacred vows of church membership, it shall be the responsibility of the local church, working through Class Leaders or Stewards or Stewardesses, to minister to that person in order that the person may reaffirm faith in Christ and the Church and return to a life of ministry and service.

¶ 508.2. Types of Church Membership

§1. *Preparatory membership* applies to all persons who are candidates for full membership but have not completed membership training and /or have completed it but have not had the membership vows administered.

§2. *Full membership* applies to persons who have been received into a local congregation by the pastor in charge. Reception may have been by:

(a) Letter or certificate of transfer of membership from another C.M.E. Church, in which instance membership vows would not be administered;

(b) Profession of faith, that is, persons having been previously baptized and held membership in another local church of a religious denomination which subscribes to belief in one God, Father, Son, and Holy Spirit; or

(c) Conversion, that is, persons who professed faith in Jesus Christ as Savior and Lord for the first time; the latter two having been instructed in membership classes, baptized where appropriate, and administered church vows.

§3. *Associate membership* is temporary and applies to persons who belong to a C.M.E. Church in one place but reside temporarily in a location different from the place where their home church is located and while living away they associate with a C.M.E. Church. Their associate membership shall be counted as a full member only in the home church. However, such persons may hold non-elective without vote office and may participate in the life and work of the church where associate membership is held. They shall be entitled to full pastoral oversight. The pastor shall notify the pastor of the person's home church of their association.

§4. *Affiliate membership* applies to persons of any other religious denomination who request membership while residing away from home, or persons who are members of one of the several denominations with which the C.M.E. Church shares "mutual recognition of members." As with Associate Members, Affiliate Members shall have the privilege of pastoral oversight and their home church pastors shall be notified of their affiliation.

¶ 508.3. Membership Rolls

§1. *Full Membership Roll.* Persons received into full membership shall be placed on the Full Membership Roll. Each entry shall include the name of each person, date received into membership, address, telephone number, date of birth, how received, baptismal date if a convert baptized by the receiving pastor, name of former church if received by transfer or on "Christian experience." All dispositions of members, deaths, transfer withdrawals and expulsions shall be recorded after the name of each person where applicable.

§2. *Cradle and Children's Roll.* Infants and small children who are baptized shall be placed on the Cradle and Children's Roll. Each entry shall include name, date of birth, parent(s) name, address, and baptismal date. This roll shall be used by pastors from time to time to notify parent(s) of their promise and responsibility toward their child or children regarding bringing them up in the Church and of teaching them the meaning of baptism. Also, it is to be used to remind parents of the need for these baptized children who are old enough to accept for themselves responsibility for church membership.

§3. *Preparatory Roll.* It shall consist of the names, addresses, telephone numbers and date of reception of persons who have not been received into full membership.

§4. *Delinquent Roll.* It shall include the names of members who willfully neglect the means of grace or fails to attend on the ordinances of the Church or support its institutions.

§5. *Associate and Affiliate Roll.* It shall include persons who hold these memberships.

CHAPTER 38
CHURCH OFFICERS, BOARDS AND AUXILIARIES

Spiritual Expectations

¶ **509.** God calls His people to various ministries. In the local congregation such ministries are fulfilled in positions of leadership. Each is vital to the church's effort to fulfill its mission as the body of Christ in every place. Accordingly, persons placed in positions of leadership should evidence the highest level of commitment to Christ and His Church by participation in public worship, Sunday Church School, opportunities for prayer and Bible study, and such spiritual disciplines as tithing of self and resources.

¶ **509.1.** Persons placed in positions of leadership in accordance with the *Discipline* should know and love Methodist doctrine and discipline. Church officers, in addition to being accountable to the Quarterly Conference, are accountable to the pastor who has the responsibility for their spiritual nurture and who shall examine each officer quarterly for progress based on the afore-mentioned expectations. Any officer failing to take part in the opportunity for means of spiritual growth shall be removed from office according to the *Discipline*.

¶ **509.2.** Each Presiding Elder shall develop or cause to be developed, and each Pastor shall implement, training classes for all persons who desire to hold an office in a local church. These classes shall be mandatory and shall be taken before officers are recommended by the pastor to the Quarterly Conference for confirmation.

¶ **509.3.** Continuing training classes, workshops, institutes, seminars and symposia shall be provided for church officers. The pastor in conjunction with the local Board of Christian Education or, in lieu of a Board, shall execute the training program.

¶ **509.4.** Lay person shall obtain a designated number of Continuing Education (CE) units per conference year in order to hold an office at the local, District or Annual Conference level.

Class Leaders

¶ **510.** Class Leaders shall be appointed by the pastor. One member from each Class shall be chosen by the pastor to serve as Class Leader.

¶ **510.1.** The moral and spiritual life of the Class Leader shall be as follows:

§1. Each of them shall be a person of sound judgment and truly devoted to God.

§2. Every one of them shall be carefully examined by the pastor at least once a quarter, concerning the method of leading the Class assigned.

¶ **510.2.** The duties of Class Leaders are:

§1. To see each person in his or her class at least once a week in order to inquire how his or her soul prospers; to advise, reprove, comfort, or exhort as occasion may require; to receive what he is willing to give toward the support of the pastor and for the relief of the poor.

§2. To meet the Ministers and the Stewards of the society once a week in order:

(a) To inform the Minister of any that are sick or of any that walk disorderly and will not be reproved.

(b) To report to the Stewards what they have received from the members of their several classes, provided, the Leaders collect class dues from each member.

Stewards

¶ 511. Election and accountability of Stewards:

§1. The Stewards shall be nominated by the Preacher in Charge to the Quarterly Conference, which reserves the authority to confirm or to reject the nominees.

§2. The Stewards are to be elected annually; each pastoral charge, or each church on an Enlarged charge, shall be entitled to one Steward for every thirty members; however, each may have at least seven Stewards.

§3. In the event that a merger of several charges is effected, the Stewards of those charges shall remain in office until the first Quarterly Conference elects a new Board of Stewards.

§4. Persons shall become stewards upon recommendation each year by the pastor and confirmation by the Quarterly Conference; provided that persons who are neither recommended nor confirmed shall not hold the office of steward; however, in the interim of the Quarterly Conference the pastor shall have the authority to name stewards *pro tempore*, subject to confirmation by the ensuing Quarterly Conference.

¶ 511.1. Stewards shall be:

§1. Persons of solid piety.

§2. Persons who both know and love the Methodist doctrine and discipline.

§3. Persons of good natural and acquired ability to transact the temporal business of the church.

¶ 511.2. It shall be the duty of the Stewards:

§1. To make, in conjunction with the Stewardesses, an estimate of appropriations for the pastor. The appropriations where practicable shall include salary, pension (C.M.E. Retirement Plan), travel allowance for automobile, travel expenses for meetings, housing (or housing allowance) and medical hospitalization insurance.

§2. To keep an accurate account of the money collected or other provisions made for the support of the ministry.

§3. To keep an accurate record of money spent by the church, for all purposes.

§4. To share their ministries with the needy and the distressed by seeking them out and by providing for them.

§5. To seek out the sick and to inform the pastor of those who are sick.

§6. To inform the pastor of the members who are disorderly, both as to who they are and what the charges are concerning them.

§7. To attend all official meetings of the church.

§8. To give advice, if asked, in planning the work of the church.

§9. To attend committees for the application of money to churches.

§10. To give counsel in matters of arbitration.

§11. To provide elements for the Lord's Supper.

§12. To appoint, in cases of necessity, persons to receive contributions for the support of the church, and to receive whatever amounts of money have been collected in order to report it to the appropriate Conference or Board of the church.

§13. To solicit and receive money quarterly, if necessary, and as a means for encouraging members to contribute, the Stewards may write letters to the members.

§14. To make a financial report to the Quarterly Conference so as to keep the members informed about the finances of the charge.

§15. To be a Standing Committee, where there is no parsonage, to provide housing for the pastor or to assist the pastor in locating houses personally.

§16. To provide for an educational paid leave for a full-time pastor in conjunction with the Stewardesses and in consultation with the pastor. A recommendation will be made to the Church Conference that it authorize and provide appropriate financial provisions for the same, which includes workshop, seminars, etc. (cf. ¶ 442.1)

§17. To elect their own chairperson, secretary and treasurer.

Recording Steward

¶ 512. The Recording Steward's election and duties shall be as follows:

§1. The Pastor shall nominate in the Quarterly Conference for Recording Steward one of the persons confirmed as a steward by the Quarterly Conference. Election shall require a majority vote of the Quarterly Conference.

§2. The Recording Steward shall preserve the records of the Quarterly Conference, where there is no office and/or storage for same.

§3. The Recording Steward shall make a quarterly financial report to the Quarterly Conference and an annual financial report of the income and expenditures of the charge of which he or she is a member. The annual financial report shall be made to the Joint Board of Finance of the Annual Conference.

§4. The Recording Steward shall apprise the pastor of the financial state of the church and provide him/her with written information or reports relative to the financial state when the pastor requests the same.

§5. The Recording Steward shall receive from the Treasurer copies of receipts and bank deposit slips and other related informational materials.

Stewardesses

¶ **513.** The number and election of Stewardesses shall be according to the following provisions:

§1. There shall be one or more Boards of Stewardesses in each Pastoral Charge.

§2. The Stewardesses shall be elected annually; each pastoral charge shall be entitled to one Stewardess for every thirty members; however each charge may have at least seven Stewardesses.

§3. The pastor shall nominate persons for the office of Stewardess to the Quarterly Conference for confirmation or rejection.

¶ **513.1.** The duties of Stewardesses are:

§1. To serve the table of the Lord.

§2. To serve the table of the poor.

§3. To serve the table of the ministry.

§4. To assist in collecting the General Funds.

§5. To assist in collecting the salaries of the Presiding Elder and the Pastor.

§6. To make, in conjunction with the Board of Stewards, an estimate of appropriations for the pastor. The appropriations where practicable shall include salary, pension (C.M.E. Retirement Plan), travel allowance for automobile, and travel expenses for meetings, housing (or housing allowance) and medical-hospitalization insurance.

§7. To provide for an educational paid leave for a full-time pastor in conjunction with the stewards and in consultation with the pastor. A recommendation will be made to the Church Conference that it authorize and provide appropriate financial provisions for the same, which includes workshops, seminars, etc. (cf. ¶ 442.1)

§8. To do other work as may be assigned to them by the pastor.

§9. To elect their own chairperson, secretary and treasurer.

Church Treasurer

¶ **514.** The Treasurer of the local church shall be elected by the Quarterly Conference. The pastor shall have the authority and right to select from among the general membership of the church a candidate for the office of Treasurer; and shall present the name of the member selected in a Quarterly Conference which has the authority and power to elect the Treasurer nominated by the Pastor.

¶ **514.1.** The duties of the Treasurer shall be:

§1. To receive all funds or monies collected by the local congregation through offerings, tithes, rallies, gifts, donations, conferences and bequests and turned over to the treasurer;

§2. To receive all funds or monies collected by local church organizations that are turned over to the Treasurer.

§3. To receipt from a receipt book all sources of all monies received.

§4. To deposit all monies received in a bank or savings and loan institution selected by the Church.

§5. To provide the Recording Steward with copies of receipts and deposit slips.

§6. To perform the duties normally related and associated with the office, provided they do not conflict with the duties of other offices or the *Discipline* of the C.M.E. Church, and such other duties as may be assigned by the Quarterly or Church Conference, the Official Board or the pastor.

Trustees

¶ **515.** The election of trustees:

§1. The pastor shall nominate persons to the Quarterly Conference for the office of trustee; provided, there is not a State or Territorial Law which prohibits or prevents this process. If there is not such a law or laws, this process shall prevail and the Quarterly Conference shall have the power of confirmation. Where there are State or Territorial Laws in conflict with the procedure, the civil laws shall prevail.

§2. The Presiding Elder shall, in the absence of a pastor, nominate persons for the office of trustee. The nominations shall be made to the Quarterly Conference, which may confirm or reject the nominee(s).

¶**515.1.** Regulations governing the eligibility, duties, limitations and removal of trustees:

§1. The minimum age for election to the office of a trustee shall be eighteen (18) years of age at the time of election.

§2. The nominees for the office of trustee shall be members of the C.M.E. Church.

§3. There shall be nine, seven, five or three trustees on a local church Board of Trustees.

§4. The vacancies occurring on the Board of Trustees for whatever reason shall be filled without delay.

§5. The trustees as a board shall hold all property, real, personal and mixed, owned by the charge; and other such property as may be committed to their keeping.

§6. The trustees shall make the property of the church to which they are trustees available and accessible to the pastor and other duly authorized ministers of the C.M.E. Church. Trustees shall neither prevent nor interfere with the pastor in the use of the property for religious services or other proper meetings which are recognized by the law and usage of the C.M.E. Church.

§7. The trustees shall be responsible to the Quarterly Conference which shall have the power to dismiss them or to remove them as individuals or as a Board, when dismissal or removal will serve the best interest of the C.M.E. Church.

§8. The trustees shall not obligate the Church financially without the consent of the Official Board, Church Conference and/or the Quarterly Conference subject to state law.

§9. No person who is a trustee shall be dismissed or removed while in joint security for money, unless such relief is given him /her as is demanded, or the creditor will accept.

§10. Failure to obey the orders of the Official Board, Church Conference, or Quarterly Conference shall mean automatic dismissal of an individual trustee or individuals or the whole Board of Trustees.

§11. The members of the Board of Trustees who are not re-elected by the Fourth Quarterly Conference are automatically removed from the Board and from acting further in such a capacity, except where state or territorial laws provide statutes to the contrary.

§12. The trustees shall present the following information to each Quarterly Conference:

(a) The number of churches and parsonages.

(b) The value of the churches and parsonages.

(c) The other property or properties held by the charge.

(d) The title(s) by which all of the above properties is/are held.

(e) The amount of income that is derived from properties; and the funds shall be reported and turned over to the Church Conference.

(f) The debts and how they were contracted.

(g) The amount of insurance on each piece of property and whether the insurance is limited or co-insured; the expiration date(s) of all insurance premiums; and the name of the company carrying the insurance.

§13. The Board of Trustees shall insure that all property of the local church is properly titled and held as follows:

(a) That titles or deeds of all new property purchased upon authorization of the Quarterly Conference, written approval of the Presiding Elder and the Presiding Bishop (cf. ¶ 602,3, § 1) for use by and for the C.M.E. Church, contain the proper trust clause, to wit:

In trust that said premises shall be kept, maintained and disposed of for the benefit of the Christian Methodist Episcopal Church and subject to the usages and the Discipline of the Christian Methodist Episcopal Church. This provision is solely for the benefit of the grantee and the grantor reserves no right or interest in said premises.

(b) That all deeds clearly show that property is held IN TRUST by the local church if incorporated, or, if unincorporated, by the local Board of Trustees who are elected from time to time, for use by the Christian Methodist Episcopal Church.

(c) That the local Board of Trustees shall have all existing deeds redrawn or rewritten where necessary to include the Trust Clause and clear wording showing that the property is held IN TRUST for the C.M.E. Connection by the local Board of Trustees who are duly elected from time to time according to the *Discipline* of the C.M.E. Church or by the local church if incorporated.

§14. The trustees shall elect their own chairperson, secretary and treasurer.

Local Board of Christian Education

¶ **516.** The Pastor and Quarterly Conference shall organize a Board of Christian Education each year.

§1. The Board shall consist of the pastor, who shall be ex-officio chairperson, the Director of Christian Education, the General Superintendent of the Sunday Church School, the President of the Youth Council and/or the President of the C.Y.F., the President of the Young Adult Council, the President of the Adult Council, a representative of the Missionary Society, Board of Stewards, Board of Trustees, Board of Stewardesses, other boards and auxiliaries as deemed necessary, and other youth (ages 17 and under) as practical. Representatives of Boards and auxiliaries should be elected by the respective organizations, nominated by the pastor, and elected by the Quarterly Conference.

§2. After election by the Quarterly Conference, the pastor shall call the members of the Board together for organization. The Board shall elect from its members a president, vice-president, secretary, and treasurer. It shall also elect chairpersons of the committees on Children's Ministry, Youth Ministry, Young Adult Ministry and Adult Ministry.

¶ 516.1. The Board of Christian Education shall have the following responsibilities:

§1. To develop and promote the program of Christian nurture of the church according to the needs of the local congregation and community, and in conjunction with the programs and policies of the General Department of Christian Education.

§2. To organize and administer the educational ministry and activities of the church including the Sunday Church School, Christian Youth Fellowship, Young Adult Council, Vacation Bible School, weekday schools, training classes for new members, Continuing education classes and institutes for church officers, boards and auxiliaries etc.

§3. To develop educational programs about the C.M.E. Church, its history, doctrine and polity.

§4. To organize and supervise the educational ministry of the church in four (4) age levels: Children's Division (Ages 1 to 11), Youth Division (ages 12 to 17), Young Adult Division (ages 18 to 35) and Adult division (ages 36 and above).

§5. To see that the Sunday Church School, Weekday Church School, Christian Youth Fellowship and other departments of the church utilize literature and curriculum materials issued or approved by the Department of Christian Education.

§6. To conduct, during the summer vacation period, a Vacation Bible School to provide Christian education programs for the children and youth of the church and community. A Superintendent appointed by the Director, approved by the pastor and confirmed by the Board shall be in charge.

§7. To sponsor Promotion Day in accordance with the plans of the General Department of Christian Education.

§8. To see that an effective ministry to the children of the church (ages 1 - 11) is provided.

§9. To be a resource for the educational ministry to Adult Work, provided by various groups, auxiliaries, organizations, and boards of the church.

§10. To see that Connectional Youth and Young Adult Week (beginning the last Sunday in January and ending the first Sunday in February) is observed.

§11. To see that Special days outlined in the *Discipline* are observed by the Sunday Church School.

§12. To organize a Committee on Scouting and, with the approval of the pastor, appoint a Scouting Coordinator.

§13. To prepare an appropriate budget for the educational ministry of the church in accordance with the total stewardship program of the church developed by the pastor and officers of the church.

§14. To see that the Sunday School and Christian Youth Fellowship observe the fourth Sunday in each month as Education Sunday, at which time an offering shall be taken for education. The offering should be sent to the General Department of Christian Education to be used for scholarship aid for C.M.E. college students according to the provisions of the *Discipline* and the Standing Committee on Christian Education.

¶516.2. The Board shall have authority to fill any office that may become vacant; and, upon the recommendation of the Director and/or pastor shall have authority to remove for cause any officer or other person to whom the Board has given responsibility within the educational program of the church.

Director of Christian Education

¶ 516.3. The Director of Christian Education shall be appointed by the Pastor and confirmed by the Quarterly Conference.

¶516.4 . The duties of the Director are as follows:

§1. Carry forward the policies and programs developed by the Board.

§2. Supervise the educational ministry of the Church in accordance with the *Discipline*.

§3. Make appropriate reports to the local church, pastor, Board of Christian Education and Quarterly Conference regarding the educational ministry of the church.

§4. Submit reports and information to the General Department of Christian Education as requested in accordance with the *Discipline*.

The Sunday Church School

¶ 517. There shall be in every church an organized Sunday Church School.

§1. The purpose of the Sunday Church School is to provide training for members of the church in the love and knowledge of God as revealed in Jesus Christ, in the meaning and understanding of the Bible as God's Word, and to help them grow in their Christian faith.

§2. The teaching ministry of the Sunday School shall be divided into the age categories of children, youth, young adults, and adults as designated by the General Department of Christian Education.

General Superintendent

¶517.1. The administrative officer of the Sunday Church School shall be a General Superintendent.

§1. The General Superintendent shall be nominated by the pastor, elected by the Board of Christian Education, and presented to the Quarterly Conference for confirmation.

§2. The Superintendent shall be under the supervision of the Director of the Board.

§3. The Superintendent shall hold meetings of teachers, committees, and other groups in the interest of the Sunday Church School.

§4. The Superintendent shall make a written report to the Quarterly Conference of the number and state of the Sunday School, and provide any information about the Sunday Church School required by the Annual Conference.

§5. The Superintendent shall report to the Board on the work of the Sunday Church School and carry out the decisions of the Board that affect and relate to the Sunday Church School.

§6. The Superintendent, in consultation with the pastor, shall nominate to the Quarterly Conference for confirmation Departmental Superintendents.

§7. The Superintendent shall report to the Director, the personnel, curriculum, facility, and material needs of the Sunday Church School as determined by the Departmental Superintendents.

¶ **517.2.** The Board of Christian Education, in cooperation with the pastor, shall elect officers and teachers of the Sunday Church School.

Christian Youth Fellowship

¶ **518.** There shall be a Christian Youth Fellowship Chapter in each Church.

§1. The purpose of the C.Y.F. is to train young people in Christian living, to enable them to enrich their lives through worship, Bible study, discussions, Christian service, and recreation; to help them solve personal and social problems in light of the life and teachings of Christ; to offer them opportunities for self-expression and exercise in the duties, functions and responsibilities of the church; and to provide opportunities for inter-action with other youth in facing social problems.

§2. The officers of the C.Y.F. shall be president, vice president, secretary, treasurer, and chaplain (See *C.Y.F. Organizational Guide* by the General Department of Christian Education for program and operation of the C.Y.F.).

Young Adult Work

¶ **519.** Young Adults are persons from the ages of 18 to 35.

§1. Ministry to young adults shall be carried out in those groups, auxiliaries, and organizations consisting of persons in that age category, including the Young Adult Fellowship, Young Adult Missionary Circle (Phyllis H. Bedford Circle), Young Adult Choir (s), Young Adult Usher Board (s), the Young Adult Division of the Sunday Church School, and other organizations established for that purpose.

§ 2. The Young Adult Fellowship may be divided into chronological age groupings such as 18-21 years of age, 22-25, and 26-30; or 18-25, 26-35; or any other groupings as determined feasible. For the purpose of ministry, it may be further divided according to social and cultural needs and interests.

§3. There may be established a Young Adult Council consisting of the officers of all Young Adult organizatons of the church.

(a) The Council shall coordinate all the activities of the Young Adult ministries.

(b) The officers of the Young Adult Council shall be president, vice-president, secretary, treasurer, and other officers deemed necessary. (See *Young Adult Council Manual* produced by the General Department of Christian Education for the program operations of Young Adults).

Commission on Membership
& Evangelism

¶ **520.** Each church shall have a Commission on Membership and Evangelism to work in cooperation with the pastor, Presiding Elder and District Director of Evangelism in spreading the "Good News" of Jesus Christ and enhance the spiritual life of the congregation.

¶ **520.1.** The Commission shall be composed of representatives of the various organizations of the church, including youth and young adults.

¶ **520.2.** The Commission should meet at least once per month.

¶ **520.3.** Officers to be elected are: chairperson, vice chairperson, recording secretary, corresponding secretary, and treasurer.

¶**520.4.** The Commission Chairperson, in consultation with the pastor, shall appoint the following committee chairpersons:
1. Prayer Committee.
2. Prospect Committee.
3. Visitation Evangelism Committee.
4. Membership Preparation and Assimilation Committee.
5. Attendance Committee.
6. Records Committee.

¶ **520.5.** Where more feasible, the six committees may be combined into three, and chairpersons be appointed accordingly.

¶ **520.6.** Committees should meet monthly, and the chairperson should report to the Commission the activities of the committee.

¶ **520.7.** The Commission shall plan its work at least one year in advance by establishing goals and special projects to be undertaken by the committees. Projects might include the following:

1. Plan "In His Presence" Meetings.
2. Organize Mid-Week Prayer Services.
3. Complete Prospect List of non-church members.
4. Make a community survey.
5. Update membership records.
6. Plan week of Visitation Evangelism.
7. Seek net increase of 10% in membership.
8. Organize Visitation Evangelism visits.
9. Organize classes for new members.
10. Reception or fellowship for new members.
11. Discover and enlist talent of new members.

The Women's Missionary Society

¶ **521.** There shall be in the Christian Methodist Episcopal Church a delegated body known as the Local Church Women's Missionary Society.

§1. There shall be in each local church only one (1) Women's Missionary Society;

§2. This body shall be organized and governed by a Constitution and By-laws in accordance with the Constitution and By-laws of the Women's Missionary Council as found in the Discipline of the Christian Methodist Episcopal Church.

¶ **521.1.** The purpose of the Local Church Women's Missionary Society shall be:

§1. To discover the mission and unity of the Women's Missionary Council.

§2. To make that mission and unity known at home and abroad.

§3. To encourage cooperation, fellowship, and mutual counsel concerning the spiritual life and religious activities of the Christian Church.

§4. To encourage the study of the Bible and to assist in spreading the Gospel.

§5. To study the needs of society in order to aid in the development of programs, people, processes, and resources that will enable the Local Church Women's Missionary Society to fulfill its mission. Such studies shall enable the Society to react cooperatively to the moral, ethical, and spiritual issues inherent in spreading the Gospel.

§6. To work closely with private and public institutions and agencies in the fulfillment of common goals, insofar as such cooperation is consistent with the

Constitution of the Women's Missionary Council.

¶ **521.2. Authority.** The Women's Missionary Society of the Local Church shall have the authority to:

§1. Recommend to the Annual Conference Women's Missionary Society By-laws in harmony with the *Discipline* of the Christian Methodist Episcopal Church.

§2. Elect its officers.

(a) The Executive Committee shall have the authority to remove any officer for a justifiable cause after due notice and hearing. Such action shall require joint consultation with the Pastor-in-Charge and two-thirds affirmative vote of the Executive Committee.

(b) Fill vacancies among the officers unless the Constitution states otherwise.

§3. Secure and administer funds for the support of all work under its charge.

§4. Be responsible for the training of the Society officers and members.

§5. Give to the members of the Christian Methodist Episcopal Church financial grants for educational purposes.

§6. Assume responsibility for the supervision of the missionary work of children, young adults, adults, and auxiliaries.

¶ **521.3 Organization**

§1. The organizational pattern of the Local Church Women's Missionary Society shall follow the pattern of the Women's Missionary Council.

§2. There shall be Circles in each Local Church Women's Missionary Society, wherever possible.

¶ **521.4** The President of the Women's Missionary Society shall be presented by the pastor to the Quarterly Conference for confirmation.

The duties of the President shall be to:

§1. Preside at meetings of the Society and at the Executive Committee meetings. She shall be a member of the Official Board, the Board of Christian Education, and the Quarterly Conference.

§2. Become personally acquainted with the members of the church and the community.

§3. Encourage the members of the Society to be active participants.

§4. Preside graciously and according to the *Newly Revised Robert's Rules of Order.*

§5. Keep the meeting moving, begin on time, and close on time.

§6. Visit Circles in local churches where there are some and cooperate with the pastor in carrying out the total program of the church.

§7. Call an Executive Committee meeting as often as is necessary to discuss and decide on plans for the advancement of the ministry.

§8. Make reports to the Quarterly Conference and the Church Conference to acquaint the officials of the church with the ministry of the Society.

§9. Make reports to the District President in all meetings of the Society.

Department of Lay Ministry

¶**522.** There shall be in each church a Department of Lay Ministry.

§1. The department shall be responsible for the program of lay ministry in the church in accordance with the objectives and structure outlined by the General Department of Lay Ministry. (cf. ¶1002.2 and ¶1135.5).

§2. Any member of the local CME Church who indicates a desire to do so may join the Department of Lay Ministry. Upon joining, such persons will be given a membership card.

§3. The department shall be under the direction of a Lay Leader elected by the Lay Department membership. The Local Lay Leader shall be a member of and subject to the Quarterly Conference. The Lay Leader shall preside at department meetings.

§4 The department membership shall elect the other officers.

§5.The department shall establish the local chapter of the Christian Methodist Men's Fellowship (cf.¶1135.2).

§6. The department shall submit a written report to the District Lay Department.

§7. The department must observe Connectional Lay Day.

§8. The membership of the Lay Department shall elect delegates to the Connectional Lay Institute.

Choirs and Personnel

¶**523.** In the worship of God, singing plays a prominent role (cf. ¶ 301, § 4 & 5; and Preface, *The CME Hymnal*, p.1). The regulations regarding church choirs and personnel are as follows:

§1. There shall be one or more choirs in every church as far as possible.

§2. There shall be a president of each choir who shall be a member of the C.M.E. Church.

§3. Each president of a choir elected by the choir must be presented by the pastor to the Quarterly Conference for confirmation or rejection.

§4. There shall be a church organist who shall be chosen from among the members of the C.M.E. Church. However, if a member of the C.M.E. Church cannot be obtained as organist, the pastor and officers may choose a person from any orthodox Christian church.

§5. In the event that the pastor and officers cannot agree on a person to serve as church organist, the pastor shall have the right to make the final decision regarding the employment of the organist.

§6. The chorister (Director of Music) must be chosen from among the members of the C.M.E. Church.

§7. The chorister must be a person of good character and must have knowledge of church music and the ability to direct the choir so as to get desired results.

§8. The chorister shall be presented by the pastor to the Quarterly Conference for confirmation or rejection.

Boards of Ushers

¶ **524.** The Boards of Ushers shall be regulated and governed in the following manner:

§1. There shall be organized in each church one or more boards of ushers.

§2. They shall elect their own officers. The president shall be a member of the Quarterly Conference.

§3 . The duties of the ushers shall be to admit people to the house of worship, attend to their comfort while they are therein, and perform any other duties assigned to them by the pastor and adhere to the usage of books on ushering that may be prescribed for use of the CME Church.

CHAPTER 39
ORGANIZING A NEW LOCAL CHURCH

¶ **525.** The procedure for organizing a new local church shall be as follows:

§ 1. A new church shall have the consent of the Presiding Bishop and the Bishop's Cabinet before it is established. The church shall be under the district administration of the Presiding Elder within whose district it is located. The Presiding Elder shall be the agent in charge of the project and shall be responsible for keeping the Bishop informed of the progress made in establishing the church.

§ 2. When the Presiding Elder receives information of persons interested in establishing a church, the Bishop shall be notified and the Presiding Elder shall meet at an appointed time with all interested persons.

§ 3. The Presiding Elder, acting as interim pastor, shall preside at the meeting and appoint a secretary. Following a period of worship, the Presiding Elder shall give opportunity for all interested persons to become members of "The proposed new C.M.E. Church of . . ." (The name of the city, town, or locality shall be used)

§ 4. The ritual for receiving members shall be used after the interested persons have been examined by the Presiding Elder as to the genuineness of their faith and purpose.

§ 5. The secretary shall compile a list of the persons who are received into the membership of the proposed church. All of those persons shall be members of the Constituting Church Conference. Except where prohibited by the Articles of Incorporation (See: Fourth Article), each member shall be entitled to a vote.

§ 6. The Constituting Church Conference shall be adjourned by the Chairperson and the Church Conference convened. A secretary shall be elected. A name of the church may be chosen by vote. The chairperson shall appoint temporary officers, trustees, stewards, stewardesses, and Sunday School Superintendent. Permanent officers shall not be elected until a pastor has been appointed by the Presiding Bishop and a Quarterly Conference convened. However, the pastor and the temporary officers shall constitute the membership of the Quarterly Conference.

§7. The Quarterly Conference shall take action on all matters related to property and, if necessary, incorporation.

§ 8. A new church organized according to these provisions shall be presented to the next session of the Annual Conference in whose bounds it is located for confirmation of its membership.

§ 9. A local church existing as an independent religious organization which expresses a written or verbal desire to unite officially with the C.M.E. Church: The Presiding Bishop and/or the Presiding Elder shall meet with the congregation in a meeting called for that purpose, the Presiding Bishop having been notified. If the members of the congregation affirm after introducing them to the beliefs, doctrine and polity of this denomination that they do accept them and will abide by them; and acknowledge their willingness to deed the property of the church according to the laws of the C.M.E. Church and to be governed by the *Discipline* of the C.M.E. Church, a formal vote shall be taken and recorded by the Secretary of the meeting.

§10. The Constituting Church Conference of the church shall proceed according to sections 4 - 6 above. If the pastor desires to become a member of the C.M.E. Church he or she must take membership vows the same as lay members. The credentials shall be recognized by the C.M.E. Church subject to the actions of the ensuing Annual Conference and in accordance with the *Discipline* of the C.M.E. Church. (For the Ordinal for Receiving a Church see *CME Book of Rituals*).

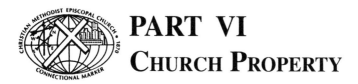

PART VI
CHURCH PROPERTY

**40. Incorporation of Local Churches
and Titles to Property**

**41. Episcopal Residences and
District Parsonages**

42. The Connectional Headquarters

43. Charitable Institutions

**44. Committee on Deeds, Titles,
and Abstracts**

CHAPTER 41
INCORPORATION OF LOCAL CHURCHES AND TITLES TO PROPERTY

¶ **601. Incorporation of Local Churches.** When so authorized and directed by the Quarterly Conference, the Board of Trustees of a Local Church shall immediately take and perform any and all necessary steps and actions to incorporate the Local Church under and in conformity with the laws of the County, State or like political unit in which it is located.

§1. The necessary articles shall be filed with proper governmental officials to secure a charter and any and all amendments thereto, that at any time may be contemplated, shall be submitted to the Presiding Bishop and the Presiding Elder of the Annual Conference and District having jurisdiction for their written approval as the conformity of the same with the provisions of the Discipline of the Christian Methodist Episcopal Church and shall contain the following provisions:

§2. The Corporation shall support the doctrine, and it and all its property, both real and personal, shall be subject to the laws, usages, ministerial appointments of the Christian Methodist Episcopal Church as are now or shall be from time to time established, made and declared by the lawful authority of the said Church.

§3. The Board of Directors of the Corporation shall be the Board of Trustees of the Local Church elected and organized as prescribed in the *Discipline* of the Christian Methodist Episcopal Church.

§4. When the local church is incorporated as provided herein, and as allowed by state law, the Pastor-in- Charge shall serve as president of the corporation,

¶ **601.1** Where local Churches were incorporated prior to the authorized incorporation of the Connection as a whole, they shall deed their property as required and set forth in the *Discipline*.

¶ **601.2.** The By-laws of the Corporation shall include the *Discipline* of the Christian Methodist Episcopal Church as from time to time enacted, authorized, and declared by the General Conference; and no other By-laws shall be adopted inconsistent with the provisions of the *Discipline*.

¶ **601.3.** The members of the Corporation shall be the members of the Quarterly

Conference or such other body of the Local Church as the local law may permit or require.

¶ 601.4. If for any reason the Corporation shall cease to exist as a legal entity and its charter shall expire or be terminated, the title to all the property, both real, mixed and personal, shall be vested in the Trustees of the Annual Conference; if the Annual Conference itself is unincorporated, in the same manner as it holds to any other real estate; or in the Annual Conference in its corporate name, if it is incorporated; and all such property shall be held, developed or disposed of by the Annual Conference within whose bounds it is located; provided, that in the event of sale, the money accruing therefrom shall be used to preserve and improve other real and personal local church properties.

¶ 601.5. Provisions as may be required by the local laws:

§1. The provisions of "The Church Board of Trustees" shall be applicable to all corporations formed hereunder as fully as to the same extent as is set forth and incorporated herein; provided, however, that Trustees and Board of Trustees shall be construed to be synonymous with Directors and Board of Directors as applied to corporations. In the event that the title of any property, real or personal, or a Local Church shall vest in the Trustees of the Annual Conference or its corporate body as a result of Corporation ceasing to exist, then and in that event the Board of Trustees of the Annual Conference, if the Annual Conference itself is unincorporated, or the Board of Directors of its corporate Body shall be and is hereby authorized and directed at the request of the Quarterly Conference of the Local Church to reconvey the title to Local Church property in such a manner as shall be requested by the Quarterly Conference with the approval of the Presiding Elder and the Presiding Bishop.

¶ 602. *All Titles in Trust.* The Christian Methodist Episcopal Church is organized and operates as a Connectional Structure. Titles to all properties held at General, Episcopal District, Annual, or District Conference levels, local churches, or an agency or institution of the church shall be held in trust for the Christian Methodist Episcopal Church and subject to the provisions of its *Discipline*. Titles not actually held by the General Conference of the Christian Methodist Episcopal Church, but instead are held in trust by local churches, Districts, Annual Conferences, Episcopal Districts, agencies or organizations of the denomination or unincorporated bodies of the denomination are held in trust by Boards of Trustees established for the purpose of holding or administering properties.

¶ **602.1.** *Use of the Denominational Name.* The words, "Christian Methodist Episcopal Church" or the "C.M.E. Church" or the denominational emblem are not to be used as, or as a part of a trade name, or trade mark, or as part of any business firm, or organization except by corporations or other business units created for the administration of work undertaken directly by the Christian Methodist Episcopal Church.

¶ 602.2. *Trust Clauses and Deeds*

§1. Except in conveyances which require that the real property conveyed shall revert to the grantor if and when its use as a place of Divine Worship has been terminated, all written instruments of conveyance by which premises are held or hereafter acquired for use as a place of Divine Worship for members of the Christian Methodist Episcopal Church or for other church activities shall contain the following trust clause: *In trust that said premises shall be used, kept and maintained as a place of Divine Worship of the Christian Methodist Episcopal Ministry and members of the Christian Methodist Episcopal Church; subject to the Discipline, usage, and ministerial appointments of said church as from time to time authorized and declared by the General Conference and by the Annual Conference within these bounds, the said premises are situated. This provision is solely for the benefit of the grantee, and the grantor reserves no right or interest in such premises.*

§2. All written instruments by which premises are held or hereafter acquired as a parsonage for the use or occupancy of the minister of the Christian Methodist Episcopal Church shall contain the following trust clause:

In trust that said premises shall be used as a place of residence for the use and occupancy of the ordained ministers of the Christian Methodist Episcopal Church who may from time to time be entitled to occupy the same by appointment; subject to the Discipline and usage of the Christian Methodist Episcopal Church, as from time to time authorized and declared by the General Conference and by the Annual Conference within whose bounds the said premises are situated. This provision is solely for the benefit of the grantee and the grantor reserves no right in said premises.

§3. In case the property so acquired is to be used for both a house of worship and a parsonage the provision of both trust clauses specified in (a and b) above shall be inserted in the conveyance.

§4. In case the property so acquired is not to be used exclusively for a place of worship or parsonage or both, all written instruments by which such premises are held or hereafter acquired shall contain the following trust clause:

In trust that said premises shall be kept, maintained and disposed of for the benefit of the Christian Methodist Episcopal Church and subject to the usages and the Disciplines of the Christian Methodist Episcopal Church. This provision is solely for the benefit of the grantee and the grantor reserves no right or interest in said premises.

§5. However, the absence of a trust clause stipulated in Article 9 (a, b, c, or d) below in deeds and conveyance previously executed shall in no way exclude a local church or church agency from or relieve it of its Connectional responsibilities to the Christian Methodist Episcopal Church. Nor shall it absolve a local congregation or church agency or Board of Trustees of its responsibility and accountability to the Christian Methodist Episcopal Church; provided that the intent and desires of the congregations or Boards of Trustees and/or later congregations or Boards of Trustees are shown by any or all of the following indications:

(a) The conveyance of the property to the trustees of a local church or agency of the Christian Methodist Episcopal Church.

(b) The use of the name, customs and polity of the Christian Methodist Episcopal Church in such a way as to be thus known to the community as a part of the Christian Methodist Episcopal Church.

(c) The acceptance of the pastorate of ordained ministers appointed by the Presiding Bishop, or use of the tax exempt privileges of the C.M.E. Church.

(d) Title to all properties of the local church, District or Annual Conference, Episcopal District, Departments, or agency of the church shall be held subject to the provisions of the Discipline, whether title to the same is taken in the name of the local church trustees, Episcopal District trustees, Departments, agencies or in the name of a corporation organized for the purpose, or otherwise.

¶ 602.3. *Restrictions Related to Church Property:* No church property shall be acquired, sold, transferred, conveyed, leased, or encumbered without the consent and approval of the appropriate authorities as herein set forth:

§1. No Local Church property, real or mixed, shall be acquired, sold, transferred, conveyed, leased, or otherwise financially encumbered, whether directly by lien or mortgage or indirectly through other financial/business transaction without prior consent of the Church Conference, Quarterly Conference and prior written approval and consent of the Presiding Elder and Presiding Bishop.

§2. No District or Annual Conference property shall be acquired, sold, transferred, conveyed, leased or encumbered without the consent of the District or Annual Conference Board of Trustees and written approval of the Presiding Elders and Presiding Bishop.

§3. No Episcopal District property shall be acquired, sold, transferred, conveyed, leased, or encumbered without the consent and written approval of the Board of Trustees and a majority of the Presiding Elders and the Presiding Bishop.

§4. No minister assigned by the Annual or General Conference in accordance with the *Discipline* shall be denied access and use of properties belonging to the C.M.E. Church in accordance with the *Discipline*.

¶ 602.4. *Authority to Bring Suit.* Any denominational unit authorized to hold title to property and to enforce trusts for the Benefit of the denomination, or the College of Bishops, may bring suit in its own name to protect the denominational interests. (This section does not conflict with ¶126, General Rules in that this has reference to the church as a legal entity.)

¶ 602.5. *Financial Obligations.* No local church, District or Annual Conference, General Department or their Administrative Officers, Presiding Elder or Bishop, agency or any other units except the General Conference or the College of Bishops by 2/3 majority vote can financially obligate the denomination.

¶ 602.6. *Discontinuation or Abandonment of Local Church Property.*

§1. When in the judgment of the Presiding Elder in consultation with the Official Board, the Church Conference and the Presiding Bishop that a local church has so declined in membership that it can no longer fulfill its mission and ministry, the Presiding Elder may recommend to the Annual Conference that the local church be discontinued. The recommendation shall include the reason for discontinuation and where the members should be transferred.

§2. When local church property(ies) is no longer used, kept, or maintained by its membership, the property shall be considered abandoned, and the Trustees of the Annual Conference in which the property is located shall assume control of the property.

¶ 603 *Rental of Parsonages*

§1. If the pastor lives in his or her own home or provides his or her place of residence, the rent from the parsonages designated for the preacher's residence shall be given to the Pastor; said rent shall not be counted as salary.

§2 Where a Church owns additional rent producing property or properties, said rent shall go to the Church and be used for the expenses of the Church.

¶ **604.** *Insurance on Church Property*

§1.The Board of Trustees of any and all property shall be required to insure such property being held by it, and to make annual reports of the insurance carried and the expiration date of each insurance policy (cf. ¶ 515.1 § 12 (g)).

§2. Subject to action by and the direction of local churches, Annual Conferences, and Episcopal Districts, incorporated and unincorporated, any and all real and personal property sufficient in value shall be insured with the C.M.E. Fire and Casualty Program.

CHAPTER 41
EPISCOPAL RESIDENCES AND
DISTRICT PARSONAGES

¶ **605.** When authorized by two-thirds of the Conferences comprising an Episcopal District, an Episcopal Residence for the Presiding Bishop may be acquired, which shall be titled to and be under the control of and management of Trustees of the Annual Conference within whose bounds the residence is located subject to approval of other Trustees of other Conferences in the Episcopal District area.

¶ **605.1.** The purchase price or the construction cost and maintenance cost thereof shall be equitably distributed by the Trustees among the several Conferences in the Episcopal District. Any such property so acquired shall not be sold or disposed of except with the consent of the majority of the Conferences in that Episcopal District and participate in the ownership. Should Annual Conferences contribute to the purchase of an Episcopal Residence and later be transferred to another Episcopal District not owning one, if it asks payment for its equity such claim shall not be denied.

¶ **605.2.** When authorized by an Annual Conference and approved by the Presiding Bishop, District parsonages may be purchased, built, maintained, and sold in accordance with the Discipline and the property regulations prescribed for an Annual Conference (cf. ¶602).

¶ **605.3.** The parsonage shall be titled to and be under the control of and management of the Trustees of the Annual Conference within whose bounds it is located.

CHAPTER 42
THE CONNECTIONAL HEADQUARTERS

¶ **606.** The Administrative offices of the Christian Methodist Episcopal Church shall be housed in the Connectional Headquarters presently located at 4466 Elvis Presley Blvd., Memphis, TN 38116.

§1. The Connectional Headquarters shall be under the supervision of a Board of Directors consisting of one representative from each Episcopal District and one of the Bishops, who will serve as chair. Said director will be recommended by the College of Bishops and elected by the General Conference.

§2. The Board of Directors shall serve for a term of four years. In the interim of the General Conference the Board will meet at least once a year at the General Connectional Board and more often if necessary. The expense shall be part of the General Connectional Board line item.

§3. The Administrator of the Connectional Headquarters shall be the Executive Secretary of the Christian Methodist Episcopal Church.

CHAPTER 43
CHARITABLE INSTITUTIONS

¶ 607. Establishing Charitable Institutions

§1. Any local church or churches, Presiding Elder's District, Annual Conference or Episcopal District desiring to fulfill the meaning of the Social Creed of the Christian Methodist Episcopal Church (cf. *The Social Creed,* "The Church and General Welfare", ¶130.4) by addressing the social conditions of people, shall have the right to minister to the physical, mental or emotional care of persons who are elderly, homeless or infirmed, by establishing and maintaining appropriate institutions or other charitable organizations, in conformity with the laws of the State in which they are located.

§2. In conformity with the laws of the resident state, a majority of the trustees of all such institutions or organizations that may be established shall be members of the Christian Methodist Episcopal Church.

§3. The authority to establish such institutions and/or organizations shall be subject to ¶602.1 and ¶602.5 of the *1998 Discipline* of the Christian Methodist Episcopal Church; and the exercise of the authority herein granted shall not conflict with the laws of the C.M.E. Church.

¶ 607.1. C.M.E. Foundation

§1. There shall be established in the Christian Methodist Episcopal Church a Christian Methodist Episcopal Church Foundation (CME Church Foundation), chartered under the laws of the State of Tennessee.

§ 2. The purpose of the C.M.E. Church Foundation shall be to receive and use funds from wills, devises, bequests, donations, gifts, offerings, etc. for and in behalf of the Christian Methodist Episcopal Church for the on-going program of education, spiritual uplift, social betterment, and general welfare of persons both in the church and in the community.

§ 3. There shall be an Advisory Board, composed of one member from each Episcopal District, named by the College of Bishops and elected by the General Conference, which shall elect the Board of Directors.

§4. The Board of Directors shall consist of five members who will serve five year staggered terms, and shall have among its members at all times an attorney and a Certified Public Accountant and/or banker.

§5. The Board of Directors shall develop By-laws deemed necessary for smooth operations. The same shall be in conformity with the CME Church Foundation's Charter of Incorporation, the Foundation Laws of the state of Tennessee and *The Book of Discipline* of The Christian Methodist Episcopal Church.

§6. The CME Foundation shall make a report each year to the General Connectional Board and to the General Conference.

CHAPTER 44
COMMITTEE ON DEEDS, TITLES AND ABSTRACTS

¶ **608.** Every Annual Conference of the C.M.E. Church shall have a Committee on Deeds, Titles and Abstracts. The duties of the Committee shall be to:

§1. Compile a brief index of the records of all deeds, titles and abstracts of all the real estate of the C.M.E. Church that exists within the bounds of the Annual Conference. In addition:

§2. Examine the deeds or instruments of record to the end that all defects in the titles or records may be known and corrected.

§3. Receive and investigate complaints concerning the purchase, use, mortgage or sale of Church property and to make the necessary recommendations to the Annual Conference for adjustments.

¶ **608.1.** The pastors of local churches shall, in connection with their annual report, present to the aforementioned Committee the papers which are necessary to aid in its operations.

PART VII
45. CONNECTIONAL DAYS, OBSERVANCES AND ORGANIZATIONS

Connectional Days
Children's Day
Mentorship Sunday
American Bible Society Day
Christian Youth Fellowship Day
Christian Ministry Sunday
Student Recognition Day
Christian Vocation Day
Social Concerns Sunday
Connectional Laymen's Day
NAACP Sunday
W. L. Graham Scholarship Day
Scout Sunday
Missions Beyond the USA Sunday
Connectional Stewardess Day
CME Founders Day

Connectional Organizations
Ministers Spouses
Connectional Lay Institute
Ministers/Laymen's Council
Connectional Young Adult Conference
Presiding Elders' Council
Connectional Christian Educators' Council
CME Historical Society
NACME Church Scouters

CHAPTER 45
CONNECTIONAL DAYS, OBSERVANCES
AND ORGANIZATIONS

In order to enable local congregtions of the Christian Methodist Episcopal Church to become more aware and supportive of programs that enhance the life of the church and extend its witness, each local congregation is called to observe the following Connectional emphases:

Children's Day

¶ **700.** Regulations governing the observance of Children's Day:

§1. There shall be held annually throughout the Church, a day to be known as Children's Day.

§2. The exercises of this day shall consist of appropriate services held in all of our congregations for the special benefit of the children.

§3. The first collection at every service on that day shall be for the cause of Education.

§4. Each Annual Conference shall decide as to which of the recognized connectional schools the money raised for education on this day shall be appropriated.

§5. Each Annual Conference shall reserve the right to fix the date for Children's Day observance.

Mentorship Sunday

¶ **701.** Children's Day, the Second Sunday in June shall be recognized as Mentorship Sunday in honor of the life and legacy of Dr. Lucius H. Pitts.

American Bible Society Day

¶ **702.** Every charge throughout the Connection shall observe American Bible Society Day, which shall be fixed by each Annual Conference.

Christian Youth Fellowship Day

¶ **703.** Every charge shall observe the fourth Sunday in July as Christian Youth Fellowship Day, at which time a collection shall be raised for the Christian Youth Fellowship Department.

Christian Ministry Sunday

¶ **704.** The second Sunday in March shall be designated as Christian Ministry Sunday in the Church for the purpose of stimulating the recruitment of Ministers in the Local Church. Each Local Church is urged to observe the celebration of Christian Ministry Sunday and receive an offering to be sent to the Ministerial Salary Supplement Program for the furtherance of services designed to mprove the living standard and quality of the Ministers of our Church. In Charges where the second Sunday is impractical, the third Sunday or the next available Sunday should be used for the celebration.

Student Recognition Day

¶ **705.** Each Church throughout the Connection is requested to observe Student Recognition Day as a day set aside to give special recognition to those persons who have received their Christian nurture in that Local Church, have completed their school requirements and are now engaged in furthering their education in some institution of higher learning. The fourth Sunday in December has been designated as Student Recognition Day and each Local Church should plan a special program of recognition for those persons who are now attending college, vocational school, or other institutions of learning.

Christian Vocation Day

¶ **706.** There should be observed Christian Vocation Day in every Local Church.

§1. This day is to be set aside to emphasize the vocations that are particularly unique to the Church. Through special programs, emphasis should be given to the various careers available to youth in the Church such as pastors, military and institutional chaplains; teacher of religion, philosophy, and theology in college and/ or seminary; secretaries, directors of Christian Education, etc.

§2. This day is also to emphasize the concept that all vocations are Christian vocations if performed by Christians as their calling in the world of work. Time for the observance of this day is to be determined by the Local Church's Board of Christian Education. However, it could be observed in conjunction with Student Recognition Day or National Youth Week.

Social Concerns Sunday

¶ **707.** There shall be observed in each charge every fourth Sunday in February Social Concerns Sunday. This observance should emphasize the Church's responsibility for the healing of brokenness in the local, regional, national and world communities. Efforts should be made to increase the Local Church's role to increase political economic and social justice, and peace and goodwill in the international community. Let the observance be planned by the Pastor-in-Charge and the Local Board of Social Concerns.

Connectional Laymen's Day

¶ **708.** There should be observed in each charge every second Sunday in October Connectional Laymen's Day. The observance should emphasize the participation of lay persons in the total program of the Church and encourage the increase of such participation.

NAACP Sunday

¶ **709.** A Connectional NAACP Sunday observance shall be developed by the General Department of Evangelism and Missions, in cooperation with the National Office of the NAACP.

W. L. Graham Scholarship Day

¶ **710.** A W. L. Graham Scholarship Day shall be held no later than the Second Sunday in October annually. The funds collected on that day shall be under the Annual Conference Lay Council for the support of the W.L. Graham Scholarship for Males in the C.M.E. Church at the Connectional Level.

Scout Sunday

¶ **711.** The first Sunday in February shall be celebrated annually in the Christian Methodist Episcopal Church as Scout Sunday. Scouting shall be highlighted and promoted.

Missions Beyond the U.S.A. Sunday

¶ **712** This emphasis shall be observed on Pentecost Sunday. On this day each local congregation shall observe Missions Beyond the U.S.A. with the receiving of special offerings and gifts. They shall be administered by the Presiding Bishop of the Tenth Episcopal District.

Connectional Stewardess Day

¶ **713.** Every local church throughout the Connection shall observe Connectional Stewardess Day on the first Sunday or any apprioreate Sunday in June. Workshops and training sessions are to be implemented as means of observing Connectional Stewardess Day.

C.M.E. Founders Day Sunday

¶ **714.** On the Sunday closest to December 16, each local church shall observe, commemorate and celebrate the beginning of the Christian Methodist Episcopal Church.

Connectional Organizations

¶ **720.** Groups and organizations established within the Christian Methodist Episcopal Church for special services, to perform specific tasks, and/or bring together persons with mutual needs, interests, and concerns that become connectional in scope, independent of any of the General Departments of the church, may be recognized by the General Conference as connectional Organizations.

§1. Connectional organizations may establish their own procedures, develop their own rules, conduct their own affairs, and elect their own officers, provided that such do not conflict with the *Discipline* of the C.M.E. Church or violate the directives of the General Conference.

§2. Connectional Departments shall under no circumstances speak for or on behalf of, neither obligate nor make any financial claim on the Christian Methodist Episcopal Church or its General Departments.

§3. Elected leaders of Connectional Organizations shall be known as Connectional Officers; provided that such leaders shall make no financial or any other claim on the Christian Methodist Episcopal Church for offices they may hold, expenses incurred as the result thereof, or the operation of the organization which they may represent.

§4. The Connectional Organizations of the C.M.E. Church are:

The Ministers Spouses Department

¶ **720.1.** The Ministers Spouses Department, authorized by the 1994 General Conference is the Connectional organization responsible for the spouses, widows, and widowers of the ministers of the Christian Methodist Episcopal Church. Its purpose is to provide at the Connectional level of the church a means by which ministers' spouses may share mutual concerns, support, communication and fellowship. It is organized at the Annual and District level and is supported by membership dues and affiliation fees. Its major program is the Widow's Mite and a scholarship fund for children of C.M.E. ministers. It meets annually at the C.M.E. Convocation and its officers are elected biannually.

The Connectional Laymen's Institute

¶ **720.2.** The Connectional Laymen's Institute began in 1965 as a program unit of the Department of Lay Activities as a means of bringing together at the national level every four years the laity of the C.M.E. Church for study, fellowship, empowerment and mutual support. Its officers are a president, one vice-president from each Episcopal District, a secretary, a treasurer and a chaplain. It has under its auspices the Connectional Steward Board, Stewardess Board and Board of Ushers, each of which shall have a president and one vice-president from each Episcopal District. The Connectional Laymen's Institute is constituted by representatives from local congregations of the denomination.

The Ministers/Laymen's Council

¶ **720.3.** The Ministers/Laymen's Council began several decades ago as an ad hoc gathering of ministers and laymen at Connectional meetings to discuss issues before the church. At the call of its president, it conducts informal worship, workshops and discussions. The officers are elected quadrennially, at the first meeting after the General Conference.

The Connectional Young Adult Conference

¶ **720.4.** The purpose of the Connectional Young Adult Conference is to assist the C.M.E. Church in planning, developing, and implementing a program of Christian mission appropriate to the needs of young adults that will assure the full involvement, participation and development of leadership capabilities of young adults in carrying out the mission of the church. It meets quadrennially and is under the auspices of the General Department of Christian Education.

The Presiding Elders Council

¶ **720.5.** The Presiding Elders Council is the Connectional organization of ministers of the C.M.E. Church who serve as district supervisors of the denomination. Its purpose is to provide a forum for discussion, sharing of ideas, fellowship and mutual support for those appointed to such leadership capacity. It meets informally at C.M.E. Connectional meetings at the call of its president. All Presiding Elders of the church are eligible for membership.

The Connectional Christian Educators' Council

¶ **720.6.** The Connectional Christian Educators' Council was established by the General Department of Christian Education to bring together persons throughout the Connection who are involved in Christian Education for the sharing of mutual concerns, fellowship, and support of the program of Christian nurture in the C.M.E. Church. The Council meets annually at the C.M.E. Convocation, quadrennially at the National Connectional Youth and Young Adult Conference, and may meet periodically at the call of the President and/or the General Secretary of Christian Education.

The C.M.E. Historical Society

¶ **720.7.** The C.M.E. Historical Society was developed by the General Department of Publications in an attempt that was to aid in the collection, organization, and preservation of historical material of the Christian Methodist Episcopal Church, as well as find ways and means to support the important work of preserving the history of the C.M.E. Church. It is responsible for the Historical Archives of the Connectional Headquarters and conducts tours and workshops on the history of the C.M.E. Church. It is under the auspices of the Commission on History and Archives of the C.M.E. Church.

The National Association of C.M.E. Church Scouters

¶ **720.8.** The purpose of the N.A.C.M.E. Church Scouters is to encourage the use of the Boy Scouts of America, Girl Scouts - U.S.A., and similar youth-serving agencies in the ministry of the church with children and youth. Membership is comprised of individuals and groups who wish to give or encourage leadership in developing the potential of the young. Use is also encouraged of the God and Country Program with modifications from the history and traditions of the Connection.

Activities, training, publicity, and working relations with the B.S.A. and G.S.U.S.A. by N.A.C.M.E.Church Scouters have been ongoing since 1992.

PART VIII
JUDICIAL ADMINISTRATION

**46.The Judicial Administration
   of the Christian Methodist
   Episcopal Church**

   **Introduction
   Practices Subject to
        Disciplinary Action
   Judicial Process
   Judicial Council**

CHAPTER 46
THE JUDICIAL ADMINISTRATION
OF THE
CHRISTIAN METHODIST EPISCOPAL CHURCH

Introduction

¶ **801.** The Bible enjoins the church to "let all things be done decently and in order" (I Cor.14:40). In keeping with the biblical mandate, Methodism, beginning with its Founder John Wesley, established "rules and regulations" for the operation of the church. Of necessity such rules and regulations contain procedures for the discipline of members, amelioration of disputes, and resolution of conflicts. Because the church is of God, the overriding intent of such procedures is to enable members of the church, again in accordance with biblical injunctions, to "do justice, love mercy, and walk humbly" before their God (Micah 6:8).

¶ **801.1.** In both administration and interpretation, judicial procedure in the Christian Methodist Episcopal Church follows three principles, namely, a) discipline is administered at the level of membership and accountability (i.e., local church for lay members, Annual Conference for preachers in Full Connection, and General Conference for bishops); b) investigation by committee; and c) the right of appeal (cf. Constitution of the C.M.E. Church, Restrictive Rule Number 5).

¶ **801.2.** Upon acceptance into full membership, members of the Christian Methodist Episcopal Church take vows to live a Christian life according to the Word of God as revealed in Jesus Christ and to be subject to the *Discipline* of the church (cf. *Constitution*, Art. 4; *Book of Ritual*, 1995, pp. 18 & 19). Any member is therefore subject to disciplinary action if, in accordance with the judicial procedures herein defined, he or she is accused and found guilty of conduct contrary to the expressed Word of God and the *Discipline*.

¶ 801.3 Members of the C.M.E. Church who, by appointment or election, might hold positions or offices of leadership, responsibility, and authority in the church are accountable for the official administration of such positions or offices as may be outlined in the *Discipline*. They are therefore subject to disciplinary action if, in accordance with procedures defined in the *Discipline*, they are accused and found guilty of violation of the *Discipline* in the administration of such positions and offices.

Practices Subject to Disciplinary Action

¶ **802.** In addition to the general expectations the C.M.E. Church has for its members and leaders as outlined above, there are particular practices and conduct for which disciplinary action might be taken, to wit:

§1. Conduct contrary to the Word of God.

§2. Conduct prohibited by the General Rules.

§ 3. Violations of vows of church membership, ordination, Admission into Full Connection, and Consecration (of bishops).

§4. Violation of the Order and *Discipline* of the church.

§5. Behavior which undermines the ministry of the church.

§6. Practicing and disseminating doctrines contrary to the doctrines of the C.M.E. Church.

§7. Sexual Harassment.

§8. Conviction of a crime of moral turpitude against the State.

Judicial Process

¶ **803. Accusation.** When members of the Christian Methodist Episcopal Church are accused of practices subject to disciplinary action listed in ¶802, the following procedure shall obtain:

§1. Report of the accusation, written or oral, shall be made to the proper official who shall make discreet inquiry into the same. If there are indications that the report might have some basis in fact, let private reproof be given. In the case of lay members, reproof shall be administered by the Pastor of the local church; if a minister in Full Connection, by the Presiding Bishop; if an Annual Conference officer, by the Presiding Bishop; if a bishop, by the Senior Bishop. (Note: in all cases where the Senior Bishop might be the offender, the official would be the next bishop in order of seniority).

§2. Should reports persist, accompanied with a written complaint, the official with one or two others shall deliver a warning to the offender. In the case of a lay member, the warning shall be administered by the Pastor and two or three church officers; for a minister in Full Connection, the Presiding Bishop, a Presiding Elder and three ministers; for an Annual Conference officer, by the Presiding Bishop, a Presiding Elder and three ministers; and for a bishop, the Senior Bishop, Chairman of the College of Bishops and the Secretary.

§3. If a third offense occurs, it shall constitute a presumption of conduct requiring disciplinary adjudication. The appropriate official (Pastor, Presiding Bishop, or Senior Bishop) shall send to the accused written notice of the accusation, copy of the accusation signed by the accuser(s), and inform the accused that a committee of investigation is to be appointed to make inquiry.

§4. If it is found that the accusation(s) concerns conduct which may have occurred more than one year previously, the matter will be dropped in its entirety and no further disciplinary action will be taken.

§5. In cases which, in the judgment of the appropriate official, the accusation is egregious and threatening on its face, e.g., imminent physical harm, civil liability, criminal culpability, etc., the official shall have authority to appoint a committee of investigation immediately.

¶ 803.1 Committee of Investigation. The responsibility of the Committee of Investigation will be to inquire into the written accusations to determine whether there be sufficient evidence to warrant a bill of charges.

§1 The committee(s) shall be constituted at the level where the membership of the accused is held, to wit: for lay members, at the local church; for ministers in Full Connection and Annual Conference officers, in the Annual Conference; and for bishops, at the Episcopal level.

§2 The committee to investigate a lay member shall be composed of three members of the local church of the accused appointed by the Pastor in Charge; for a minister in Full Connection, five clergy members of the Annual Conference to which the accused belongs appointed by the Presiding Bishop; for an Annual Conference officer, three lay and two ministers appointed by the Presiding Bishop; and for a bishop, seven ministers in Full Connection within the Episcopal District over which the bishop presides appointed by the College of Bishops upon nomination by the Senior Bishop.

§3. The proceedings of the Committee of Investigation shall be informal, and no oaths shall be taken.

§4. The committee shall begin its inquiry on the presumption that the accused is innocent and that the burden is on the accuser(s) to prove the accusation(s). It shall examine the written accusation and supporting evidence of the accuser(s). After the committee has heard from the accuser(s) to its satisfaction, the accuser(s) will no longer have a justiciable interest in the matter.

§5. The committee shall grant the accused his/her right to confront the accuser(s) face to face, provide ample opportunity to respond to and refute the accusations, and shall hear any supporting evidence the accused might present.

§6. The committee may hear other witnesses who might have evidence relevant to the truth or falsity of the accusation(s).

§7. If in the judgment of the Committee of Investigation there is reasonable grounds for the accusation, the committee shall prepare appropriate Bill(s) of Charges and forward the same to the proper official.

¶803.3. Bill(s) of Charges. The Bill(s) of Charges prepared by the Committee of Investigation shall define the offense for which the offender is accused as follows:

§1 The Bill(s) of Charges must be submitted in writing and signed by the chairperson and secretary of the Committee of Investigation.

§2 A separate Bill must be submitted for each alleged offense, setting forth the approximate time, date, place, and specific circumstances of the offense.

§3 The Charge must cite the specific rule or regulation in the Discipline which has been violated, stating the paragraph, section, and page.

¶ 803.4. Tribunal. A tribunal is a formal hearing within the church at which it is determined whether the charges which have been preferred against a member are with or without merit, and censure awarded accordingly. A Tribunal, in distinction from a trial, seeks healing, reconciliation, and rehabilitation.

§1. The official in charge of the Tribunal, to be called "The Presiding Official", shall be the Pastor, Presiding Bishop, or Senior Bishop as appropriate. The Presiding Official shall appoint a secretary, select a member of the Committee of Investigation to present the evidence against the accused, choose the members of the Tribunal, and summon witnesses whose testimony might have a bearing on the case.

§2. The Tribunal for a lay member shall consist of five members of the church of which the accused is a member; for a minister in Full Connection, seven members of the Annual Conference of which the accused is a member; for an Annual Conference officer, four lay persons and three ministers who are members of the

Annual Conference; for a bishop, nine ministers in Full Connection within the Episcopal District over which the bishop presides.

§3. Upon receipt of a Bill of Charges, the Presiding Official shall, as soon as practicable but no later than thirty days, give written notice to the accused and all parties involved of the time and place of the Tribunal.

§4. The accused has the right to be present at the Tribunal and every effort is to be made to accommodate that right. Accordingly,upon showing cause a continuance for the accused might be granted. However, the refusal of the accused to be present or participate in the Tribunal shall not obviate the charges, keep evidence from being presented, or censure awarded.

§5. The accused shall have the right to be heard in oral or written presentation, to call witnesses, and to cross-examine opposing witnesses. He/she may select any member of the C.M.E. Church, other than an Attorney-at-Law, to speak on his/her behalf.

§6. When the Tribunal convenes, the accused shall state whether he/she denies the accusations specified in the Bill of Charges. The accused may admit to the charges, deny the charges, or plead mitigating circumstances.

(a) If the accused admits to the charges, the members of the Tribunal shall be excused and the Presiding Official shall assess appropriate censure.

(b) If the accused pleads mitigating circumstances, he/she shall be allowed to explain those circumstances to the members of the Tribunal. If a majority of the members of the Tribunal believes that the circumstances justify the accused, the case is dismissed.

(c) If the accused denies the charges, the Tribunal proceeds to hear evidence.

¶ **803.5. Tribunal Decisions**. After all the evidence has been heard, members of the Tribunal shall retire to deliberate their judgment.

§1. If the judgment is that the accusation(s) is "Without Merit" the accused shall be exonerated.

§2. If the judgement is that the accusation(s) is "With Merit," the members of the Tribunal shall recommend censure appropriate to the charges. In the case of lay members and ministers in Full Connection, any censure other than expulsion shall be pronounced by the Presiding Official. (The censure of expulsion can only be awarded by the Church Conference or Annual Conference.) In the case of bishops, censures other than expulsion shall be pronounced by the College of Bishops. (Expulsion can only be awarded by the General Conference).

§3. If a minister in Full Connection against whom the accusation(s) is found to be "With Merit" is receiving a salary from a local church, and the censure is suspension, he/she shall be entitled to full salary until the end of the Annual Conference year in which the suspension takes place. If a bishop is suspended under the same conditions, he shall be entitled to full salary until the ensuing General Conference has reviewed the case.

¶ **803.6. Appeal Process.** Any member against whom it is determined by a Tribunal that charges brought are "With Merit" and who may have been censured accordingly has the right to have that determination and/or censure reviewed by another properly constituted body within the church. The process of review is called an "appeal."

§1. Within fifteen days (15) of the determination, the accused must notify the Presiding Official of the Tribunal of the intention to appeal.

§2. The appeal for a lay member shall be to the Quarterly Conference; for a minister in Full Connection, the Annual Conference; and for a bishop, the General Conference.

Judicial Council

¶ **804.** There shall be a Judicial Council of the Christian Methodist Episcopal Church with membership, authority, and procedure as herein set forth.

¶ **804.1. Membership.** The Judicial Council shall be composed of nine (9) members, four (4) of whom shall be clergy persons in Full Connection; and five (5) of whom shall be lay persons who shall have been members of the C.M.E. Church for at least eight years prior to their election.

¶ **804.2.** Members of the Judicial Council shall be elected by the General Conference in regular session as follows:

§1. The College of Bishops shall nominate at least twice the number of clergy and lay persons that are to be elected at that session. Other persons may be nominated from the floor.

§2. Preparation of ballots and voting shall be in accordance with procedures adopted by the General Conference, provided that the age(s) of persons nominated will be filed with the Secretary of the General Conference; and provided further that a person must receive a simple majority of votes cast to be elected.

§3. Members of the Judicial Council shall not be eligible to be delegates to the General Conference or members of the General Connectional Board.

¶804.3. Members of the Judicial Council shall be elected for a term of eight years, and shall be eligible for re-election.

¶804.4. Members of the Judicial Council shall be automatically retired at the age of seventy-four (74), provided that when such retirement occurs during the interim of the General Conference, the retiring member shall be replaced by an Alternate.

¶ 804.5. There shall be three clergy and three lay Alternate Members of the Judicial Council whose eligibility and mode of election shall be the same as members of the Council, provided that the clergy and lay categories shall be respectively maintained.

§1. The Alternate Members shall be elected from among those persons nominated but not elected in the balloting for regular members.

§2.The term of Alternate Members shall be for four years.

§3. The Alternate Members shall fill vacancies in the Council in the order in which they were elected, provided that the Alternate filling a vacancy shall serve the unexpired term of the member the Alternate succeeds.

§804.6. Vacancies due to death, resignation, removal or retirement shall be filled as described in the previous paragraph; provided that the voluntary retirement of a clergy member from the active itinerancy shall be treated as if it were mandatory; and provided further that any member may be removed if convicted of any offenses listed in ¶802.

¶805. Jurisdiction. The Judicial Council is the final adjudicator of the rules and regulations of the Christian Methodist Episcopal Church, its jurisdiction is appellate and declaratory to be exercised solely within the province of the denomination. Its decisions are final.

§1. It shall not exercise original jurisdiction.

§2. It shall exercise no jurisdiction over theological or doctrinal matters.

§3. It shall exercise no jurisdiction over political or civil affairs; nor shall it take judicial notice of any action which may come within the realm of any civil magistracy.

§4. It shall exercise appellate jurisdiction, including Declaratory Judgment specifically; no petition for Declaratory Judgment or Bill of Charge may be presented nor shall it be considered by the Council until all other steps of the judicial process, including appeals have been exhausted (cf. ¶ 805.2).

¶ 805.1. Authority. The Judicial Council shall have authority as follows:

§1. To hear and decide appeals from the ruling of a bishop on questions of law as defined under ¶ 803.4 (cf. ¶ 428, §10 §11).

§2. To determine the constitutionality of an action of the General Conference upon appeal of one-sixth of the delegates or upon appeal of a majority of the College of Bishops.

§3. To hear and determine the legality of any act of an Annual Conference or the General Connectional Board upon appeal of one-sixth of the members thereof or a majority of the College of Bishops.

¶ 805.2. The Judicial Council may, under conditions herein set forth, render Declaratory Decisions, i.e., interpretations of specific rules and regulations of the church which may appear ambiguous or of doubtful meaning.

§1. Members of the C.M.E. Church with a justiciable interest in the meaning and application of a specific paragraph(s) or section of the Discipline may petition the Judicial Council for a declaratory decision.

§2. Petitions shall specify the paragraph, article and/or section of the Discipline for which the decision is sought, be dated, signed by the petitioner(s), and forwarded to the President and Clerk of the Council.

§3. The rationale, motivation, circumstances, etc. out of which petitions might arise shall not be included in the petition(s) since the facts regarding the laws for which clarification is sought might later become issues in formal adjudication; and the Judicial Council, as the final adjudicator, shall take official notice of such facts only after formal charges have been filed and adjudicated at the Tribunal level.

§4. Petitioner(s), other members or official bodies who may be affected by the issue raised in the petition, shall have the right to be heard before the Council either in person, through a representative and/or by written documentation.

§5. The Legal Counsel for the Christian Methodist Episcopal Church shall have the right to apprise the Council of issues any given petition might raise which affect the legal status and liability of the C.M.E. Church.

§6. Because Declaratory Decisions are final, interpretive in nature, and not subject to appeal, the Judicial Council shall make the following determinations prior to hearing a petition.

(a) Whether rendering a decision on a given petition will clothe the Council with original jurisdiction in conflict with ¶ 805 §1.

(b) Whether its decision will embroil the Judicial Council in civil affairs in conflict with ¶ 805 §3 and place the actions of the Council outside its proper jurisdiction.

(c) Whether hearing a given petition would by-pass the appellate process as outlined in ¶ 803.6and thereby compromise the neutrality of the Council as the final adjudicator as described in ¶ 801 and ¶ 805.

(d) Whether a given petition is a guise for making allegations or insinuating charges against other members of the church in lieu of due process of the C.M.E. Church as outlined in ¶ 803 of the Judicial Procedure.

(e) Whether the Judicial Process for filing a given petition or questions of interpretation has been followed accordingly, to wit:

1) Petitions or questions of interpretations are to be heard in the Church Conference: Authority to interpret: Preacher in Charge.

2) Appeal from interpretation of pastor is to Quarterly Conference: Authority to interpret: Presiding Elder.

3) Appeal from interpretation made by Presiding Elder is to the Annual Conference: Authority to interpret: Presiding Bishop.

4) Appeal from interpretation made by Presiding Bishop is to Judicial Council: Authority to interpret: Judicial Council.

When any step of the appeal process as outlined above is by-passed, the person, group or entity receiving such a petition shall not have the authority to hear nor shall it hear or render any decision in the matter until received by and through the appropriate manner. Certified copies of previous decisions/interpretations shall be submitted to the appellate body by the petitioner as proof of adherence to the process.

¶ **806. Organization.** The Judicial Council shall meet during the sessions of the General Connectional Board, the General Conference, and at any other times deemed necessary by the Council upon call of the President and concurrence of at least three other members.

¶ **806.1.** The Officers of the Judicial Council shall be a President, Vice-President, and a Clerk elected quadrennially by the Council.

§1. The President shall convene and preside over the sessions of the Council.

§2. The Vice-President shall assume the duties of the President in case of inability or absence.

§3. The Clerk shall receive all matters submitted to the Council and notify the President of the same, keep the docket, record the actions of the Council, and furnish appropriate parties as well as the Secretary of the College of Bishops and the Legal Counsel of the C.M.E. Church, official copies of actions and/or decisions of the Judicial Council.

¶ **806.2.** A quorum for the Judicial Council shall be six members, and a two/thirds affirmative vote of the entire Council shall be required for all actions and decisions.

¶ **806.3.** The Judicial Council shall consider appeals, petitions for Declaratory Decision, questions of legality of actions of the Annual Conference, constitutionality of actions of the General Conference and any other matters within its jurisdiction in the following manner:

§1. Documents prepared for subject matter before the Council shall be furnished to all members of the Council.

§2. Parties involved shall be given opportunity to be heard, the number and time allotted will be determined by the Council. All hearings shall be public. Members of the Council may ask questions.

§3. The Council may hear other interested parties as it deems appropriate.

§4. Members of the Judicial Council shall not discuss with persons other than Council members any subject matter pending before the Council.

§5. The deliberations of the Council shall be in Executive Session.

¶ **806.7. Decisions.** The decisions of the Council shall be written and shall indicate the names of members of the Council who concurred.

§1. Decisions on constitutionality of acts of the General Conference or General Connectional Board shall become effective when announced.

§2. Decisions on appeals shall be sent to the parties involved.

§3. Declaratory decisions shall be filed with the Secretary of the General Conference for depositing with the official records of the denomination, and published in the official publication of the denomination, provided that the Legal Counsel has made a determination that such publication will not expose the C.M.E. Church to liability.

PART IX
CLERGY CREDENTIALS

47. Certification of Ordination
and Full Connection
48. Deprivation of Credentials

Traveling Preachers
Local Preachers

CHAPTER 47
CERTIFICATION OF ORDINATION AND FULL CONNECTION

¶ **901.** Ordination by the Christian Methodist Episcopal Church and Admission into the Full Connection of the itinerancy of the church is a high and sacred trust. When a preacher has been elected to the Orders of Deacon and Elder and has been ordained to the same by the Bishop and when a preacher has been admitted into Full Connection in accordance with the rules of the Christian Methodist Episcopal Church, the preacher shall be given credentials signed by the Presiding Bishop certifying such ordination and admission.

¶ **902.** Should the credentials of any Deacon or Elder be destroyed or lost, the Bishop who ordained him or her, or the Presiding Bishop of the Annual Conference of which the preacher is a member, upon ascertaining the necessary information bearing on the date and place of the ordination, shall reissue the proper credentials.

¶ **903.** In the event that an ordained Elder, Deacon, Member in Full Connection with an Annual Conference or Probationer on Trial shall be expelled after due process in accordance with the *Discipline* of the C.M.E. Church (cf. ¶ 803.5, § 2) the credentials of said preacher shall be revoked, and the minutes of the Annual Conference shall faithfully record the date of and reason for the revocation. An orderly transfer of credentials shall be made for ministers in good standing that withdraw from the C.M.E. Church upon contacting their presiding Bishop (cf. ¶ 420.4)

¶ **904.** Upon revocation of credentials, the Presiding Bishop of the Annual Conference shall request from the involved preacher in writing by certified mail that he/she surrender to the Bishop certificates of ordination and/or Full Connection. Where applicable, the Bishop shall give public notice and announcement that the involved preacher is no longer an ordained minister in the Christian Methodist Episcopal Church.

CHAPTER 48

DEPRIVATION OF CREDENTIALS

Traveling Preachers

¶ **905.** When a Traveling Elder or Deacon is deprived of his or her Credentials of Ordination by expulsion or otherwise, they shall be filed with the papers of the Annual Conference of which that person was a member.

¶ **905.1**. Should the person, at any future time, give satisfactory evidence to said Conference of amendment or innocence, and procure a certificate from the Quarterly Conference of the charge of residence or of the Annual Conference of which he or she was formerly a member, for the restoration of the Credentials, said Conference may restore them.

Local Preachers

¶ **906.** When any Local Elder or Deacon is deprived of Credentials of Ordination by expulsion or otherwise, it shall be the duty of the Presiding Elder to require said Credentials of the person, and to file them with the papers of the Annual Conference within the limits of which the said Local Preacher resides.

¶ **906.1.** Should the person at any future time produce to the Annual Conference a Certificate of Restoration by the Quarterly Conference, signed by the President and Secretary thereof, his/her Credentials may be restored to him or her.

PART X
THE GENERAL
CONNECTIONAL BOARD

49. The General Connectional Board

The Executive Secretary
Editor, The Christian Index

CHAPTER 49
THE GENERAL CONNECTIONAL BOARD

¶ **1000.** The administration of the Connectional program of the Christian Methodist Episcopal Church shall be under the supervision of a *General Connectional Board* which shall have the following composition, authority, and responsibilities:

¶ **1000.1.** The General Connectional Board shall be composed of representatives from the several districts of the church in accordance with the following ratio: one clergy and one lay representative for every five thousand (5,000) members of each Episcopal District as reported to the General Conference plus one additional representative, either clergy or lay, for a major fraction of five thousand such members. Provided that the Haitian Annual Conference and the Jamaican Mission Annual Conference shall each have the right to elect one clergy and one lay representative to the General Connectional Board.

¶ **1000.2.** Members of the General Connectional Board shall be elected by the delegates from the several Annual Conferences of each Episcopal District to the General Conference. Any person who is a member of the C.M.E. Church within the Episcopal District is eligible for election. Said delegates may come together for the election of said representatives either before or during the session of the General Conference. Upon election, the names of the representatives shall be submitted to the General Conference in session for certification. With the exceptions noted in the next paragraph, persons not thusly certified will not be members of the General Connectional Board. Members of the General Connectional Board will be responsible for attending all meetings of the Board and of the committee(s) to which they may be assigned.

¶ **1000.3.** Upon the death, resignation, or removal of a representative from an Episcopal District, another representative from that Episcopal District shall be nominated by the Presiding Bishop and approved by the General Connectional Board.

¶ **1000.4.** The officers of the General Connectional Board shall be: a Chairman who shall be the Senior Bishop of the Christian Methodist Episcopal Church; a Vice-Chairman who shall be one of the bishops of the church elected by the College of Bishops; and a Secretary who shall be elected by the General Conference.

¶ **1000.5.** The General Connectional Board shall have authority to:

§1. Serve as a screening committee to evaluate the qualifications of persons seeking to be elected to a General Office by the General Conference.

§2. Discipline, suspend, and/or remove from office any General Officer after proper hearing and due process according to the *Discipline* when the General Connectional Board deems such officer guilty of malfeasance, neglect of duty, inefficiency in performance of duty, or conduct of such nature that it reflects negatively upon the office or upon the church.

§3. Allocate to the several departments of the church that portion of the connectional budget appropriated for General Church Administration in accordance with program projections and needs assessments of such departments.

§4. Supervise and direct the expenditure of any funds which may accrue to any Connectional department and/or agency in the name of and for the intended use of the C.M.E. Church, with the exception of any funds that might be restricted by civil law.

§5. Review and appropriate annually the budgets of each department and/or agency of the church. The General Secretaries of the General Departments shall give official receipts for money collected from all sources. They shall submit all required financial records to a Certified Public Accountant to be audited at the close of the fiscal year.

§6. Supervise and direct the programs and activities of departments and agencies responsible for the connectional programs of the C.M.E. Church; and periodically review and evaluate such programs and activities.

§7. Exercise any other administrative duties or fulfill other responsibilities that may be given to it by the General Conference or the College of Bishops.

¶ **1000.6. Meetings.**

§1. The General Connectional Board shall meet annually the First Wednesday in May, except in the year of the General Conference.

§2. The time of the meetings of the General Connectional Board shall be determined by the Chairman (or the vice-chairman if the chairman is unable to do so). The place will be set by the Board. The call for the meeting shall be made no less than nine months before the date of the meeting.

§3. Other meetings of the Board may be called by a majority of the College of Bishops.

¶ 1000.7. Standing Committees

§1. The General Connectional Board will be divided into Standing Committees as follows: Christian Education; Lay Ministry; Evangelism and Missions; Finance, Publications, *The Christian Index*, and Personnel Services.

§2. Members of the General Connectional Board will be assigned to one of the Standing Committees by a special committee established by the General Connectional Board composed of two bishops, two general officers, and three members of the board.

§3. The Chairperson for each of the Standing Committees shall be one of the bishops assigned by the College of Bishops, and each Standing Committee shall elect a Vice-Chairperson.

§4. Each of the Standing Committees shall have the responsibility for supervising the General Department and the General Officer designated in its name. Said Commitee shall have the following authority in order to carry out such responsibility:

(a) To screen and evaluate the qualification of persons seeking positions that are within the purview of the procedure and authority established for elections involving the General Connectional Board in the screening and evaluating.

(b) To recommend through the appropriate General Secretary the budget needs and program projections of the department to the General Connectional Board.

(c) To initiate any necessary disciplinary action against the General Secretary.

§5. The Standing Committee on Connectional Budget shall review requests and make recommendations to the General Connectional Board budgetary allocations of the General Departments each year.

§6. The Executive Secretary of the C.M.E. Church shall be responsible to the College of Bishops (cf. 1001.7, § 1).

§7. The General Connectional Board shall have authority to establish Special Task Forces to carry out particular assignments, the members of which may be persons who are not members of the General Connectional Board.

The General Officers

¶ **1001.** The Connectional program of the Christian Methodist Episcopal Church shall be administered by General Officers. The General Officers will be those persons holding offices designated by the General Conference as General Offices. General Officers will serve as the chief executive officers of the department or office to which they are elected in accordance with a job description established by the General Connectional Board.

¶ **1001.1.** The General Officers of the Christian Methodist Episcopal Church shall be:

The Executive Secretary of the C.M.E. Church
The Editor of *The Christian Index*
The General Secretary of Christian Education
The General Secretary of Lay Ministry
The General Secretary of Evangelism and Missions
The General Secretary of Finance
The General Secretary of Publications
The General Secretary of Personnel Services
The President of the Women's Missionary Council

¶ **1001.2.** The salary, pension, housing allowance, and fringe benefits for the General Officers shall be paid from the portion of the Connectional Budget designated for such.

¶ **1001.3.** Funds for the administration of the work of the General Officers, including travel expenses, shall be made available in accordance with an allocation determined by the General Connectional Board from the portion of the Connectional Budget for connectional administration, and shall be based upon program projections and needs assessments for each department or office on an annual basis.

¶ **1001.4.** Funds for office rent and office utilities for General Officers shall be a part of the operational budget for the C.M.E. Connectional Headquarters.

¶ **1001.5.** General Officers shall be responsible and amenable to the General Connectional Board for their conduct and the administration of their respective offices in accordance with the provisions of the *Discipline*.

¶ **1001.6.** General Officers who have their positions or the Department which they are executive officers affected by actions of the General Conference shall prepare a summary of the changes and submit them to *The Christian Index* within sixty days (60) of the close of the General Conference.

¶1001.7. The Executive Secretary

§1. The Executive Secretary shall be elected by the General Conference and shall report to the College of Bishops.

§2. The Executive Secretary shall have the following duties and responsibilities:

(a) To administer the operations of the Connectional Headquarters as directed by the Board of Directors.

(b) To assist in the planning and coordinate the meetings of the General Conference, the General Connectional Board, the C.M.E. Convocation and other meetings of the denomination as might be requested by General Departments.

(c) To be a liaison between the C.M.E. Church and other ecumenical bodies and agencies as directed by the College of Bishops.

(d) To facilitate with the Episcopal Districts the identification and solicitation of community development program grants and other such funding resources to assist the various Annual Conferences.

(e) To facilitate administrative functions for the Christian Methodist Episcopal Church as directed by the College of Bishops.

¶ 1001.8. Editor, *The Christian Index*

§1. The Editor of *The Christian Index* shall be elected quadrennially according to laws enacted by the General Conference.

§2. The duties of the Editor shall be:

(a) Preparing the manuscripts of *The Christian Index* for publication; including format, selection of materials, and editing of materials.

(b) Supervising all details related to the publication, except printing and mailing as directed by the Standing Committee on *The Christian Index*.

(c) Distributing news and informational public relations materials to promote *The Christian Index* and the Christian Methodist Episcopal Church.

(d) Seeking membership in the appropriate news services and associations for the Editor and *The Christian Index* on behalf of the Christian Methodist Episcopal Church.

Division of Connectional Ministries

¶ 1002. Connectional departments that are designed to minister directly to the local congregations and annual conferences of the Christian Methodist Episcopal Church are: General Department of Christian Education, General Department of Lay Ministry, and General Department of Evangelism and Missions. These departments shall function together in the church as the Division of Connectional Ministries. The overall purpose and general functions of each of these departments shall be as follows:

¶ 1002.1. General Department of Christian Education

§1. *Purpose:* The purpose of the General Department of Christian Education shall be to provide "cradle to the grave" nurture in the Christian faith for the members of the C.M.E. Church.

§2. *Function:* In addition to those activities normally associated with Christian nurture, this department shall perform these specific functions:

(a) Prepare, select, and recommend all literature and materials that are to be used in C.M.E. Churches or authorized for the C.M.E. Church, especially for Sunday Church Schools, membership training classes, and children, youth and young adults.

(b) Prepare, select, and recommend leadership training and promotional literature for *all* the areas of the life and witness of the C.M.E. Church.

(c) Promote programs of Christian nurture by keeping the C.M.E. Church informed about such activities as Christian Education Week, National Youth and Young Adult Week.

(d) Promote Sunday Church Schools, Christian Youth and Young Adult Fellowships, Vacation Bible Schools, Adult Education Courses, Bible Study Courses, etc.

(e) Through the General Secretary of the department, be the official liaison between the Christian Methodist Episcopal Church and those colleges under the auspices of the C.M.E. Church and the theological school under the auspices of the C.M.E. Church.

¶ 1002.2. General Department of Lay Ministry

§1. *Purpose:* It shall be the purpose of the General Department of Lay Ministry to aid the Christian Methodist Episcopal Church in equipping and enabling the members of the church to engage in more effective ministry in the Name of Jesus Christ.

§2. *Function:* As the department of the church with a focus primarily on the whole people of God, the specific function of this department shall be:

(a) To develop programs that will strengthen the ministry of the *laos* (the "people of God") who, as the "saints" of the Household of God are "building up the body of Christ."

(b) To aid the local congregations of the Christian Methodist Episcopal Church to "equip" the members of the congregation to be more effective witnesses of Jesus Christ in stewardship and service.

(c) To provide materials and leadership to insure that the local congregations of the C.M.E. Church who are engaged in leadership and service roles as stewards, stewardesses, trustees, choir members, ushers, and other organizational leaders might be more effective in those roles.

(d) To help local congregations address the needs and concerns of men, especially those men served primarily by the C.M.E. Church, as they confront the hostility of the present society, through the development of a *C.M.E. Men's Fellowship* throughout the Christian Methodist Episcopal Church.

(e) To strengthen the ministry of local congregations to women, especially those women served primarily by the C.M.E. Church, as women face increased poverty, desertion, sexism, and aging.

(f) To provide direction to the presidents of the Connectional Boards of Stewards, Stewardesses, Trustees, and Ushers.

¶ 1002.3. General Department of Evangelism and Missions

§1. *Purpose:* It shall be the purpose of the General Department of Evangelism and Missions to keep before the Christian Methodist Episcopal Church its evangelistic and social concerns as these concerns are expressive of the Mission of the Church.

§2. *Function:* As the center of the church's mission thrust in evangelism and social ministry, this department shall have as its specific functions:

(a) To develop and promote programs that will help local congregations become more aware of and involved in evangelism and mission concerns.

(b) To direct workshops, seminars, etc. at annual, district, and local congregational levels on the meaning of and strategies for evangelism and the mission ministry of the church.

(c) To prepare position papers and statements on the vital social, political, and moral issues before the church and the world.

(d) To represent the C.M.E. Church when necessary at conferences, seminars, etc. as such representation enhances the purposes of the department.

(e) To be the focal point of the ecumenical witness and involvement of the C.M.E. Church on matters of evangelism and missions.

Division of Connectional Operations

¶ **1003.** The Connectional Departments designed to serve the Christian Methodist Episcopal Church at the connectional level in order to keep the denomination operational are: General Department of Finance, General Department of Publications, and General Board of Personnel Services. These departments shall function together as the Division of Connectional Operations as follows:

¶ 1003.1. General Department of Finance

It shall be the function of the General Department of Finance to administer the Connectional Budget as approved by the General Conference in accordance with the *Discipline.*

¶ l003.2. General Department of Publications

It shall be the function of the General Department of Publications to provide the publishing services for the Christian Methodist Episcopal Church, publish *The Christian Index,* and to administer all of the publishing interests of the church. It shall be administered by the appropriate Standing Committee of the General Connectional Board.

¶ 1003.3. General Department of *The Christian Index.*

It shall be the function of the General Department of *The Christian Index* to promote the editing, circulation, and support of *The Christian Index* in providing appropriate news and informational services for the Christian Methodist Episcopal Church.

¶ 1003.4. General Board of Personnel Services

It shall be the function of the General Board of Personnel Services to administer those programs of the Christian Methodist Episcopal Church that were related to the Department of Superannuated Preachers, Widows & Orphans (SPWO), Department of Personnel Services, the Ministerial Salary Supplement Program, the C.M.E. Fire and Casualty Program, and any other programs of pensions and insurance that may be established by the C.M.E. Church.

Connectional Commissions

¶ **1003.5.** The total program of the Christian Methodist Episcopal Church shall be projected and evaluated by five Connectional Commissions which shall operate in the following manner:

§1. Each commission shall be composed of ten members recommended by the College of Bishops and confirmed by the General Connectional Board. Members should be selected according to ability and interest in the particular commission and not necessarily as representatives of Episcopal Districts or Annual Conferences. Vacancies by death or resignation shall be filled by the College of Bishops.

§2. One of the bishops, as designated by the College of Bishops, shall be the Chair of each Connectional Commission.

§3. The Connectional Commissions shall meet at least every two years. The expenses for such meetings will be a part of the Connectional Budget.

¶ **1003.6.** *Commission on Faith and Order*

Purpose: To keep before the Christian Methodist Episcopal Church its biblical, theological, and historical heritage; to inform the church on any theological concerns that may be referred to it by either the church or one of its agencies.

¶ **1003.7.** *Commission on Life and Witness*

Purpose: To monitor the denominational life of the church and determine the extent to which the connectional administration of the church is in keeping with its established missions, goals, and purpose; and to plan for the future of the church in every area of its life and witness.

¶ **1003.8.** *Commission on Social Justice and Human Concerns*

Purpose: To determine the witness of the Christian Methodist Episcopal Church in terms of the social, economic, and political issues of the day.

¶ **1003.9.** *Commission on Ecumenicity*

Purpose: To evaluate the nature of the relationship the Christian Methodist Episcopal Church should have with other Christian denominations and religious organizations.

¶**1003.10.** *Commission on Concerns of Women in the Ministry*

Purpose: Set goals and seek avenues to deal effectively with issues concerning the work of women in the ministry; and to develop a plan of action to implement said goals at every level of the Connection.

PART XI
GENERAL CHURCH ADMINISTRATION: CONNECTIONAL OPERATIONS

50. The General Department of Finance
51. The General Department of Publications
52. *The Christian Index*
53. The General Board of Personnel Services

CHAPTER 50
THE GENERAL DEPARTMENT OF FINANCE

¶ **1004.** There shall be a General Department of Finance of the Christian Methodist Episcopal Church with the authority to administer the General Funds of the church in accordance with the Connectional Budget approved by the General Conference and the provisions of the *Discipline*. The department shall be under the supervision of the General Connectional Board as provided by the *Discipline*.

¶ **1004.1.** The executive officer of the General Department of Finance shall be a General Secretary elected for that purpose in accordance with the Discipline. The General Secretary of Finance will be amenable to the General Connectional Board as provided in the *Discipline*.

¶ **1005.** The fiscal year for the Christian Methodist Episcopal Church shall be January 1 to December 31.

¶ **1006.** All connectional funds, including the apportionments to the several Annual Conferences approved by the General Conference, shall be forwarded to the General Secretary of the Department of Finance with the exception of the 12% Pastors' Salaries for the C.M.E. Retirement Plan and funds derived from the C.M.E. Fire and Casualty Program which shall be received by the General Secretary of the General Board of Personnel Services, the income of the General Department of Publications, subscription income from The Christian Index and The Missionary Messenger, and funds that may be restricted by civil law or previous commitments. The General Department of Finance shall be and is designated, effective January 1, 1996, as the Business Department of the C.M.E. Church.

¶ **1007.** The General Secretary of Finance shall expend the connectional funds in accordance with the Connectional Budget. The schedule for expenditures shall be established by the General Connectional Board in light of provisions of the budget and expected schedule of income. At no time shall the General Secretary of Finance be required to overdraw the allocations in any fund after it has been established.

¶ **1008.** The General Secretary of Finance shall make an annual report of the work of the General Department of Finance for the fiscal year ended. Said report shall include all income, disbursements, investments, fund balances, and other pertinent data as may be required by the Discipline to the General Connectional Board, which report shall be accompanied by the report of a Certified Public Accountant approved by the General Connectional Board. In addition, a quadrennial report covering each year shall be made to the General Conference.

¶ **1009.** The allocation for the work of the General Departments of the church (cf. Connectional Budget, Schedule "B") shall be disbursed to the General Departments in accordance with a budget for each department based on a needs analysis and program projections of each department approved annually by the General Connectional Board.

¶ **1010.** The allocation for Episcopal Supervision of Non-U.S. Areas shall be under the authority of the bishop assigned to the designated area. Funds for the work in the Non-U.S. Areas of the Church (termed "Missions to Non-U.S. Areas" in the budget) shall be on this ratio: Africa: 60%; Haiti: 25%; and Jamaica:15%, and shall be under the supervision of the bishop assigned to that area.

¶ **1011.** The terms "expense" or "travel expense" shall be used for transportation costs, room, board, and necessary incidentals involved on the part of persons designated by proper authority to represent the C.M.E. Church or attend a meeting in the interest of the church. The General Connectional Board shall establish a uniform policy and procedure for such expenses which shall include a reasonable mileage cost, per diem, etc., and said policy and procedure shall apply to all persons whenever the church is expected to pay such expenses. The General Secretary of Finance shall pay such expenses in accordance with the provisions of the budget, the established policy, and upon presentation of appropriate voucher.

¶ **1012.** Expenses for bishops, both active and retired, shall be provided for official meetings of the College of Bishops, but shall be limited to no more than three such meetings per fiscal year. Expenses for the bishops, both active and retired, and the wives and widows of bishops shall be provided for attendance at the General Conference and the Quadrennial Assembly of the Women's Connectional Council.

¶ **1013.** The management of the General Headquarters of the Christian Methodist Episcopal Church shall be under the supervision of the Executive Secretary of the C.M.E. Church, and the allocation for the headquarters shall be under the authority of the Executive Secretary.

¶ **1014.** The allocation for Professional Fees and Services (cf. Connectional Budget, Schedule "C")includes as its primary expenditure a retainer fee for the Legal Counsel of the C.M.E. Church, which allocation shall be under the authority of the College of Bishops.

¶ **1015.** The allocation for C.M.E. Colleges includes funds for the resolution of the financial problems of Mississippi Industrial College. Upon resolution of such problems, as determined by the General Connectional Board, the allocation shall be divided equally among the remaining colleges.

¶ **1016.** The Department of Finance shall have authority to invest any funds on hand not for immediate use or otherwise designated in savings certificates or other preferred securities, provided that one-half of interest accrued therefrom shall be used for the Reserve Fund and one-half for the Contingency Fund.

¶ **1016.1.** The Standing Committee on Finance has the responsibility to adopt an investment policy for the C.M.E. Church and it shall be their responsibility to implement and monitor the investments of the Church. It shall handle and monitor all matters related to finance.

¶ **1016.2.** The Department of Finance in consultation with the College of Bishops shall explore alternate sources of revenue to aid in underwriting the operational costs of the Christian Methodist Episcopal Church. A recommendation shall be presented annually to the General Connectional Board for action.

The Christian Methodist Episcopal Church
General Connectional Budget

¶ 1017. Connectional Budget January, 1999 – December, 2002

Schedule "A" - Episcopal Fund

Categories		Per Annum
Episcopal Salaries	10 @45,000	450,000
Episcopal Travel	10 @6,500	65,000
Episcopal Administration	10 @6,500	65,000
Senior Bishop's Office Expense		6,000
Secretary - College of Bishops		3,000
Total Schedule A		**$589,000**

Schedule "B" - Connectional Ministries

General Officers Salaries	9 @30,000	270,000
General Officers Housing	9 @ 6,500	58,500
Program - General Departments		
Lay		45,000
Evangelism & Missions		50,000
Christian Education		85,000
(Programs 70,000)		
(Young Adult 10,000*)		
(Scouting 5,000*)		

Total Schedule B   **$508,000**

*Requisitions must be made through the General Secretary of Christian Education.

Schedule "C" - Connectional Operations

Categories	Per Annum
Operational Fund	55,000
General Connectional Board Expense	60,000
Inter-Church Delegates	25,000
Headquarters Mortgage Note	160,000
Executive Secretary Expense	16,000
Department of Finance Expense	67,000
The Christian Index	28,100
Subscriptions to *Christian Index* for Retired Preachers/Widows	21,000
Connectional Commissions and Committees	7,000
Commission on Human Concerns	10,000
General Conference Expense	20,000
Judicial Council	10,000
Reserve Fund	33,500
Collins Chapel Hospital	28,000
Women's Missionary Council	48,300
General Counsel	75,000
(Legal Retainer 65,000)	
(Office Expense and Travel 10,000)	
Directors and Officers Liability Insurance	13,000
Mississippi Industrial College Properties	50,000
Total Schedule C	**$726,900**

Schedule "D" - Educational Ministries

Lane College	141,000
Miles College	141,000
Paine College	141,000
Texas College	141,000
Phillips School of Theology	175,000
Ministerial Scholarships	60,000
Total Schedule D	**$799,000**

Schedule "E" Ecumenical Affiliations

World Methodist Council	5,000
National Council of Churches	5,000
World Council of Churches	5,000
Consultation on Church Union	6,500
Congress of National Black Churches	10,000
American Bible Society	2,000
NAACP	10,000
SCLC	5,000
Church Union of Pan Methodist Bodies	3,750
Commission on Pan Methodism	1,855
Operation PUSH	1,000
One Church - One School	500
Commission on Religion in Appalachia	2,500
Total Schedule E	**$58,105**

Schedule "F" - Pension Ministries

Categories		Per Annum
C.M.E. Gift Fund		400,000
Retired Bishops Pensions	4 @18,000	72,000
Episcopal Annuity	10 @5,400	54,000
Widows of Bishops	5 @8,000	40,000
General Officers Annuity	9 @3,600	32,400
Retired General Officers Pension	2 @13,000	26,000
Total Schedule F		**$624,4000**

Schedule "G" - Missions to Non - U. S. Areas

Africa

Travel in Continental Africa	15,000
African Housing Allowance	12,500
Operations	25,000
P. R. Shy Hospital	7,000
Breeding-Montgomery Bible College	10,000
General Conference Delegate Expense	7,000

Jamaica

Operations	13,000
General Conference Delegate Expense	2,000

Haiti

Operations	13,000
General Conference Delegate Expense	2,000
Total Schedule G	**$106,500**

Recapitulation of Connectional Budget
January, 1999 - December, 2002

Schedules	Per Annum
"A" - Epsicopal Fund	589,000
"B" - Connectional Ministries	508,500
"C" - Connectional Operations	726,900
"D" - Educational Ministries	799,000
"E" - Ecumenical Affiliations	58,105
"F" - Pension/Ministries	624,400
"G" - Foreign Work/Missions	106,500
Grand Total	**$3,412,405**

¶ 1017.1. Connectional Assessments Per Episcopal District
January, 1999 - December, 2002

Episcopal Districts	Per Annum
First Episcopal District	475,274
Second Episcopal District	222,230
Third Episcopal District	500,305
Fourth Episcopal District	367,318
Fifth Episcopal District	354,392
Sixth Episcopal District	423,889
Seventh Episcopal District	332,095
Eighth Episcopal District	430,649
Ninth Episcopal District	305,163
Tenth Episcopal District	1,000
Grand Total	**$3,412,405**

CHAPTER 51
THE GENERAL DEPARTMENT
OF PUBLICATIONS

¶ **1018.** The name for the publishing interests shall be the General Department of Publications. This Department comprises the publishing interests of the Christian Methodist Episcopal Church.

¶ **1018.1.** The objective of the General Department of Publications shall be: the advancement of the cause of Christianity by disseminating religious knowledge and useful literary and scientific information in the form of books, tracts and periodicals; the promotion of Christian Education; the transaction of any business properly connected with the publishing, manufacturing and distribution of books, tracts, periodicals, materials and supplies for Churches, Church Schools and such other business as the Committee On Publications may authorize and direct.

¶ **1018.2.** The General Department of Publications shall be under the direction and control of the General Connectional Board and the Committee On Publications, acting through the General Secretary, who shall be elected according to the laws of the General Conference, and through other officers as the General Connectional Board may find necessary or expedient to select.

¶ **1018.3.** The net proceeds of the General Department of Publications, after setting up proper reserve funds for efficient operation of the business and necessary expansion, shall be paid to the General Board of Personnel Services to be distributed to the Claimants of that Department.

¶ **1018.4.** The income of the General Department of Publications shall be appropriated to no other purpose than its own legitimate business and the distribution of the net proceeds set forth above.

¶ **1018.5.** The General Department of Publications shall have charge of exhibit space at all national and connectional meetings of the Christian Methodist Episcopal Church. All negotiations and agreements for use of the exhibit space must be done and made with the General Secretary of the Department of Publications.

¶ **1019.** There shall be a Connectional Historical Library which is the Woodruff Library at Clark Atlanta University, Atlanta, Georgia to preserve and keep the records of the Christian Methodist Episcopal Church and all data referring to its organization, its past history, its heroes and achievements. The Historical Library shall contain the archives for periodicals, books, and literature written or published by members of the C.M.E. Church. It shall preserve pictures, minutes, reports, letters and all data of historical value for the use of the Connection. The artifacts shall be located in the Connectional Headquarters under the care of the Historical Society and shall be an auxiliary of the Commission on History and Archives. Its personnel shall be appointed jointly by the General Department of Publications and the Commission on History and Archives.

¶ **1020.** The General Conference shall elect a General Secretary of Publications who shall be the executive officer of the C.M.E. Church Publishing House, under the supervision and direction of the Committee on Publications subject to the power and authority of the General Connectional Board.

¶ **1020.1.** The General Secretary of Publications shall submit written report to each session of the General Connectional Board. The report shall include an audit of the funds of the General Department of Publications by a Certified Public Accountant.

¶ **1020.2.** The General Secretary of Publications shall have authority to extend the business of the General Department of Publications, with the approval of the General Connectional Board, in such manner as he or she judges to be for the best interest of the Church.

Church School Publications
¶ **1021.** The manuscript for the various Church School publications shall be furnished by the General Department of Christian Education, printed and sold by the General Department of Publications of the C.M.E. Church.

¶ **1021.1.** At the beginning of the quadrennium, the General Secretary of Publications and the General Secretary of Christian Education shall prepare a budget covering the costs for Lesson Outlines and cuts to be used for the publication of literature.

¶ **1021.2.** In matters involving financial responsibility in the manufacturing and distributing of literature, the final determination in every case shall lie with the Department of Publications.

¶ **1021.3.** The General Secretary of Publications and the Editor of Church School Publications of the General Department of Christian Education shall prepare a schedule for all manuscripts to be printed by the General Department of Publications, so that each publication may be mailed 15 days before the date it is to be used.

¶ **1021.4.** The Editor of the Church School publications shall have the right to sit with the Committee on Publications for the consideration of matters pertaining to the joint interests of the Committee on Publications and the Committee on Christian Education and shall have the privilege of voice without vote.

¶ **1021.5.** It shall be the duty of the Bishops, Presiding Elders, and Pastors, to see to it that all of CME Annual Conferences, Districts, Charges and Mission Charges use the Sunday Church School literature from the C.M.E. Publishing House and give full support to all other enterprises of the Department of Publications.

Printing for Church Agencies

¶ **1022.** It is recommended that all of the Departments under the General Connectional Board, institutions, commissions, colleges and Annual Conferences of the C.M.E. Church have their printing done by the C.M.E. Publishing House.

¶ **1022.1.** The rights and responsibility for selling and distributing religious literature, books and other supplies at District, Annual, General meetings and Leadership Schools shall rest with the General Department of Publications.

Commission on Records and Statistical Blanks

¶ **1023.** The General Conference shall elect quadrennially a Commission on Records and Statistical Blanks, consisting of five members, of which the General Secretary of Publications, the General Secretary of Christian Education, and the Chairman of the Committee on Publications shall be ex-officio members.

Annual Conference Board

¶ **1024.** There shall be, in each Annual Conference, an Annual Conference Board of Publication Services. The Board shall:

§1. Consist of an equal number of ministers and laymen elected from the respective Presiding Elder Districts by the Annual Conference; the number and mode of election to be determined by the Annual Conference.

§2. Immediately after election, the Board shall meet and elect such officers and committees as it may deem necessary.

§3. Make an annual report of its work to the Annual Conference and to the office of the General Secretary of Publications.

§4. Annually nominate a Conference Agent of Publication Services, who shall be confirmed by the Annual Conference. He or she shall be the Executive Officer of the Annual Conference Board of Publication Services.

§5. Direct, promote, and distribute religious literature within the bounds of the Annual Conference.

§6. Cooperate with all other agencies in distributing to all Local Churches sufficient Sunday School and Christian Youth Fellowship literature published by the C.M.E. Church Publishing House.

§7. Compile or secure an itemized report on the amount of literature purchased by each Local Church.

§8. Cooperate with the General Department of Publications, the various Annual Conference agencies and the Pastors in distributing and securing subscriptions for The Christian Index and other literature of the Church.

§9. Encourage the writing of books, pamphlets, and other religious literature to be published by the Publishing House. The Annual Conference Board of Publication Services shall supervise and encourage the sales of books and other literature from the Publishing House at the Annual Conference. It shall assist the General Secretary of Publications in securing competent persons for distributing religious literature.

§10. Through its Annual Conference, assist the Publishing Department in locating and establishing branch depositories within the bounds of the Annual Conference.

¶ **1025.** The General Department of Publications shall sponsor, in each Annual Conference, a Historical Society, the members of which shall be appointed or elected in whatever manner the Conference may decide. Its duty shall be to help preserve the records of the Church.

¶ **1025.1.** The Annual Conference Historical Society shall gather all data of historical interest, such as pictures, letters, Minutes, relics, and other data pertaining the organization of the Church's early development and past history of the denomination. It shall also preserve and keep a record of current items of importance, and keep before the people the glorious deeds of the heroes of the past.

¶ **1025.2.** The Historical Society under the supervision of the Annual Conference, and in cooperation with other agencies, should secure such historical data and submit it to the Historical Library of the C.M.E. Church at the Headquarters of the Church.

CHAPTER 52

THE CHRISTIAN INDEX

¶ **1026.** *The Christian Index* shall be the Official Publication of the Christian Methodist Episcopal Church; and shall publish all official announcements, notices, communications, and decisions of the Church as directed by the General Connectional Board, and/or the College of Bishops.

¶ **1026.1.** *The Christian Index* shall be published on a regular schedule and special publications may be advisable. The editing of *The Christian Index* shall be under the supervision of the General Connectional Board's Standing Committee on *The Christian Index* which shall be constituted according to the *Discipline of the C.M.E. Church.*

¶ **1026.2.** The cost of publishing *The Christian Index*, including printing, mailing, and circulation management, shall be defrayed by subscriptions to it; the rate of said subscriptions shall be determined by the General Connectional Board.

¶ **1026.3.** The printing, mailing, and circulation management of *The Christian Index* shall be the responsibility of the General Department of Publications, which shall bear full printing and mailing costs.

¶ **1027.** The preparation and editing of *The Christian Index* shall be the responsibility of the Editor who shall be elected quadrennially according to the laws enacted by the General Conference and shall be one of the General Officers of the Church (cf. ¶ 1001.8).

¶ **1028.** The expense of the editorial office in the preparation of the manuscripts, travels, telephone, etc., shall be derived from the allocation of the Connectional Budget.

¶ **1029.** Circulation income (i.e., income from subscriptions) in excess of the printing, mailing and circulation expense shall be turned over to the General Secretary of the General Board of Personnel Services to be distributed to the Claimants of that Department.

¶ 1030. Correspondents

§1. Each Annual Conference shall have a Correspondent to *The Christian Index* who shall be named by the Presiding Bishop of the Conference. The Correspondent shall report events of the Annual Conference to the Editor.

§ 2. Each Presiding Elder's District will have a Reporter to *The Christian Index* who will report events of the District to the paper and obtain subscriptions and promote it throughout the District. The Reporter will be appointed by the Presiding Elder.

¶ 1031. Each Local Church will have an Index Agent, who will serve as the Agent for *The Christian Index* in the Local Church. He/she will be named by the Preacher-in-Charge at the Quarterly Conference and will secure subscriptions, promote the paper within the Local Church, and handle problems with subscriptions that might arise.

¶ 1032. Each Local Preacher and Traveling Preacher of the Christian Methodist Episcopal Church shall subscribe to *The Christian Index* annually.

¶ 1033. Retired preachers and widows/widowers of ministers who were in Full Connection shall receive subscriptions to *The Christian Index* without charge. Within 30 days of the close of the Annual Conference the secretary of each Annual Conference shall forward to the General Secretary of Publications a list of such persons. Said susbscriptions shall be included in the Connectional Budget and paid to the Department of Publications by the General Secretary of Finance.

CHAPTER 53
THE GENERAL BOARD OF
PERSONNEL SERVICES

Article 1 — Organization

¶ **1034.** There shall be a Department known as the General Board of Personnel Services (formerly known as the General Board of Pensions) of the Christian Methodist Episcopal Church.

¶ **1034.1.** The objectives of the General Board of Personnel Services shall be the following:

§1. To develop an expanded program which includes concerns of and for the ministry in terms of support and maintenance, counseling, welfare relief, pre-retirement assistance, retirement and survivors' benefits of C.M.E. ministers.

§2. To oversee and coordinate all pension funds, insurance programs, health services, retirement plans and other related personnel services for ordained ministers in Full Connection and lay personnel working full time for the Church.

§3. To keep records and vital statistics of all clergy personnel in Full Connection such as date of birth, Social Security numbers, baptismal data, education, special skills, ordinations, consecration, marriages, divorces, remarriages, beneficiaries and date of death.

¶ **1034.2.** The Board shall have the following authority:

§1. To make By-laws in harmony with the Constitution and Discipline of the C.M.E. Church.

§2. To regulate its own proceedings in accordance with its own By-laws.

§3. To buy, acquire, receive by gift, devise or bequest, property, real, personal, and mixed; and to hold, sell and dispose of property.

§4. To secure appropriate counsel and administer funds for its work.

§5. To elect necessary officers and members of its staff, remove them for cause, and fill vacancies.

§6. To do any and all things which shall be authorized by its By-laws and Board of Directors.

§7. To name trustees for the purpose of receiving and taking title to such gifts or devises to the benefit of the Board.

¶ **1034.3.** The General Board of Personnel Services shall have a General Secretary and such other staff persons as the governing Board may deem necessary to select from time to time, to carry out an expanded role in its efforts to address the general welfare and needs of ministers and full time lay personnel of the Christian Methodist Episcopal Church. The allocation in the Connectional Budget for this department for administration shall not exceed the average allocation to the other General Departments for administrative purposes.

¶ **1034.4.** The General Board of Personnel Services shall be under the management of a Committee of the General Connectional Board, consisting of a Bishop, who shall be elected by the College of Bishops and shall serve as Chairman, the General Secretary of the General Board of Personnel Services, as ex-officio, and members assigned to it by the Special Committee established by the General Connectional Board.

¶ **1034.5.** This Committee shall meet annually during the meeting of the General Connectional Board, or at such times as business shall require, and then upon the call of the Chairman.

¶ **1034.6.** The General Connectional Board shall supervise the work of the Board, hear and receive the audited reports of the General Secretary.

¶ **1034.7.** The General Board of Personnel Services is divided into the following component areas:

§1. Retirement Benefits: C.M.E. Church Retirement Plan and Gift Ministry (to designated recipients).

§2. Ministerial Care: Ministerial support, consultation and counseling services, Christian Ministry Sunday, records.

§3. Economic Development: economic generation projects, donations, gifts, wills and bequests.

§4. Insurances: Group Life, Group AD and D, Group Safety Plan (Fire and Casualty Coverage), Group Health Insurance and Health Care.

§5. Fiscal Affairs: Investment income, endowment program.

Article 2 — Operational Procedure

¶ 1035. The General Secretary shall receive all monies of the Department, and give an official receipt for the same. The Secretary shall report annually to the General Connectional Board, and quadrennially to the General Conference.

¶ 1035.1. All money received by the General Secretary shall be turned over to the General Secretary of Finance, except that which accrues from the General Fund, twelve percent (12%) of employees' salaries, and any direct gifts, donations, solicitations, bequests and funds generated from interest and economic development projects.

¶ 1035.2. The General Secretary shall keep a record of the retired ministers and families of deceased ministers in each Annual Conference, showing the time each retired minister served the active ministry after being admitted into full connection. The General Secretary shall also give the number and age of the children of each deceased minister's family, if any.

¶ 1035.3. The Superannuated Preacher, Widows, & Orphans (S. P. W. & O) Plan, having been abolished by the General Conference of 1982, has been replaced by a periodic Gift Plan. The General Secretary of Personnel Services shall, as funds become available from time to time, distribute periodic gifts to the existing recipients of the old S.P.W. & O. Plan, and the General Secretary is authorized to do all things necessary to carry out the intent of the original S.P.W. & O. Plan wherever possible.

¶ 1035.4. The periodic gift distribution for the recipients shall accrue from the General Fund and from net income of the operation of the General Department of Publications.

Article 3—Annual Conference Board

¶ 1036. It shall be the duty of the Annual Conference to elect an Annual Conference Board of Personnel Services.

¶ 1036.1. The Board shall be constituted of the Presiding Elders and a layperson from each District, who shall collect and send to the General Secretary of the Department the following information through the Records Clerk:

§1. The name of each retired minister.

§2. The number of years spent in active service after the minister was admitted into Full Connection.

§3. The name of each widow(er), the number of years the spouse served after admission into Full Connection, when the minister died, and a certified copy of the death certificate; the number and age of each child of the deceased preacher and the proper address of all recipients.

§4. The roll of Gift Plan recipients of the Annual Conference and other neccessary information as may be requested by the General Board of Personnel Services. Recipients shall not claim or be eligible to receive benefits unless their names have been officially reported to the General Secretary by the Conference.

¶ **1036.2.** Each recipient shall report annually to his or her Annual Conference, the name, address, present status; and name, age and status of all recipients who are minors.

Article 4—Endowment Fund

¶ **1037.** There should be an Endowment Fund connected with the General Board of Personnel Services.

¶ **1037.1.** The General Board of Personnel Services is hereby authorized by the General Conference to raise one million dollars for the Pension Endowment Fund. This drive is to cover a period of ten to twenty years.

¶ **1037.2.** The funds for the Endowment Program shall accrue from plans and devices instituted and promoted by the General Secretary and his or her assistant(s).

¶ **1037.3.** All monies accruing from interest on endowment, net income from real estate investments, or otherwise, will be added to the funds in the hands of the General Secretary of Personnel Services for annual appropriation and distribution.

¶ **1037.4.** The General Secretary shall secure such help as shall be necessary to expedite the business of the department and devise such other plans among the ministers and members of the church that will work best in raising the endowment (not to interfere with the program of the church.)

Article 5 —Revenue and Accountability

¶ **1038.** Revenue for the support of the Board of Personnel Services shall be derived from:

§1. The percentage allotted by the General Conference.

§2. The interest on the Endowment Fund.

§3. From funds solicited by the General Secretary from corporations, firms, institutions and individuals; from Annual Conferences, district meetings and local charges which the General Secretary may visit to devise plans among ministers, members and friends for the support of this department.

¶ **1038.1.** The General Secretary of Personnel Services shall be required to keep an accurate and itemized account of all receipts and disbursements and turn over to a Certified Public Accountant the books, vouchers and canceled checks for audit any time after the first of January preceding the meeting of the General Connectional Board in May of each year when the General Conference is not in session.

The Retirement Plan of the C.M.E. Church

Article 1- Name

¶ **1039.** There shall be and is hereby established a Retirement Plan for the salaried servants of the Christian Methodist Episcopal Church.

¶ **1039.1.** It is hereby mandated and directed that all active Bishops, General Officers, Presidents and Deans of Theological Seminaries, Presiding Elders and salaried Pastors of the Christian Methodist Episcopal Church, who are under 74 years of age, shall mandatorily enroll in the Christian Methodist Church Episcopal Retirement Plan.

§1. All lay employees, who are salaried and full-time, may, at their and their employer's option, be included in said plan upon request in writing, conforming to the regulations, and making annual contributions to said plan.

¶ **1039.2.** After funds have been paid by the local church to the Joint Board of Finance, Annual Conference and to the Department of Finance and/or Department of Personnel Services in 60 days as required by the Discipline of the Christian Methodist Episcopal Church, the enrollment time shall begin for a period of three years thereafter. If enrollment has not been completed after three (3) years from the above conditions, the paid-in funds shall be forfeited and will inure to the use and benefit of the plan and are not refundable or returnable to the source.

¶ **1039.3.** During the three year period in which a minister fails to enroll, the General Secretary of Personnel Services shall escrow the funds paid by the local church in an interest bearing account.

¶ **1039.4.** A serving General Officer who retires in office, pursuant to the retirement laws of the Christian Methodist Episcopal Church, shall be entitled to benefits as follows:

§1. A General Officer who serves twelve (12) consecutive years or more, and retires while actively in office as such General Officer, shall be entitled to a sum equal to one-half (1/2) of a General Officer's salary at the time of retirement.

§2. A General Officer who serves a minimum of eight (8) consecutive years or more, and retires while still acting as such General Officer, shall be entitled to a sum equal to one-third (1/3) of the salary of a General Officer at the time of retirement.

¶1039.5 The Trustee/Fiduciary holding the retirement contributions for the General Officer shall pay according to the amount of retirement benefits held to the credit of the participant. The Financial Secretary of the Christian Methodist Episcopal Church shall pay the amount of benefits due to be paid by the Church, according to the benefit schedule heretofore stated.

Article 2—Revenue
¶ **1040.** Revenue for the contributions of the Retirement Plan participants shall be derived from:

§1. The source of salaries of the Bishops, General Officers, Deans of Seminaries, Presiding Elders, Church Pastors and Ordained Ministers of the Christian Methodist Episcopal Church on authorized leave of absence or special assignment shall pay an amount equal to 12% of their annual reported salary; active employees on authorized leave of absence or on special assignment should pay an amount equal to 12% of their annual reported salary. (The 1986 General Conference froze the contribution at 12%.) All salaried full-time lay employees may be included in the Christian Methodist Episcopal Church Retirement Plan upon opting to do so, conforming to the plan regulations and making the required contributions annually.

§2. For the Pastor, the source of the twelve percent (12%) of salary shall be the local church he or she serves.

§3. For the Presiding Elder, the source of the twelve percent (12%) of salary shall be the Annual Conference he or she serves, which shall be reported to the respective Annual Conference.

§4. For the General Officers and Bishops, the source of the twelve percent (12%) of salary shall be the Department of Finance of the Christian Methodist Episcopal Church.

§5. For the salaried lay personnel, the source of the twelve percent (12%) shall be the employer if said employer has opted to participate in the Christian Methodist Episcopal Church Retirement Plan on behalf of the said employees.

¶ **1040.1.** The twelve percent (12%) of salaries are to be paid annually, during each Annual Conference.

¶ **1040.2.** The pension reports and retirement contributions collected by each Annual Conference shall be reported, subject to penalty, sixty (60) days following the collection of said funds in the sessions of each Annual Conference and its Winter Council, but not later than December l, of each fiscal year which shall be the deadline for completing and reporting of all funds.

Article 3- *Method of Payment and Enrollment*

¶ **1041.** The twelve percent (12%) of salaries of each pastor shall be paid at the Annual Conferences to the Joint Board and Cabinet and/or other designated agencies.

¶ **1041.1.** Each Annual Conference or source of salary for General Officers, College Presidents, Deans, and salaried lay personnel shall forward the entire amount paid and the retirement reports to the General Secretary of the General Board of Personnel Services of the Christian Methodist Episcopal Church within sixty (60) days following the collection of said funds but not later than December 1 of each fiscal year.

¶ **1041.2.** A penalty shall be assessed against the Annual Conference, Department of Finance, and other sources of retirement contributions at a rate equal to the annual earnings rate of the guaranteed investment fund when retirement reports and payments are received after December 1.

¶ **1041.3.** It shall be the duty of each Presiding Bishop, Presiding Elder and Annual Conference Board of Personnel Services to assist the Annual Conference Joint Board in assuring the enrollment of each eligible participant into the Retirement Plan and the reporting of salaries and payments.

¶ **1041.4.** The Bishop of an Episcopal District shall use the same diligence and have the same authority and obligation in the collection of the twelve percent (12%) of salaries for the Retirement Plan as in the collection of the General Funds.

Article 4 - Operations
¶ **1042.** The General Secretary of the General Board of Personnel Services shall file for and maintain in good standing a Charter of Incorporation in the name of the General Board of Personnel Services (Christian Methodist Episcopal Church), Inc.

¶ **1042.1.** The General Secretary of the Board of Personnel Services or its Contract Administrator, within thirty (30) days following the receipt of contributions, shall forward each participant a receipt showing the amount of salary on the participant's report and the amount of contributions paid.

¶ **1042.2.** The General Secretary of the General Board of Personnel Services shall maintain a Fidelity Bond in the amount of ten percent (10%) of twelve percent of salaries reported and paid.

Article 5 - Charter of Incorporation
¶ **1043.** The General Secretary of the General Board of Personnel Services shall file for and maintain in good standing a Charter of Incorporation in the name of the Christian Methodist Episcopal Church Retirement Trust.

¶ **1043.1.** The officers of the General Board of Personnel Services of the Christian Methodist Episcopal Church, Inc, shall be:

§1. President, the Bishop elected by the College of Bishops.

§2. Secretary-Treasurer, the General Officer elected by the General Conference.

¶ **1043.2.** The members of the Retirement Trust Board shall be assigned by the Special Committee of the General Connectional Board. The initial officers and Board shall be the present members of the Board of Personnel Services of the Christian Methodist Episcopal Church.

¶ **1043.3.** The aforesaid, officers and members of the Retirement Trust shall serve as like members of the Board of Trustees or Directors of the Corporation.

¶ **1043.4.** The General Secretary of the Board of Personnel Services and the aforesaid officers and Board members are subject to the General Connectional Board and/or the General Conference of the Christian Methodist Episcopal Church.

Article 6 - The Plan

¶ **1044.** The plan is a qualified Money Purchase Plan for the exclusive benefit of eligible employees and their beneficiaries.

¶ **1044.1.** Employees are eligible to participate in the Plan after completing one (1) year of service and having attained age 18, provided the General Board of Personnel Services has received a properly executed enrollment form and contributions of at least $180 have been made.

¶ **1044.2.** An employee shall become a member of the earlier of the first day of the Plan Year or the first day of the seventh month of the Plan Year coinciding with or next following the date the employee satisfies the Plan eligibility requirements, provided an enrollment form is completed.

¶ **1044.3.** If a person fails to enroll within three (3) years from the time contributions were reported, the contributions plus accrued interest shall be forfeited.

¶ **1044.4.** Distributions of benefits shall be made no later than one year after termination due to retirement, official withdrawal from the Christian Methodist Episcopal Church, or death.

¶ **1044.5.** Members shall be entitled to 100% of their account balance except when employment is terminated by withdrawal from the Christian Methodist Episcopal Church before becoming fully vested in the account.

¶ **1044.6.** A copy of the Plan shall be on file at the office of the Secretary-Treasurer of the Retirement Plan and Trust and may be read by members, their beneficiaries or legal representatives at any reasonable time.

¶ **1044.7.** Copies of the summary plan description, a brief description of the Plan and member rights, obligations, and benefits shall be forwarded to each member by the Secretary-Treasurer.

¶ **1044.8.** The Secretary-Treasurer of the Retirement Plan and Trust shall submit to the Internal Revenue Service, and other appropriate agencies, all amendments and documents required.

The C.M.E. Church Group Fire & Casualty Insurance Plan

Article 1 - Name
¶ **1046.** There shall be and there is a program known as the Christian Methodist Episcopal Church Group Fire & Casualty Insurance plan.

¶ **1046.1.** The C.M.E. Group Fire & Casualty Insurance plan shall serve as a risk management agency to negotiate premiums, claims and loss prevention needs for all C.M.E. Church properties throughout the Connection.

¶ **1046.2.** All C.M.E. Church properties shall be insured with the C.M.E. Church Group Fire & Casualty Insurance Plan.

Article 2—Management
¶ **1047.** The General Board of Personnel Services shall be charged with the risk management responsibility and that of collecting premiums and negotiating coverage for C.M.E. Church properties, including colleges, departments, housing projects, hospitals, nursing homes and other properties owned and leased by the Christian Methodist Episcopal Church.

Article 3 - Design of Plan

¶ **1048.** The Christian Methodist Episcopal Church Group Fire and Casualty Insurance Plan is designed to accomplish the following:

(a) Cover all properties of the C.M.E. Church regardless of location, conditions of previous history or Insurability.

(b) Give the C.M.E. Church an element of self-determination in dealing with rates and limits of coverage.

(c) Give the C.M.E. Church a place in the insurance market of the nation.

Article 4 - Brokerage

¶ **1049.** The General Secretary, with the approval of the Chairman of the Committee of Personnel Services and the Committee thereof, shall select the liability carrier and/or broker herein, to insure said C.M.E. Church property in said plan.

Article 5 - Loss Prevention

¶ **1050.** The C.M.E. Church Group Fire & Casualty Plan shall provide a Loss Prevention Program to each participant in the Group Plan for the purpose of minimizing the loss potential and protecting against unnecessary claims. This program should result in stabilizing rates and eventually decreasing premiums.

Article 6 - Trust Fund

¶ **1051.** A Trust Account shall be maintained for the collection and transmittal of premiums from the C.M.E. Church properties to the brokerage firm at such times and in such amounts as may be mutually agreed upon by the College of Bishops, General Board of Personnel Services and the primary broker.

¶ **1052.** All laws and parts of laws in conflict with the foregoing are hereby repealed.

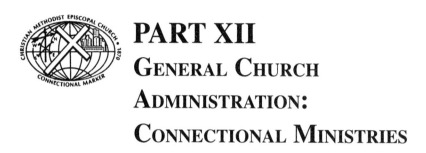

PART XII
GENERAL CHURCH ADMINISTRATION: CONNECTIONAL MINISTRIES

54. The General Department of Christian Education

55. The Women's Missionary Council

56. The General Department of Lay Ministry

57. The General Department of Evangelism and Missions

CHAPTER 54
THE GENERAL DEPARTMENT
OF CHRISTIAN EDUCATION

Organization and Duties

¶ **1100.** The General Department of Christian Education shall be under the supervision of the Standing Committee on Christian Education of the General Connectional Board.

¶ **1100.1.** The Committee shall be constituted as provided by the *Discipline* of the C.M.E. Church.

¶ **1100.2.** The Committee membership shall consist of both clerical and lay representatives.

¶ **1100.3.** Vacancies during the quadrennium shall be filled in accordance with the provisions of the *Discipline* as set forth in the section on the General Connectional Board.

¶ **1100.4.** The Presidents of the recognized C.M.E. institutions of higher education, including the Dean of Phillips School of Theology, shall be ex-officio members of the Committee on Christian Education.

¶ **1100.5.** At its initial meeting the Committee shall organize by electing a Vice - Chair, Recording Seretary. The Chair shall be a Bishop elected by the College of Bishops.

¶ **1101.** There shall be an Executive Committee of the Standing Committee on Christian Education composed of the President, Vice President, Recording Secretary, General Secretary of the Board of Christian Education, and any other persons deemed desirable by the Committee.

¶ **1101.1.** The Presidents of the recognized C.M.E. institutions of higher education shall meet with the Executive Committee when matters affecting the institutions are being considered.

¶ **1101.2.** The Executive Committee shall meet at such times and places as may be designated by the President and the General Secretary.

¶ **1101.3.** The Standing Committee may commit to the Executive Committee such powers and duties as it may determine. The Recording Secretary of the Executive Committee shall send to each member of the Standing Committee a copy of the minutes of the Executive Committee meeting.

¶ **1102.** The Standing Committee shall meet annually during the meeting of the General Connectional Board. The majority of the members shall constitute a quorum.

¶ **1102.1.** A special meeting of the Standing Committee may be held when deemed necessary by the President and the General Secretary or when requested in writing by a majority of the members of the Committee.

¶ **1103.** The expense of the meetings of the Committee on Christian Education and its Executive Committee shall be paid in accordance with the Connectional Budget.

¶ **1103.1.** Members whose expenses are paid in part or otherwise provided for shall receive only the remaining part of the expenses from the General Board of Christian Education.

¶ **1104.** The work of the General Department of Christian Education shall be conducted under such rules and regulations as may be prescribed by the General Conference from time to time. The operation of the Department shall be conducted under the Charter of the Department according to the laws of the state in which the principle offices of the General Department of Christian Education are located. It shall have power to regulate its own proceedings and pass By-laws for its own operations providing such By-laws do not conflict with the *Discipline of the Christian Methodist Episcopal Church* nor with the revisions of the Charter under which the Board operates.

¶ **1104.1.** The Department shall have authority to receive and apply donations, devises, bequests, to own, buy, and sell real estate; to do all other things provided for in said Charter, or subject to and under the provision of charter under which said Department shall operate.

¶ **1104.2.** The Department, with the approval of the General Connectional Board, shall have authority to promote religious educational conferences, pastors institutes, and other training activities in the interest of Christian training, nurture, and development of children, youth, young adults, and adults.

¶ **1105.** The General Conference shall provide for the quadrennial election of the General Secretary of the General Department of Christian Education whose term of office shall be for four (4) years or until his successor is elected or appointed.

¶ **1105.1.** The General Connectional Board, in the interim of the General Conference, shall have the right and power, when cause is sufficient, to suspend the General Secretary and to fill the vacancy caused by such suspension until the ensuing General Conference. A vacancy caused by death, resignation, or suspension of the General Secretary shall be filled by the General Connectional Board.

¶ **1105.2.** The General Secretary shall be the Executive Officer of the Department and shall fulfill the duty of the office according to the job description as provided by the Committee on Christian Education or the General Connectional Board.

Division of General Christian Education

¶ **1106.** The purpose of the Division of General Christian Education is to provide opportunities for educational ministry to the various agencies, boards, departments, and age groupings of the Church, to promote Christian nurture, growth, and development at all levels.

¶ **1107.** *Church School Administration.* The General Department of Christian Education, through the Church School Department, shall promote programs in church school administration, curriculum development, and other needed subjects whereby the age groupings of the local church schools will provide adequate Christian growth.

¶ **1107.1.** The Department shall direct and promote a total program for the development of the Church School Department.

¶ **1107.2.** The Department shall provide or approve Sunday School, weekday Church School and vacation school charters, manuals, guides, song books, promotion certificates, programs for special days, and any other materials and supplies that are to be used in our Church Schools.

¶ **1107.3.** The Department of Christian Education shall have general supervision in the determination of the curriculum to be used in all Vacation Bible Schools and other weekday schools in our churches.

¶ **1107.4.** The Department shall promote, supervise, and provide suggestions for programs on the District, Annual Conference, Regional and Connectional levels for youth conferences, assemblies, Jubilees, and conventions.

¶ **1107.5.** The Department shall promote the scouting program and recommend the agencies for boys and girls as youth serving. In promoting scouting the *God and Country* award shall be developed.

¶ **1107.6** The General Department of Christian Education is the administrative unit for the ministry of Scouting.

§1. *Structure.* Two directors of Scouting exist beyond the Annual Conference.

(a) The National Director of Scouting, appointed by and supervised by the General Secretary of Christian Education, administers a national program of scouting and supervises Episcopal Directors of Scouting Ministries.

(b) The Episcopal Directors of Scouting Ministries, recommended by the Presiding Bishop, shall coordinate the programs within their respective districts. The appointment will be made by the National Directors of Scouting with approval of the General Secretary of Christian Education.

§2. *Operations.* For the *God and Country Awards* and *God and Service Award*, the materials and medals shall be those which are provided in the God and Country series of Programs of Religious Activities with Youth (P.R.A.Y.) under the general category Protestant.

§3 Girl Scouts of the USA within the CME Church shall be administered by an Associate Director of Scouting Ministries for Girl Scouts. The Associate will be a member of the Girl Scouts of the U.S.A. and the C.M.E. Church. Upon recommendation by the Director of Scouting Ministries, the Associate shall be appointed by the General Secretary of Christian Education and reimbursed for expenses through that Department. Other responsibilities and procedures will be developed and published by the Director of Scouting and the General Secretary (cf. ¶ 711 Scout Sunday).

¶ **1107.7** The Department of Christian Education shall develop a uniform course of study and continuing education for ministers, and a uniform course of study for lay persons subject to revisions by the College of Bishops (cf. ¶ 442.1); and shall in conjunction with the General Department of Evangelism and Missions administer a course of study for new members (cf. ¶ 1152.1).

¶ **1108.** *Editorial Department.* The Editorial Department of the General Department of Christian Education shall develop, endorse, or recommend all curriculum materials used by the church schools (Sunday Church Schools, Weekday Schools, and Vacation Bible Schools), Christian Youth Fellowship Chapters and leadership training schools and classes.

¶ **1108.1.** Materials produced by the General Department shall be, where feasible and practical, printed by the General Department of Publications. In instance in which it is impractical or impossible to do so, material shall be printed by company selected by the General Department of Christian Education.

¶ **1108.2.** The General Secretary of Publications shall sit with the General Department of Christian Education for the consideration of matters pertaining to the printing and handling of publications and shall have the privilege of the floor for discussion.

¶ **1108.3.** The General Secretary-Editor of the General Department of Christian Education shall sit with the Committee on Publications on matters issued or approved by the Committee on Christian Education, and shall have the privilege of the floor for discussion of the same.

¶ **1108.4.** The Publishing Department shall furnish cuts and lithographs for manuscripts supplied by the Editorial Department in the Sunday Church School and Christian Youth Fellowship publications.

¶ **1108.5.** The General Department of Publications shall share equally with the General Department of Christian Education the expense incurred in sending representatives to the several meetings of the Committee on Uniform Series in the preparation and development of Sunday School curriculum outlines as sponsored by the National Council of Churches in Christ in the U.S.A.

¶ **1108.6.** The General Department of Christian Education is to receive from the General Department of Publications an equitable sum of the net funds received from the sale of those publications used in the Church Schools (Sunday church schools, weekday schools, vacation Bible schools) that were developed by the General Department of Christian Education.

¶ **1109.** *Leadership Training Department.* The General Department of Christian Education through its Leadership Training Department, shall have supervision of all the religious educational training ministry of the Church except where definite authority has been delegated to other Boards. In these cases, the General Department of Christian Education shall have a consultatory relationship to these Boards to assure that these Boards maintain a high quality of religious educational training.

¶ **1109.1.** The Department shall make provisions for the organizing and conducting of training schools and classes to meet the needs of the various groups of the church. It shall also have power to establish and conduct correspondence courses for religious educational training.

¶ **1110.** *Regional Committees.* In many cases it is both convenient and profitable for one or more Episcopal District, Annual Conference, or Presiding Elder's District to cooperate in the promotion of regional leadership education schools, youth conferences, conventions, Jubilees and assemblies. In such cases these enterprises should be sponsored by a Regional Committee composed of representatives of the cooperating agencies.

¶ **1110.1.** Duties of Regional Leadership Education Committees shall be as follows:

§1. To make plans for regional leadership education schools including the selection of date, place, courses of study, instructors, and other administrative officers.

§2. To nominate persons to the General Department of Christian Education for approval and accreditation as deans of such schools.

§3. To develop a budget for such schools.

§4. To attend to administrative matters related thereto.

§5. To establish appropriate committees to carry through the plans for the schools.

Annual Conference Board

¶ **1111.** There shall be organized in each Annual Conference a Board of Christian Education which shall be related to the Department of Christian Education.

¶ **1111.1.** The Board shall consist of a Director appointed by the Bishop, the Annual Conference General Sunday School Superintendent, Departmental Superintendents, the District Conference Directors and Presidents of Boards of Christian Education, the Annual and District Conference Presidents of Youth Councils and C.Y.F. chapters, a representative of the Annual Conference Board of Stewardesses, the Annual Conference President of Lay Activities or his/her designee, at least two representatives from the clergy and any other persons appointed by the Bishop. The Bishop and Presiding Elders are ex-officio members of the Board.

¶ **1111.2.** The Board shall have nine standing committees.

§ 1. Committee on Children's Ministry which shall

(a) Develop an education program on the C.M.E. Church, its history, beliefs, polity, institutions, etc.

(b) Develop programs for the recognition of young people.

(c) Promote the involvement of young people in the administration and business of the church.

§2. Committee on Youth Ministry.

§3. Committee on Young Adult Ministry.

§4. Committee on Adult Ministry.

§5. Committee on Family Ministry.

§6. Committee on Leadership Education.

§7. Committee on Literature and Audio-Visuals.

§8. Committee on Boy Scouting and Scouting Coordinator appointed by the Presiding Bishop.

§9 Committee on Communications and Information Technology. This Committee shall identify and execute goals and objectives of using and advancing technology in the church.

¶ **1111.3.** Immediately after the organization of the Annual Conference Board of Christian Education, the elected Secretary of the Board shall file with the Secretary of the Annual Conference a statement of the organization consisting of the names and addresses of all officers and members. The Secretary of the Board shall also send a copy of this statement to the office of the General Department of Christian Education, Memphis, Tennessee.

¶ **1112.** The Annual Conference Board shall meet as frequently as necessary in order to accomplish its purposes and shall seek to fulfill the following duties:

§1 To promote the organization and development of the program of Christian Education in harmony with the policies and standards of the Gernal Department of Christian Education and the Discipline of the Christian Methodist Episcopal Church.

§2. To appoint a committee to meet with similar committees of other organizations of the Annual Conference to coordinate the educational programs of the several Boards and organizations of the church.

§3. Make an annual report of its ministry to the Annual Conference and the General Department of Christian Education.

§4. Organize a Committee on Children, Youth, Young Adult, and Adult Ministries.

§5. Sponsor a Youth Conference annually in each Annual Conference, or where desired and is feasible, the Annual Youth Conference can be sponsored jointly by the Boards of Christian Education of two or more Annual Conferences.

§ 6. Encourage each local church to have an education offering each fourth Sunday which shall be forwarded to the treasurer of the Board of Christian Education. The Board shall make recommendations at the Annual Conference regarding the expenditures of the funds occurring from this offering and from any other contributions made to the Board.

§ 7. Develop and promote a program of leadership training in the Districts and local churches for the training of leaders.

¶ **1113.** The Director of Christian Education shall be appointed annually by the Presiding Bishop.

¶ **1113.1.** The Annual Conference Director of Christian Education shall be the recognized representative of the General Department of Christian Education and shall be charged with the responsibility, through the Annual Conference Board of

Christian Education, of implementing the program of the Department of Christian Education.

¶ **1113.2.** The Director shall encourage the use of the literature developed or recommended by the General Department of Christian Education; and the purchase of all materials and supplies from the General Department of Publications.

District Board

¶ **1114.** In each Presiding Elder's District there should be a District Board of Christian Education.

¶ **1114.1.** The District Board shall be composed of the Presiding Elder, the District Director of Christian Education, who is appointed by the Presiding Elder, the Sunday Church School Superintendent, the Christian Youth Fellowship President, the President of the Young Adult Council, the President or an elected representative of the Women's Missionary Society, the Chairman or an elected representative of the Board of Lay Activities, the President or an elected representative of the Board of Stewardesses, and other persons as are deemed necessary,

¶ **1114.2.** Subsequent to being constituted, the Board should, at its first meeting, elect a President, Vice-President, Secretary, and Treasurer. Chairpersons for committees on Leadership Training, Children's Ministry, Youth Ministry, Young Adult Ministry, and Literature and Audio-Visuals should be nominated by the President and elected by the Board. In all cases, the Board shall consist of the Committees on Children's Ministry, Youth Ministry, Young Adult Ministry, and Adult Ministry.

¶ **1114.3.** The District Director of Christian Education shall be appointed by the Presiding Elder.

¶ **1114.4.** The duties of District Board of Christian Education shall be as follows:

§1. To develop and promote the program of leadership training for all Christian workers in the District.

§2. To develop and promote a program of Christian nurture and growth for the children, youth, young adults, and adults in the District.

§3. To sponsor District youth meetings and at least one annual District Youth and Young Adult Convention. (The District Sunday School and C.Y.F. Convention may meet in conjunction with the District Youth and Young Adult Convention).

§4. To work in cooperation with the Presiding Elder in formulating and implementing the program for the training of District Sunday Church School and C.Y.F. workers.

§5. To organize a Committee on Scouting and, in consultation with the Presiding Elder, appoint a Scouting Coordinator.

¶ **1115.** Local Church Boards of Christian Education (cf. ¶ 516 - 519).

¶ **1125. The Connectional Young Adult Constitution**

Article l—Name
§1. This organization shall be known as the Connectional Young Adult Conference of the Christian Methodist Episcopal Church.

Article 2 – Purpose
§1. The purpose of the Connectional Young Adult Conference of the C.M.E. Church is to assist the church in planning, developing, and implementing a program of Christian mission appropriate to the needs of young adults that will assure the full involvement, participation and development of leadership capabilities of young adults in carrying out the mission of the church.

Article 3 – Organization
§1. Any person who is in good standing with the C.M.E. Church and between the ages of 18 and 35, inclusive, shall be known as a member of the Connectional Young Adult Conference.

§2. The Connectional Young Adult Conference shall be the governing body of all local, district, and Annual Conference young adult councils.

§3. The administrative division of the Connectional Young Adult Conference shall be known as the executive board.

§4. The organizations of the Connectional Young Adult Conference shall be grouped according to each Episcopal District of the C.M.E. Church, their Annual Conferences, District Conferences and Local Church conferences.

§5. The Young Adult Conference shall be comprised of organizations of equal rank, representing each church in the C.M.E. connection.

§6. The organizations at the Annual Conference, district conference, and local church conference levels shall be called Young Adult Councils.

Article 4 - Conference

§1. The Connectional Young Adult Conference shall have the power to organize, constitute, provide leadership and consultation for its organizations; to write, compile, and promulgate the ritualistic ministry; to make decisions on questions referred to it in consultation with the Secretary of the General Board of Christian Education; and to perform every lawful act necessary or expedient for efficiently conducting the business of the group as authorized in the *Discipline* of the C.M.E. Church. It shall have the power to make recommendations to the General Department of Christian Education and to have the recommendations forwarded to the General Conference of the C.M.E. Church for consideration, when necessary.

§2. The Connectional Young Adult Conference shall meet quadrennially in the summer.

§3. The quorum for the Conference shall be according to *Robert's Rules of Order.*

Article 5—The Executive Board

§1. The officers of the Conference shall be: the President, Vice-President, Secretary, Assistant Secretary, Treasurer, Parliamentarian and Chaplain. All officers must be members of the C.M.E. Church.

§2. The officers of the Conference and one representative from each Episcopal District shall compose the Executive Board.

(a) The Executive Board shall have the power to act upon all issues brought before it by members and groups of the episcopal, annual, and district conference levels. It shall have the power to make recommendations to the Conference and to submit for circulation proposed amendments to the Constitution and By-laws.

(b) The Executive Board shall have the power to carry on the business of the Conference when the Conference is not in session.

(c) In the absence of the President, the Vice-President shall preside at the meetings.

§3. Election of the Executive Board of the Connectional Young Adult Conference shall follow the procedures prescribed in the By-laws.

§4. With the exception of the Parliamentarian and Episcopal District representatives, the members of the Executive Board shall be elected by a simple majority vote at the regular meeting of the Conference.

Article 6—Districts

§1. The Connectional Young Adult Conference shall be divided geographically into districts, the number and levels set forth by the General Conference of the C.M.E. Church—episcopal, annual, and district levels.

§2. Each Episcopal District shall have representation and hold meetings according to their established meeting schedule.

§3. Each Episcopal District shall select its Episcopal District representative, according to the policies within that district.

§4. The Episcopal District shall also select a member to serve on the Elections Committee.

§5. The Episcopal District shall have the power to make recommendations to the Executive Board or to the Conference, and to propose amendments to the Constitution and By-laws of the Conference.

Article 7- Councils

§1. Each group at the local church level shall have the power to recruit and select its members, subject to the rules and regulations of the Connectional Young Adult Conference.

§2. Each group shall have the power to make its own By-laws. The By-laws must not conflict with the Constitution or By-laws of the Connectional Young Adult Conference.

Article 8- Amending the Constitution

§1. This Constitution may be amended by the following procedure:

(a) Any member wishing to amend the Constitution shall forward, in writing, the proposed change to the local level, district level, and the Annual Conference for consideration. If favorably acted upon by two-thirds of the votes cast, the proposed change shall be sent to the Episcopal District Representative who will then forward same to the Connectional Conference Headquarters within Forty-five (45) days following the Annual Conference.

(b) Any changes proposed by the Executive Board, Standing or Special Committees, shall be forwarded to the Connectional Conference office at least five months prior to the Connectional Conference.

(c) The proposed amendments shall be read and discussed at the regular meeting of the Connectional Conference.

(d) Voting upon the proposed constitutional amendments shall be by ballot by registered conference, at the Connectional Young Adult Conference. Designated tellers shall open and count the votes at the Conference. Each registered conferee will vote on proposed changes. Two-thirds of the total number of votes cast shall be required for adoption.

Division of Higher Education

¶ **1126.** The several colleges and the theological school under the auspices of the Christian Methodist Episcopal Church are institutions designed to provide opportunity for higher education for all members throughout the CME connection. Accordingly, they shall receive support and maintenance from the entire C.M.E. Church. Those colleges are: Lane College in Jackson, TN; Paine College in Augusta, GA; Texas College in Tyler, TX; and Miles College in Birmingham, AL. The theological school is Phillips School of Theology which is a part of the Interdenominational Theological Center in Atlanta, Georgia.

¶ **1126.1.** The Committee on Christian Education shall have general authority to superintend the Connectional interest in the affairs of all colleges and schools of the C.M.E. Church. However, this authority should not usurp or violate the authority and responsibility that the Local Boards of Trustees have in administering the individual and specific affairs of individual institutions.

¶ **1127.** The General Department of Christian Education shall review all matters affecting the status of the educational standing of the several schools of the Connection related to the achievements of the goals, mission, philosophy, and objectives of the Committee, and shall assist the institutions in maintaining academic quality and compliance with appropriate accrediting agency mandates.

¶ **1127.1.** The Committee on Christian Education, in conjunction with the Board of Trustees of each educational institution, shall have the authority to determine the need to merge, federate, or close those institutions under the auspices of the C.M.E. Church.

¶ **1127.2.** The General Department of Christian Education shall seek to promote diversity and quality in the academic programs of institutions of the Connection. It shall collect statistics and data from the institutions and shall cause the same to be published and disseminated to the constituency.

¶ **1127.3.** The further objectives and duties of the General Department of Christian Education shall be:

§1. To recommend institutions for Connectional relations.

§2. To classify the educational institutions of the Church.

§3. To assist in raising endowment funds.

§4. To sponsor rallies and meetings where the needs of higher education in the Connection are addressed.

§5. To equitably prorate funds which may accrue to the Board.

§6. To advance the cause of higher education throughout the church.

¶ **1128.** *Educational Senate.* There shall be an Educational Senate established by and shall report to the Standing Committee on Christian Education at its annual meeting. Its purpose shall be to:

§1. Promote the academic interest of colleges and seminaries. The Senate shall be charged with the responsibility for insuring quality of academic standards and performance of the C.M.E. Church or state accrediting agencies.

§2. Monitor and evaluate the organizational structure of higher education in the Christian Methodist Episcopal Church.

§3. Establish minimum academic standards.

§4. Promote curriculum diversity.

§5. Visit and evaluate the C.M.E. Church's institutions of higher education at least every two years.

§6. Develop and recommend, to the General Department of Christian Education, and the various institutions, plans of operation, cooperation, and coordination.

¶ **1128.1.** The Senate shall meet annually at the call of the General Secretary of the Department of Christian Education and shall be constituted as follows: Chief Administrators of the Christian Methodist Episcopal Church's educational institutions of higher learning; one representative from each Episcopal District, providing that each Board of Trustees is represented; a representative from the College of Bishops; the Executive Committee of the Standing Committee on Christian Education; and one representative at large from each institution of higher learning, with special competency in some area of institutional or academic development and administration.

¶ **1128.2.** A Commission on Educational Standards, shall be established by the Educational Senate. This Commission shall meet at least once every two years and shall make appropriate reports and recommendations to the General Department of Christian Education and the College of Bishops for the furtherance of higher education and for the Christian Methodist Episcopal Church. Membership of this Commission shall be determined by the Educational Senate.

¶ **1129.** The Department of Christian Education and Educational Senate shall determine the need for and approve the organization and location of any new Connectional educational institutions. Final approval of any new school will be made by the General Conference.

¶ **1129.1** No more Connectional schools shall be authorized by the church until existing ones are endowed adequately and have achieved a sound and permanent fiscal base.

¶ **1130.** *School and College Administration.* The revenue of the Division of Higher Education is derived from the Connectional Budget; from Special Collections by the Secretary and Bishops; and from other sources, including gifts, bequeaths, etc.

¶ **1130.1.** The educational institutions established or maintained by the General or Annual Conferences of the Christian Methodist Episcopal Church shall be managed, operated, or conducted by a Board of Trustees of which the Bishop of this Church in charge of the Annual Conference in whose bounds the same is located, and the General Secretary of the General Department of Christian Education, shall be members. The Trustees shall be elected and held in accordance with the laws of the State or Territory in which the educational institution for which they were elected is located.

¶ **1131.** The election of the President of the Board of Trustees of each school and college of the C.M.E. Church shall be vested in the several Boards of Trustees. The office of President shall not be confined to the Presiding Bishop. However, the Bishop in charge of the Annual Conference in whose bounds a school is located shall be a member of the Board of Trustees of said school.

¶ **1132.** The Board of Trustees, of which the Bishop in charge of the Annual Conference is a member, shall appoint or elect such officers and teachers for same as are necessary and proper and as are usually employed by like institutions.

¶ **1132.1.** The Board of Trustees, of which the Bishop in charge of the Annual Conference in which any school, college or university is located, shall be a member, conducting or operating any school, college or university established or maintained by the General Conference or Annual Conferences of the Christian Methodist Episcopal Church, shall make all necessary and proper rules and regulations for governing same, and may grant diplomas to students thereof who have pursued the prescribed course of study, and confer degrees of every nature as are usually conferred by like institutions.

¶ **1132.2.** The Board of Trustees may acquire, by purchase or gift, necessary land and erect necessary buildings thereon and purchase the necessary equipment for any School, College or University operated by them for the General or Annual Conference or Conferences and to this end contract indebtedness and borrow money and pledge or mortgage any property held by them for the use of or benefit of the General Conference or Annual Conference or Conferences, establishing and maintaining such, provided, however, that no property held by said trustees, shall be pledged or mortgaged without the endorsement in writing on the instrument pledging or mortgaging the same, of the Bishop in charge of the Annual Conference in whose bounds such School, College, or University is located, which shall be witnessed acknowledged by him in accordance with the law of the State or Territory in which said property is located. Nor shall such property be pledged or mortgaged without the written agreement of the General Department of Christian Education if the school is a claimant on the Connectional Fund for Education administered by the General Department of Christian Education.

¶ **1132.3.** The Board of Trustees of any School, College, or University established or maintained by the General or Annual Conference or Conferences of the Christian Methodist Episcopal Church may acquire by purchase and hold, or receive by gift or bequest any real, mixed, or personal property.

¶ **1132.4.** All deeds of conveyance or any property conveyed for the General or Annual Conference or Conferences of the Christian Methodist Episcopal Church for educational purposes shall have the following clause inserted in the proper place: *"In trust that said premises shall be used, kept, and maintained and disposed of for educational purposes for the Christian Methodist Episcopal Church subject to the usage, and ministerial appointments of said Church, as from time to time authorized and declared by the General Conference of said Church and Annual Conference or Conferences operating and maintaining such School, College, or University."*

¶ **1133.** All schools, colleges or universities established, and under the auspices of the General Conference or any Annual Conference or Conferences of the Christian Methodist Episcopal Church and all property held for the use and benefit of, or subject to the Discipline, usage and ministerial appointments of said Church, come under the operation hereof and shall be governed hereby and the Trustees thereof shall have all authority and power herein conferred, by law, or by charter or by instrument conveying property so as to prevent this chapter from becoming effective, and all Trustees of such wherever it can reasonably be done are hereby directed, required, authorized and empowered to take such steps and adopt such measures as are necessary to bring into effect this chapter.

CHAPTER 55
THE WOMEN'S MISSIONARY COUNCIL

¶ 1134. Constitution

Article 1 - Name

§1. There shall be in the Christian Methodist Episcopal Church a delegated body known as the Women's Missionary Council. Such delegates shall be elected by the Annual Conference Women's Missionary Society the year preceding the Quadrennial meeting of the Assembly.

§2. This body and the Annual Conference and District Conference and the local Missionary Societies shall be organized and governed by the Constitution and By-laws in accordance with the Constitution and By-laws of the Women's Missionary Council as found in the Discipline of the Christian Methodist Episcopal Church.

Article 2-Purpose

§1. The purpose of the Women's Missionary Council shall be:

(a) To implement the mission and unity of the Women's Missionary Council.

(b) To make that mission and unity known at home and abroad.

(c) To encourage cooperation, fellowship, and mutual counsel concerning the spiritual life and religious activities of the Christian Church .

(d) To encourage the study of the Bible and to assist in spreading the Gospel.

(e) To study the need of society in order to aid in the development of programs, people, processes, and resources that will enable the Women's Missionary Council to fulfill its mission. Such studies shall enable the Council to react cooperatively to the moral, ethical, and spiritual issues inherent in spreading the Gospel.

(f) To work closely with private and public institutions and agencies in the fulfillment of common goals, insofar as such cooperation is consistent with the Council.

Article 3-Authority

The Women's Missionary Council shall have the authority as follows:

§1. To add, amend, delete and approve the By-laws of the Women's Missionary Council and to present its final constitution to the General Conference for approval.

§2. To elect its officers.

The Executive Committee shall have the authority to remove any officer for justifiable cause after due notice and hearing. Such action shall require joint consultation with the Patron Bishop and two-thirds affirmative vote of the Executive Committee.

§3. To fill vacancies among the officers unless the Constitution states otherwise.

§4. To secure and administer funds for the support of all ministry under its charge.

§5. To be responsible for the training of the Council officers and members.

§6. To give to the members of the Christian Methodist Episcopal Church financial grants for educational purposes.

§7. To assume responsibility for the supervision of the Missionary work of adults, young adults, youth, children, and auxiliaries.

Article 4 - Organization

§1. The Women's Missionary Council shall be composed of members from the Local Church, District Conference, and Annual Conference Women's Missionary Societies of the Christian Methodist Episcopal Church, the Bishops presiding over the several Episcopal Districts, members of the Executive Board, and elected officers of the Council.

§2. The Executive Board of the Women's Missionary Council shall have as its patron a Bishop elected by the College of Bishops (cf. ¶ 1135).

§3. The organizational pattern of the Women's Missionary Council shall be the Missionary Societies at three (3) levels, namely: the Annual Conference, the District, and the Local Church.

Article 5 - Membership

§1. *Qualifications.* Membership shall be open to any member of the Christian Methodist Episcopal Church who has indicated a desire to participate in the mission of the Church through the Women's Missionary Society.

§2. *Officers.* The officers of the Women's Missionary Council shall be the President, who is a General Officer, the Vice President, the Secretary, the Assistant Secretary, the Treasurer, and the Editor of *The Missionary Messenger.* All officers of the Women's Missionary Council shall be elected by ballot.

§3. *The Executive Committee.* The Executive Committee shall be composed of the President, the Vice President, the Secretary, the Assistant Secretary, the

Treasurer, and the Editor of *The Missionary Messenger*. The Patron Bishop shall be a member ex-officio. Other persons designated as Consultants may serve as ex-officio members without vote.

§4. *The Executive Board.* The Executive Board shall be composed of the Patron Bishop, the President, the Vice President, the Secretary, the Assistant Secretary, the Treasurer, the Editor of *The Missionary Messenger*, the Division Leaders of Structure, Program, Service and Outreach, the Past Presidents of the Council and the Annual Conference Presidents.

§5. Also, the Chairpersons of Standing Committees, namely; the Executive Committee, Constitution and By-laws, Finance, Nominating and Resolutions.

§6. Also the Department Secretaries of the Division of Structure, namely; Rossie T. Hollis Children, Mattie E. Coleman, Phyllis H. Bedford Young Adults, Organization and Promotions, and Status of Women.

§7. Also, the Department Secretaries of the Division of Program, namely: Literature and Publications, Fine Arts, Missionary Education, and Spiritual Life and Message.

§8. Also, the Department Secretaries of the Division of Service and Outreach, namely: Educational Services, Overseas Missions and Hunger and Meals for Millions.

§9. Also, the Chairpersons of Commissions, namely: Historical, Communications, Christian Social Relations, and Education.

§10. Also the Chairpersons of Compilation and Statistics, Life Membership and Credentials.

§11. The President and the Executive Committee shall have the power to call upon such consultants as may be needed to carry out the program of the organization. Such consultants shall be ex-officio, without vote, as well as other chairpersons of other committees.

§12. *The Assembly.* The Assembly shall be composed of the Presiding Bishops of the several Episcopal Districts, ex-officio, without vote, the Executive Committee, the Executive Board, the Retired Presidents of the Women's Missionary Council, and the duly elected delegates.

§13. *The Annual Conference.* The Annual Conference Women's Missionary Society of the Christian Methodist Episcopal Church shall be composed of the Local Societies within the bounds of the Annual Conference. The Presiding Bishop shall be a member ex-officio, without vote.

§14. *The District Conference.* The District Conference Women's Missionary

Society of the Christian Methodist Episcopal Church shall be composed of organized units of the Women's Missionary Societies in the Local Churches of the District. The Presiding Elder shall be a member, ex-officio, without vote.

§15. *The Local Church.* Membership shall be open to any member of the Christian Methodist Episcopal Church who desires to participate in the mission of the Local Church through the Women's Missionary Society. The Pastor-in-Charge shall be a member, ex-officio, without vote.

§16. *The Standing Committees.* The Standing Committees of the Women's Missionary Council shall be Constitution and By-laws, Finance, Nominating and Resolutions.

§17. *The Commissions.* The Commissions of the Women's Missionary Council shall be Christian Social Relations, Communications, Education, and Historical.

Article 6 - Meetings

§1. The Women's Missionary Council, in delegate assembly, shall meet quadrennially the last week in July or the first week in August during the year subsequent to the General Conference. The Assembly shall meet for four (4) consecutive days, not to exceed five (5) days.

§2. The Executive Board of the Women's Missionary Council shall meet annually, except in the year of the Quadrennial Delegate Assembly, the last weekend in February or the first weekend in March for at least two and one half (2 1/2) days, the first day of which shall be for training.

§3. Special meetings for the Executive Board of the Women's Missionary Council may be called by the President in consultation with the Patron Bishop, Council Officers, and Standing Committee Chairpersons.

§4. The Executive Committee of the Women's Missionary Council shall meet on call of the President and Patron Bishop in consultation with the other members of the Executive Committee.

Article 7 - Funds

§1. The funds for the maintenance of the Women's Missionary Council shall be derived from the total membership of the Local Churches, the General Church budget allocation, annual donations, and such funds as may be secured from other sources. One such source shall be personal pledges.

§2. There shall be a retirement fund for Council Presidents, Treasurers, and The Missionary Messenger Editors, which shall be given after two (2) terms in office.

The amounts shall be one hundred dollars ($100.00) per month for retired Presidents and seventy-five dollars ($75.00) per month for retired Treasurers and Editors. This fund shall come from Life Memberships once per quadrennium.

§3. The Chairperson of Finance shall be given per diem, effective after ratification by the 1986 General Conference of the Christian Methodist Episcopal Church, for any Council meeting that occurs.

§4. There shall be given to the Vice President of the Council a salary of one hundred dollars ($100.00) per month, effective after ratification by the 1986 General Conference of the Christian Methodist Episcopal Church.

Article 8 - Amendments

§1. Proposed amendments to the Constitution and By-laws of the Women's Missionary Council shall be made from the recommendations of the Executive Committee, one or more of the Standing Committees, or one or more of the Departments of the Women's Missionary Council by two-thirds (2/3) vote of the members present and voting, provided a thirty (30) day notice is given in writing to all members of the Executive Board.

Article 9 - Government

§1. Robert's Rules of Order shall govern the parliamentary procedure at all meetings of the Women's Missionary Council where no other procedure is in the Constitution and By-laws.

§2. This revised Constitution shall be in effect immediately upon ratification by the 1998 General Conference of the Christian Methodist Episcopal Church.

Ratified July 3, 1998.

§3. (Reserved for future enactments.)

¶ 1135. The Patron Bishop of the Women's Missionary Council

By the legislative action of the General Conference, the Bishop elected by the College of Bishops to serve as the Patron Bishop of the Women's Missionary Council shall be officially related to the Council as follows:

§1. An ex-officio member of the Quadrennial Assembly, the Executive Board and its Executive Committee with voice but without vote.

§ 2. Consulted by the President of the Women's Missionary Council prior to any meeting of the bodies listed under ¶ 1134, Art. 6, Sections 1 -4, or any Connectional officer of the Women's Missionary Council taking action of a disciplinary or legal nature against another officer, or any person or entity within or without the Christian Methodist Episcopal Church.

§ 3. Consulted prior to the formulation of worship service bulletins involving members of the College of Bishops.

§ 4. Consulted prior to the selection of sites for holding Connectional meetings. In order that the Bishop presiding over the Episcopal District encompassing said meetingmay have advance knowledge of the events in time to participate in making the final selection and have input in planning related to local matters.

§ 5. The official liaison between the Women's Missionary Council and the College of Bishops.

§ 6. The Presiding Officer during Women's Missionary Council elections in the Assembly, unless he/she selects another bishop to preside at that time.

CHAPTER 56
THE GENERAL DEPARTMENT OF LAY MINISTRY

¶ 1135. The General Department of Lay Ministry

§1. There shall be in the Christian Methodist Episcopal Church an organization known as the General Department of Lay Ministry.

§2. The Department shall be organized and governed according to by-laws consistent with the Discipline of the Christian Methodist Episcopal Church.

§3. The Executive Officer shall be a General Secretary elected according to the provision set forth by General Conference.

§4. The General Department of Lay Ministry shall seek to achieve the following objectives:

(a) To introduce positive role models for males through enrichment programs, i. e., scouting, career days, net-working with mentoring organizations such as Big Brothers, etc.

(b) To seek, daily, Christ's Way of Life, to bear witness to the Way in business dealings and in social contacts.

(c) To develop leadership for participation in politics and civic affairs so as to become more effective in the local community.

(d) To study the doctrine, policy, history, and traditions of Christian Methodism.

(e) To enhance Christian fellowship in the local church among the lay by promoting responsible Christian living.

(f) To design and disseminate resource materials for workshops and study courses meaningful to the needs and concerns of lay people.

(g) To encourage out-reach ministry in the local church.

(h) To promote Christian stewardship through programs of nurture, leading to commitment of time, talents and resources.

(i) To participate in the observance of Connectional Lay Day on the second (2nd) Sunday in October.

(j) To promote and provide recreational facilities and equipment for children and youth of the church.

(k) To establish a scouting program.

¶ 1135.1. Organization

§1. *Standing Committee on Lay Ministry.* The Committee shall have as its chairman a Bishop elected by the College of Bishops. Other officers shall be elected by the Committee. The members of the Standing Committee shall be assigned to it by the special committee established for that purpose by the General Connectional Board.

§2. The authority and responsibility of the Committee shall be that as given by the General Conference.

¶ 1135.2. Christian Methodist Men's Fellowship

§1. A distinctive men's organization known as The Christian Methodist Men's Fellowship is established within the Department of Lay Ministry at all levels.

§2. The purpose of this ministry shall be to help the Christian Methodist Episcopal Church:

(a) Minister to the needs and concerns of men in the C.M.E.
Church.

(b) Address the systemic problems African-American males
face under the social, economic, and political conditions of the
nation and the world.

¶ 1135.3. Connectional Lay Council

§1. This organization shall meet once every four years simultaneously with the Connectional Lay Institute Meeting (cf. 1135,10).

§2. Delegates to the Council shall be:

(a) Elected lay members with full membership status at any CME Church, provided said member is in good standing and is at least eighteen (18) years of age or has been emancipated by marriage, at the time of the election of delegates by said local council. The number of delegates shall be unlimited.

(b) "Voting Delegates" shall be limited to two (2) from each local Lay Council and shall be elected by the local council, then certified by the Quarterly Conference meeting immediately prior to the Annual Conference which immediately precedes the Connectional Lay Institute. Local Lay Councils may elect one (1) additional "voting delegate" to the Connectional Lay Institute in the same manner as in the *Book of Discipline* for the election of additional Annual Conference delegates. The Local Lay Leader shall be authorized to substitute a voting delegate with other local Lay Council members in the event of delegate absence from the

Connectional Lay Institute.

(c) All delegates to the Connectional Lay Institute may participate in all deliberative actions of the Connectional Lay Council (Connectional Lay Institute), providing only voting delegates shall cast ballots for final actions or adoption of resolutions.

§3. The voting delegates to the Connectional Lay Institute shall elect a President, Secretary, Assistant Secretary, Treasurer and ten (10) vice presidents elected by their respective Episcopal District delegations convening at the Connectional Lay Institute.

§4. This body shall have the authority to make its own By-laws which shall conform to the *Discipline* of the CME Church.

§5. The purpose of this body shall be:

(a) To make a serious study as to how lay programs are implemented.

(b) To recommend ways of improving the role and image of the laity.

(c) To assist the Department of Lay Ministry in involving more laity in its programs.

§6. Resolutions for consideration by the Connectional Lay Institute shall be signed for the purpose of confirmation and must conform to the Methodist tradition and the *Discipline* of the CME Church.

§7. Copies of all resolutions must be sent to the General Secretary of the Department of Lay Ministry and the Connectional Lay Council thirty (30) days prior to the meeting of the Connectional Lay Institute.

¶ 1135.4. Conference Lay Council

§1. There shall be in every Annual Conference a Lay Council. The Conference Lay Leader shall be elected at the Annual Conference by the Lay delgates to the Conference.

§2. *Officers:* The Conference Lay Leader shall be nominated by the District Lay Leaders in joint consultation with the Presiding Elders. Nominations from the floor can be made by delegates. The other conference lay officers shall be 1st Vice Lay Leader, 2nd Vice Lay Leader, Secretary, Assistant Secretary, Treasurer, and Worship Leader. The District Lay Leaders and the Presiding Elders in joint session shall have the authority to fill vacancies at interim (in the office of District Lay Leader).

§3. This Department shall hold one annual meeting in conjunction with the Annual Conference and such other meetings deemed necessary and/or upon the call of the Lay Leader.

§4. This Department shall submit a written report to the Annual Conference and to the Department of Lay Ministry.

§5. The minutes of all meetings of the Department/Board shall be kept in a permanent journal by the Secretary.

§6 The lay members of the Christian Methodist Episcopal Church were authorized by the 1958 General Conference to organize the fellowship and larger service in the work of the church. The official organization of the work of the church (formerly known as the Connectional Laymen's Council) is known as the General Department of Lay Ministry.

¶ 1135.5. The Department shall carry out the program of lay activities as outlined under the direction of the General Department of Lay Ministry by promoting the following objectives:

(a) Establishing a vigorous lay teaching ministry.

(b) Organizing studies in Christian stewardship.

(c) Lay people's work in general.

(d) Developing and maintaining a sound and workable financial system in every local church.

(e) Fostering adequate support for the ministry.

(f) Making full payment of budget assessments.

(g) Assuring the proper financial and budgetary provision for all other church obligations.

(h) Promoting personal evangelism.

(i) Establishing a Lay Speaking Bureau.

(j) Adhering to parliamentary procedures.

(k) Developing a Bible Study Program.

(l) Studying the history of our Great Zion.

(m) Initiating programs to develop more committed lay persons.

(n) Training church officers in the full understanding and discharge of the duties inherent in their office.

(o) Work cooperatively with members of the Department of Christian Education at every level of the church to promote and support the activities of the Division of Scouting Ministries, which Division shall be a part of the quadrennial meeting of the Lay Institute.

¶ 1135.6. District Lay Board

§1. The District shall be organized into zones.

§2. The Zone Leaders shall submit a written report to the District Council.

§3. The District Board shall submit an annual written report to the Conference Lay Department.

§4. The District Lay Leader shall preside at District Board Meetings. The Lay Leader shall be elected by the Lay delegates to the District Conference in session. Other officers shall be elected by the District Board.

§5. The District Board shall meet as often as necessary to effectively carry out the work of the Board.

§6. The Board shall conduct the program of lay activities as outlined under the direction of the Department of Lay Ministry by promoting the listed objectives.

§7. The minutes of all meetings of the Board shall be kept in a permanent journal by the Secretary.

¶ 1135.7. Local Lay Council (cf. ¶ 522)

¶ 1135.8. Connectional Laity Day

§1. The Conference Lay Department, the District Lay Department, and the Local Lay Department shall observe Connectional Laity Day on the second Sunday in October.

§2. Newly elected local lay officers shall be presented to the local churches (and with the Pastor's consent, the presentation ceremony can be used).

§3. All local church Lay Departments shall take a free-will offering on Connectional Laity Day to the Department of Lay Ministry.

§4. Local Lay membership cards must be renewed by or on Connectional Laity Day.

¶ 1135.9. Workshops

§1. The Conference Lay Department, the District Lay Board, and the Local Church Lay Department must have workshops to continue the lay vigorous teaching ministry in accordance with the listed objectives.

¶ 1135.10. Connectional Lay Institute

§1. The General Department of Lay Ministry of the Christian Methodist Church Episcopal Church shall sponsor a Connectional Institute which shall be incorporated into the Annual CME Convocation in the year preceding the General Conference.

§2. The theme for the Connectional Lay Institute shall be the quadrennial theme for the General Department of Lay Ministry.

§3. The officers of the Connectional Laymen's Council shall participate in all planning aspects of the Connectional Lay Institute and shall specifically formulate the agenda for the Institute in cooperation with the General Secretary of Lay Ministry and the Standing Committee on Lay Ministry.

¶ 1135.11. Charters. Each local church shall have a Local Lay Council with a charter issued by the General Department of Lay Ministry.

¶ 1135.12. Emblem and Logo. The Lay Logo Lapel Pin is the official identification symbol of the General Department of Lay Ministry.

CHAPTER 57
THE GENERAL DEPARTMENT OF EVANGELISM
AND MISSIONS

¶ **1150.** *Purpose.* It shall be the purpose of the General Department of Evangelism and Missions to keep before the Christian Methodist Episcopal Church its evangelistic and social ministries, as these concerns are expressive of the mission of the church.

¶ **1151.** The General Department of Evangelism and Missions, and its General Secretary, shall be supervised by a Standing Committee the Chair of which shall be a Bishop elected by the College of Bishops and the members of the committee assigned by a Special Committee of the General Connectional Board.

¶ **1152. Aims and Definitions**

§1. *Evangelism.* The aim of evangelism is to bring all persons into living active fellowship with God through Jesus Christ as Divine Savior and through the regenerating power of the Holy Spirit; to gather them into the fellowship of the Church; to lead them to express their Christian discipleship in every area of human life that the kingdom of God may be realized.

§2. *Missions.* The objectives of the Missions ministry shall be evangelical and educational, designed to promote Christian missions, Church extension, Missionary education and interest throughout the Connection in the United States and in other countries in which the C.M.E. Church conducts missionary activity.

The Ministry of Evangelism
Episcopal District Board

¶ **1153.** Each Episcopal District shall have an Episcopal District Board of Evangelism, which shall promote the program of evangelism in the District in cooperation with the Committee on Evangelism and Missions,

¶ **1153.1.** Each Episcopal District Board of Evangelism shall include in its membership all members of the Committee on Evangelism who reside within the bounds of the Episcopal District, and the Episcopal District President of the Women's Missionary Society. The Episcopal District Board shall further the organization and financial support of the Episcopal District through the guidance of the

General Board of Evangelism in keeping with the constitution.

¶ **1153.2.** There shall be an Episcopal District Director selected by the Committee on Evangelism in cooperation with the Presiding Bishop.

Annual Conference Board
¶ **1154.** Each Annual Conference of the Church shall provide for a Conference Board of Evangelism, which shall promote the program of evangelism as outlined by the Board of Evangelism and in cooperation with the Episcopal District Board.

¶ **1154.1.** Each Conference Board of Evangelism shall include in its membership the Presiding Elders, one Pastor and one lay member for each District in the bounds of the Annual Conference, the Missionary President, the Annual Conference C.Y.F. President and the Conference Director of Evangelism, and other organizations as the Annual Conference may desire; provided that no salaried officer, employee, or anyone receiving remuneration from the Conference Board of Evangelism, be a member thereof.

¶ **1154.2.** Each Annual Conference, upon organization of its Board of Evangelism, shall annually elect a Conference Director of Evangelism to promote the policies and program of the Connectional, Episcopal District and Conference Boards of Evangelism under direction of the General Department of Evangelism and Missions.

District Board of Evangelism
¶ **1155.** Each District of each Annual Conference shall promote the program of evangelism as outlined by the General Department and in cooperation with the Conference Board of Evangelism.

¶ **1155.1.** The District Board of Evangelism shall include in its membership such members of the conference Board as may reside within the bounds of the District, the President of the District Women's Missionary Society, District Lay Leader, the Presiding Elder, and three Pastors, three lay women and three young people to be elected by the District Conference.

¶ **1155.2.** There shall be a District Director of Evangelism in each District, nominated by the Presiding Elder and properly assigned by the Bishop. He or she shall work in cooperation with the Presiding Elder and the Conference Director of Evangelism.

The Ministry of Missions

¶ **1156.** The Ministry of Missions as part of the function of the Department of Evangelism and Missions and operating under the aegis of a Standing committee and the administrative direction of the General Secretary is sub-divided into several components.

The Division of Overseas Missions

¶ **1157.** Within the Department there shall be a Division of Overseas Missions which shall be one of the coordinated divisions or departments of the Board.

§ 1. The Director of the Division of Overseas Missions shall be nominated by the General Secretary and elected by the Committee. The Director may or may not be a member of the General Connectional Board.

§ 2. The Division shall administer and promote the work of Missions outside the United States, provided such work has been approved by the General Conference or the College of Bishops.

§ 3. The Division is to formulate policies for Overseas Missions; to promote efforts for securing funds for Missions; to assist in training and supervising missionary personnel for Overseas Missions.

§ 4. In coordination with the Committee, the General Secretary, the President, the Director of the Division of Overseas Missions shall have authority to cooperate with interchurch agencies in securing full cooperation, assistance, and counsel of the other denominations both within and outside the United States.

The Division of National Mission and Church Expansion

¶ **1158.** Within the Department, there shall be the Division of National Missions and Church Expansion (work formerly referred to as Home Missions and Church Extension) which shall be one of the divisions of the Department and under the general supervision of the General Secretary.

¶ **1159.** There shall be a Director of the Division of National Mission and Church Expansion who shall be nominated by the General Secretary and elected by the Committee. The Director may or may not be a member of the General Connectional Board.

¶ **1160.** The Director in cooperation with the General Secretary, shall nominate the personnel or staff members of this Division, who shall be elected or approved by the Committee.

¶ **1161. The function of this Division shall be as follows:**

§1. To develop and administer the work of Missions in the United States.

§2. To administer and develop Church expansion.

§3. To counsel, advise, and aid in planning, architecture, building, and securing financing of church buildings.

§4. To search ways and means to cooperate more fully with agencies sponsoring Ministry to Migrant workers.

§5. To encourage the erection of churches in new communities not already supplied.

§6. To assist in building churches, parsonages and other church buildings where assistance is most needed, subject to the approval of the Presiding Bishop and the Annual Conference.

Establishing Mission Annual Conferences

¶ **1162.** Mission work in areas outside the United States may be organized into a Mission (local churches, schools, or other projects) under the supervision of the Bishop assigned to the area and the Standing Committee on Evangelism and Missions, provided such work has been approved by the College of Bishops.

¶ **1162.1.** The work of the Mission shall be divided, when necessary, into areas over which an Elder or a mission area supervisor may be assigned to take general supervision of the work under the direction of the Presiding Bishop and to report the state of that work and its needs to the Bishop.

¶ **1162.2.** Regularly appointed missionaries, both lay and clergy, and mission traveling preachers and other lay members shall determine the number of lay members and mode of their appointment to the Annual Mission Meeting.

¶ **1162.3.** A Bishop shall preside in the Annual Meeting, or, in his or her absence, a representative appointed by him or her. The Board of Missions in its Annual Meeting shall have the power to license suitable persons to preach upon recommendation of their Local Church; to pass the character of preachers not members of an Annual Conference; to receive mission preachers, and recommend to an Annual Conference proper persons for Admission on Trial and for Deacon's and Elder's orders. The Mission shall receive and consider reports from churches, schools, and projects organized within its area.

¶ **1162.4.** The Bishop or President shall, at the Annual Meeting of the Mission, assign Missionaries and Preachers to the several charges.

¶ **1162.5.** Any Mission containing eight or more pastoral charges, outside the United States, established under the provision of the *Discipline*, may be constituted as an Annual Conference by the General Conference; provided that no such Mission Annual Conference shall be continued with fewer than six ministerial members.

¶ **1162.6.** The Bishop having Episcopal supervision of a foreign mission field may appoint a representative as Administrative Missionary or Mission Supervisor. to whom may be committed specific responsibilities.

§1. Such duties shall be exercised so as not to interfere with the work of the Presiding Elder of a Mission District.

§2. This Administrative Missionary or Mission Supervisor may also be a Presiding Elder, provided that the person is a member of that Mission Conference. In either case, he/she shall be directly responsible to the Bishop appointed to administer the work in the Episcopal District.

§3. The Supervisor shall make reports of the work and needs of the mission field to the Bishop, said reports may be transmitted to the Standing Committee on Evangelism and Missions.

¶ **1162.7.** Rules and regulations of established Annual Conferences of the Church shall apply to the administration of a Mission Conference, with the exception that the minimum number of delegates from a Mission Conference elected to the General Conference shall be one clerical and one lay delegate.

Rural Work Department

¶ **1163.** There shall be a Rural Work Department, the Director of which shall be nominated by the General Secretary and elected by the Standing Committee. The Director may or may not be a member of the General Connectional Board.

¶ **1163.1.** The Director of Rural Work shall nominate the personnel of the Department and they shall be elected by the Standing Committee.

Annual Conference Board

¶ **1164.** There shall be a Board of Missions organized in each Annual Conference following the General Conference which shall function until the Annual Conference succeeding the next General Conference.

¶ **1164.1** The Annual Conference Board of Missions shall consist of an equal number of clergy and lay members.

District Board of Missions

¶ **1165.** It shall be the duty of the Presiding Elder to see that a Board of Missions is organized in his District, which shall consist of an equal number of clergy and lay members.

Local Church Board of Missions

¶ **1166.** It shall be the duty of the Preacher-in-Charge to organize a Board of Missions in each church of his/her charge.

¶ **1166.1.** The Local Church Board of Missions shall have representatives from each department of the church. One member may be a Local Preacher.

PART XIII

58. ANNUAL CONFERENCE BOUNDARIES

CHAPTER 58
ANNUAL CONFERENCE BOUNDARIES

¶ **1201.** Alaska-Pacific Conference shall consist of the states of Oregon, Washington, Utah, Idaho and Alaska (with future possibility of the development of Hawaii); which states heretofore were a part of the California Conference.

¶ **1202.** Arizona-New Mexico Conference shall consist of the states of Arizona and New Mexico.

¶ **1203.** Birmingham Conference shall consist of the Birmingham District, the West Birmingham District, the Anniston District which heretofore has been included within the bounds of the East Alabama Conference, and the South Birmingham District which heretofore has been included within the bounds of the Central Alabama Conference.

¶ **1204.** Carolina Conference shall consist of the states of North and South Carolina and Galax in Virginia which heretofore were two separate conferences.

¶ **1205.** The Central Georgia Conference shall be bounded on the east by South Carolina state line and the Atlantic Ocean; on the west by the Flint River to the southern boundaries of Macon and Houston counties and the western boundaries of Pulaski and Wilcox counties; on the north by the northern boundaries of the following counties; Burke, Jefferson, Glascock, Washington, Baldwin, Jones, Monroe, and Spalding; and on the south by the southern boundary of the following counties: McIntosh, Long, Tattnall, Emanuel, Treutlen, Laurens, Dodge, and Wilcox.

¶ **1206.** Central Texas Conference beginning at the northeast corner of Rockwall County, running thence East at parallel 33, across Hunt County, thence southeast to the M.K. & T. Railroad (including South Greenville and Lone Oak in Central Texas Conference) down to the T. & P. Railroad, thence East on the T. & P. Railroad to the 95th meridian, thence South to Troupe, leaving out the Winona Circuit. Thence North from Troupe, up the I . & G.N . Railroad to Longview, thence southeast down to Teneha leaving Beckville Circuit, Carthage Circuit and Post Oak in the East Texas Conference; thence East to the Louisiana State Line, beginning from Logansport, Louisiana, running West along the northern boundary lines of the Shelby and Nacogdoches Counties and in imaginary line running across Cherokee County to the Natchez River (including Lynnat Circuit), thence South of the I. & G.N. Railroad, to Galveston (Houston, Galveston, Trinity and Sunnyside Circuit not included in the Central Conference.) The Southern boundary shall be the Gulf of Mexico and the Rio Grande. The Western boundary of the Central Texas Conference begins at the northeast corner of Rockwall County and follows the eastern boundary of the West Texas Conference to Corsicana, thence along the southern boundary of the West Texas Conference to the Rio Grande River.

¶ **1207.** Dallas-Fort Worth Conference bounded on the East by Grayson, Collins, Rockwall and Dallas counties, down to the southern boundary line of Dallas Country to Trinity River, down to Cotton Belt Railroad; south by the East Boundary line of Vavara and Freestone counties to the 1. & G.N. Railroad to San Antonio and Austin (San Antonio to be included in the West Texas Conference) on the Southern Pacific to the Rio Grande River; north by Red River to the northern corner of Grayson Country.

¶ **1208.** East Tennessee Conference bounded on the West and Northwest by the line of the Kentucky Conference; on the South by Highway 45 East; on the North by Kentucky and Virginia state lines.

¶ **1209.** East Texas Conference bounded on the North by Oklahoma; East by Arkansas and Louisiana to the H. E. & W.T. Railroad; West by the H. E. & W.T. Railroad to Lufkin, thence West by an imaginary line to the East boundary line of Anderson County to Trinity River, Texarkana not included in the East Texas Conference. The H. E. & W.T. Railroad shall not include any part of the Timpson Circuit.

¶ **1210.** Florida Conference shall be composed of all territory within the bounds of the state of Florida.

¶ **1211.** The Georgia, North, Annual Conference shall be bounded on the north by the Tennessee state line on the east by the South Carolina state line; on the west by the Alabama state line, and on the southern boundaries of the following counties:

Richmond, McDuffie, Warren, Hancock, Putnam, Jasper, Butts, Henry, Clayton, Fayette, Coweta, and Heard.

¶ **1212.** Kansas-Missouri Conference bounded on the East by the Southeast Missouri, Illinois and Wisconsin Conference; West by the western Boundary line of the State of Colorado; north by Wyoming; South by Oklahoma; said Conference to include the states of Colorado, Iowa and Nebraska, but excluding Davidson Chapel Congregation in Coffeyville, Kansas.

¶ **1213.** Kentucky Conference shall comprise what formerly was the Kentucky and West Kentucky Conferences which excluded Covington and Carrollton, Kentucky across the Ohio River from Cincinnati, Ohio and including Evansville, Indiana and other Missions that might be established in Indiana south of the Baltimore and Ohio Railroad; provided that Terre Haute and Indianapolis, Indiana, shall not be included.

¶ **1214.** Louisiana Conference bounded on the North by Arkansas; on the East by the Mississippi River; on the West by Texas; on the south by an imaginary line beginning at the mouth of the Red River and running West across the state.

¶ **1215.** Michigan-Indiana Conference shall include the state of Michigan and the following cities in Illinois: Joliet, Robbins, and Chicago Heights, and the northern section of Indiana.

¶ **1216.** Mississippi-South Annual Conference shall be bounded on the north by the North-East Mississippi Conference; on the east by the Alabama State Line and on the south by the Gulf of Mexico and on the west by the Pearl River up to the 31 st. Parallel line, thence west along the Louisiana State Line to the Mississippi River and north along the River bounding Louisiana and Arkansas to the southwestern corner boundary of the North-East Mississippi Conference.

¶ **1217.** New York-Washington Conference shall embrace the New England States, the States of New York, New Jersey and Pennsylvania, with the exception of the Pittsburgh area; and the States of Maryland, Delaware, Virginia and District of Columbia.

¶ **1218.** North Arkansas Conference bounded on the North by Southeast Missouri, Illinois and Wisconsin Conference; bounded on the East by the Mississippi River; bounded on the South by South Arkansas Conference; bounded on the West by the State line.

¶ **1219.** North Central Alabama Conference shall be bounded on the West by the Mississippi State line; on the south by the Frisco Railroad, including Guin and Carbon Hill. From Jasper by an imaginary line running northwest to the line of the East Alabama Conference (not including Jasper), and on the north by the line of Tennessee (but including Iron City).

¶ **1220.** North-East Mississippi Conference shall be bounded on the north by the Tennessee State Line, except Saulters Chapel C.M.E. Church located in Acton, Tennessee which shall be included within said conference; on the east by the Alabama State Line; on the south by a point three-fourth distance to the 33rd parallel line from the 34th parallel then by a line running northwest of West Point, Mississippi and west of Grenada, Mississippi and continuing north of Charleston, Mississippi along the 34th Parallel; there turning south along Highway 35 to the Mississippi-South Conference; and bounded on the west by the Mississippi River and the Arkansas State Line.

¶ **1221.** Northern California Annual Conference shall be bounded on the north by the State of Oregon, on the east by the State of Nevada, on the west by the Pacific Ocean, and on the south by an imaginary line extending east and west across the state half way between the cities of Fresno and Bakersfield, California.

¶ **1222.** Northwest Texas Conference is bounded on the East by the Red River directly north of Henrietta, thence South from said point on an imaginary line to Dublin, thence along an imaginary line to Lampassas with Del Rio, and on the southeast by the Dallas-FortWorth, Central East Texas, and Southeast Texas Conferences, on the north by Oklahoma, west and southwest by Mexico and Arizona-New Mexico Conference, and on the south by the Rio Grande.

¶ **1223.** Ohio-Central Indiana Conference shall include the states of Ohio, West Virginia, the Central portions of Indiana, and the Pittsburgh area of Pennsylvania.

¶ **1224.** Oklahoma-Muskogee Conference shall be composed of all territory within the bounds of the state of Oklahoma.

¶ **1225.** South Arkansas Conference is bounded on the south by Louisiana. North by a line beginning due west of Dequeen, Arkansas, through Murfreesboro, Pine Bluff, Delophia and Lake Villa. And on the East by the Mississippi River.

¶ **1226.** The South Georgia Conference shall be bounded on the east by the Atlantic Ocean, on the west by the Alabama state line, on the south by the Florida state line, and on the north by the northern boundary of the following counties: Glynn, Wayne, Appling, Toombs, Montgomery, Wheeler, Telfair, Ben Hill, Turner, Worth, Dougherty, Calhoun, and Early.

¶ **1227.** South Louisiana Conference bounded on the North by the Louisiana Conference; on the East by the Mississippi River, on the West by Texas; on the South by the Gulf of Mexico.

¶ **1228.** Southeast Alabama Conference bounded on the North by the Southern Railroad, running from Meredith, Mississippi, to Selma, Alabama, and thence on a straight line to Georgia; on the South by the Gulf of Mexico and Florida; and shall include Opelika District and the Phoenix City District.

¶ **1229.** Southeast Missouri, Illinois and Wisconsin Conference includes St. Louis, the states of Wisconsin, Minnesota and Illinois, except Robbins, Joliet, Chicago Heights.

¶ **1230.** Southeast Texas Conference bounded on the east by the state line of Texas and Louisiana running North to Panola County, on the North by Panola County, Rusk County, Cherokee County, with an imaginary line running to the northwest of San Antonio and Austin included. On the West by San Antonio and Austin, the Gulf of Mexico and bounded on the South by the Gulf of Mexico.

¶ **1231.** Southern California Annual Conference shall be bounded on the north by the Northern California Conference, on the east by the border of California with the exception of that area around El Centro California that is in the Arizona-New Mexico Conference, and on the south by the boundary between Mexico and California, and on the west by the Pacific Ocean.

¶ **1232.** Southern Zone (Nigeria) Annual Conference shall cover the Ikot Abasi District and Central District and shall embrace Mkpat Eknin Local Government Area and Ukanafun Local Government Area of Akwa Ibom State.

¶ **1233.** The West Georgia Conference shall be bounded on the west by the Alabama state line, on the north by the northern boundary of Troup and Merriweather counties, on the east by the contours of the Flint River to the northern boundary of Dooley County, the eastern boundary of Dooley, Crisp and Lee counties; and on the south by the southern boundary of Crisp, Lee, Terrell, Randolph, and Clay counties.

¶ **1234.** West Tennessee Conference is bounded on the West by the Mississippi River; on the South by the Mississippi State line; on the North by Highway 45 East; and on the West by Highway 45.

¶ **1235.** Western Zone (Nigeria) Annual Conference shall consist of Eket District, Etinan District, Oniong Nung Ndem District, and Aba/ Port Harcourt District of the C.M.E. Church and shall cover Eket Local Government Area, ONNA Local Government Area, Etinan Local Government Area, Nait-Ubium Local Government Area in Aka Ibom State, Imo State, Anambra State and Rivers State.

PART XIV: APPENDIX

59. Biography of Bishops Elected in 1998

60. Episcopal Supervision 1998 -2002

61. Addresses of the Bishops

62. Members of the Judicial Council

63. Connectional Administration

> The General Officers
> Members of General Connectional Board
> Members of Connectonal Commissions

**64. Members of the Committee
on Episcopacy**

**65. Resolution on Pan-Methodist
Cooperation**

66. The Bishops' Course of Study

**67. Rules and Procedures of the 1998
General Conference**

CHAPTER 59
BIOGRAPHIES OF BISHOPS ELECTED IN 1998

¶ **1300.** Biographical sketches of the 50th and 51st bishops elected in the 1998 General Conference:

§ 1. Paul A. G. Stewart, Sr., 50th Bishop of the CME Church

Paul A. G. Stewart, Sr. was elected the 50th Bishop of the Christian Methodist Episcopal Church on July 1, 1998, in the Thirty-Third Quadrennial Session and the Thirty-Fourth General Conference meeting in Birmingham, Alabama. He was born June 21, 1941, in Baldwyn, Mississippi, the youngest of six children born to Leroy and Bessie Stewart. Bishop Stewart's elementary and secondary education was in the schools of Baldwyn, and his B. S. Degree was earned from Mississippi Industrial College. In 1965 he graduated from the Phillips School of Theology of the Interdenominational Theological Center with the Master of Divinity Degree, received a Master's Degree from the University of Mississippi in 1975, and graduated from the U. S. Military Academy for Chaplains.

The ministry of Paul A. G. Stewart in the CME Church has been extensive as a local pastor, instructor in religion at the college level, chaplain in the U. S. military, dean of students at Miles College, and Presiding Elder. His most noted pastorates were the Russell Memorial CME Church of Durham, North Carolina, and the Phillips Temple CME Church of Los Angeles, California, from which he was elected bishop.

Throughout his ministry Bishop Stewart has been an active participant in community, ecumenical, civic, social, and Civil Rights affairs. He has worked exstensively with the NAACP, served as President of the Los Angeles Council of Churches, President of the Interdenominational Ministerial Alliance of Durham and Vicinity, President of the Alumni Association of the Phillips School of Theology, and a member of the Coordinating Council of Hope in Youth Gang Prevention Program of Los Angeles.

The 50th Bishop is married to Mattie Earlene (nee) Gardner, and they are the parents of three children, Gloria Jean, Paul, Jr., and Shinar La Donna. Upon his election and consecration he was assigned to the Fifth Episcopal District, named the Ecumenical Officer and the Chaplaincy Endorsing Agent for the CME Church.

§2. Lawrence L. Reddick III, 51st Bishop of the CME Church

The 51st Bishop of the Christian Methodist Episcopal Church elected in the Thirty-Third Quadrennial Session and the Thirty-Fourth General Conference meeting in Birmingham, Alabama, in 1998 was Lawrence L. Reddick III. He was born June 20, 1952, and is the son of Reverend Lawrence L. and Elizabeth Reddick, Jr. He was born in Huntsville, Alabama. His formative education was in the schools of Huntsville. He earned the B. A. degree from Ohio Wesleyan University, Master of Divinity from Duke University, and the honorary Doctor of Divinity from the United Theological Seminary and Bible College.

Bishop Reddick was licensed to preach in 1966, ordained Deacon in 1968, and ordained Elder in 1969. He was admitted into Full Connection in 1972. His itinerant ministry was extensive, including Antioch CME Church of Paint Rock, Alabama, youth minister of Lane Metropolitan CME Church, Cleveland, Ohio, under the pastorate of Reverend Anzo Montgomery, Scruggs Memorial CME Church of St. Louis, Missouri, and Presiding Elder in the North-East Mississippi Conference. He was elected Editor of The Christian Index, the official publication of the CME Church in 1982, a position he held until his elevation to the Episcopacy in 1998 — making him the longest serving Editor in the history of the denomination.

The Connectional responsibilities and services of the 51st Bishop have been numerous. He served as Secretary of the Carolina Annual Conference as well as the Southeast Missouri, Illinois and Wisconsin Annual Conference; member of the Commission on Hymnal and Ritual; Research Assistant to Bishop Bertram W. Doyle as head of the Division of Research and History of the CME Church; a member of the Commission on Cooperation and Counsel Between the CME Church and the United Methodist Church; and a member of the World Methodist Council for the 1996 — 2001 quinquennium.

He is married to Robin (nee) Shyne, and is the father of five children — Jon Bradley, Janice Patrice, twins Iris Lucille and Rose Elizabeth, and Samuel Lawrence. He is the grandfather of Jesiree Dillon.

Upon his election Bishop Reddick was assigned to the Tenth Episcopal District, and named Chair of the Commission on Ritual and Worship and Vice-Chair of the Committee on Compilation.

Chapter 60
Episcopal Supervision 1998 — 2002

¶ 1301. **The assignments for Episcopal Supervision for the 1998 - 2002 Quadrennium is as follows:**

FIRST EPISCOPAL DISTRICT — North Arkansas; South Arkansas; West Tennessee; East Tennessee Conferences — Bishop William H. Graves, Sr., Presiding Bishop.

SECOND EPISCOPAL DISTRICT — Ohio-Central Indiana; Kentucky Conferences — Bishop Nathaniel L. Linsey, Presiding Bishop.

THIRD EPISCOPAL DISTRICT — Michigan-Indiana; Kansas-Missouri; Southeast Missouri, Illinois and Wisconsin Conferences — Bishop Dotcy I. Isom, Jr., Presiding Bishop.

FOURTH EPISCOPAL DISTRICT— Louisiana; Mississippi-South; North-East Mississippi; South Louisiana Conferences — Bishop Thomas L. Hoyt, Jr., Presiding Bishop.

FIFTH EPISCOPAL DISTRICT — Birmingham; North Central Alabama; Southeast Alabama; Florida Conferences — Bishop Paul A. G. Stewart, Sr., Presiding Bishop.

SIXTH EPISCOPAL DISTRICT — Georgia, North; Central Georgia; South Georgia; West Georgia Conferences — Bishop Othal H. Lakey, Presiding Bishop.

SEVENTH EPISCOPAL DISTRICT — New York-Washington; Carolina Conferences — Bishop Charles L. Helton, Presiding Bishop.

EIGHTH EPISCOPAL DISTRICT — Dallas-Fort Worth; Southeast Texas; East Texas; Central Texas; Northwest Texas Conferences — Bishop Marshall Gilmore, Presiding Bishop.

NINTH EPISCOPAL DISTRICT —Northern California; Southern California; Arizona-New Mexico; Oklahoma-Muskogee; Alaska-Pacific Conferences — Bishop E. Lynn Brown, Presiding Bishop.

TENTH EPISCOPAL DISTRICT — Eastern Zone (Nigeria); Ghana; Haiti; Jamaica; Lagos (Nigeria); Liberia; Southern Zone (Nigeria); Western Zone (Nigeria) — Bishop Lawrence L. Reddick III, Presiding Bishop.

Chapter 61
Addresses of the Bishops

¶ 1302

Bishop Nathaniel L. Linsey, Senior Bishop
Second Episcopal District
5115 Rollman Estate Dr.
Cincinnati, OH 45236

Bishop William H. Graves
First Episcopal District
1374 Farrow Road
Memphis, TN 38116

Bishop Othal Hawthorne Lakey
Sixth Episcopal District
2001 M. L. King, Jr. Drive, S. W.
Suite 423
Atlanta, GA 30310

Bishop Thomas L. Hoyt, Jr.
Fourth Episcopal District
109 Holcomb Dr.
Shreveport, LA 71103

Bishop Paul A. G. Stewart, Sr.
Fifth Episcopal District
310 18th St., No., Suite 400D
Birmingham, AL 35203

Bishop Marshall Gilmore
Eighth Episcopal District
1616 E. Illinois Ave.
Dallas, TX 75216

Bishop Dotcy I. Isom, Jr.
Third Episcopal District
5925 W. Florissant Ave
St. Louis, MO 63136

Bishop E. Lynn Brown
Ninth Episcopal District
3844 W. Slauson Ave.
Suite 1
Los Angeles, CA 90043

Bishop Charles L. Helton
Seventh Episcopal District
6524 16th St., NW
Washington, DC 20012

Bishop L. L. Reddick III
Tenth Episcopal District
P.O. Box 27147
Memphis, TN 38167

Retired Bishops

Bishop Henry C. Bunton
853 E. Dempster Ave.
Memphis, TN 38106

Bishop Oree Broomfield, Sr.
3505 Springrun Dr.
Decatur, GA 30032

Bishop C. D. Coleman
1000 Longmeadow Lane
DeSoto, TX 75115

Bishop Richard O. Bass, Sr.
1556 Delton Pl.
Midfield, AL 35228

Chapter 62
The Judicial Council

¶ 1303. Members of the Judicial Council

Reveverend James A. Hawkins, Sr.
(Class of 1994)
President
6329 DuPree Dr.
Columbus, GA 31907

Honorable Bertina Lampkin
(Class of 1994)
Clerk
10004 S. Peoria
Chicago, IL 60643

Honorable Emma I. Darnell
(Class of 1994)
284 Peyton Rd., S. W.
Atlanta, GA 30311

Commissioner Harold Watkins
(Class of 1994)
571 New Town St.
Detroit, MI 48215

Reverend O'Neal Shyne, Sr.
(Class of 1994)
3754 Parkfield Pl.
Dayton, OH 45416

Dr. Joseph Capers
(Class of 1998)
Vice President
110 Adams Ave.
Grambling, LA 71245

Reverend Claude Johnson
(Class of 1998)
775 Lincoln Ave.
Pasadena, CA 91103

Reverend Dr. Charles L. Johnson
(Class of 1998)
1404 Blueberry Dr.
Memphis, TN 38116.

Dr. Barbara Boyd
(Class of 1998)
2222 McDaniel Ave.
Anniston, AL 36201

¶1303.1 Alternate Members

Clergy
Franklin M. Easterly
H. C. Wilkes

Lay
Barbara Nichols
Carter Curtis

Chapter 63
Connectional Administration

¶1304. The General Officers

Executive Secretary
Attorney Juanita Bryant
3675 Runnymeade
Cleveland, OH 44121

General Secretary Finance
Dr. Joseph C. Neal, Jr.
P. O. Box 75085
Los Angeles, CA 90075

Editor, *The Christian Index*
Dr. Kenneth E. Jones
P.O. Box 431
Fairfield, AL 35064

General Secretary Publications
Reverend William E. George
P. O. Box 2018
Memphis, TN 38101

General Secretary
Christian Education
Dr. Ronald M. Cunningham
4466 Elvis Presley Blvd.
Box 193
Memphis, TN 38116 -7100

General Secretary
Evangelism and Missions
Dr. Willie C. Champion
102 Pearly Top Dr.
Glenn Heights, TX 75154

General Secretary
Lay Ministry
Mr. Victor Taylor
9560 Drake Ave.
Evanston, IL 60203

General Secretary
Personnel Services
Dr. N. Charles Thomas
P. O. Box 74
Memphis, TN 38101-0074

President
Women's Missionary Council
Dr. Judith E. Grant
723 E. Upsal St.
Philadelphia, PA 19119

¶1304.1 The General Connectional Board 1998 — 2002

Bishop Nathaniel L. Linsey, Senior Bishop, Chair
Bishop Marshall Gilmore, Vice-Chair

First Episcopal District

Clergy	Lay
James Brown	Phyllis Barlow
Thurston Callier	Brinder Bursey
Arthur David	Matthew Davis, III
William Gant	Claudette Harris
Walter Hurt, Jr.	Juanita Johnson
Louis T. Purham	Wesley McClure
Edgar L. Wade	Freeman McKindra
Charles E. Winfrey, Sr.	Leonard Mitchell

Second Episcopal District

Arthur Green	Marshall Franklin
Charles King	Michael Morgan
James Washington	Betty Ruth Stephens

Third Episcopal District

David Bryant	Barbara Bouknight
Carrell K. Cargle, Sr.	Earl Bryant
Julius Clay	Velma Fulks
Daniel L. Fitten	Cephus Johnson
Tony C. Henderson	Phedonia Johnson
Jerome Price	Evelyn Moore
Anthony Robinson	L. C. Strayhorn
O'Neal Shyne, Jr.	Martenis Tyiska
Henry Williamson, Sr.	Albert Ward

Fourth Episcopal District

Clergy	Lay
Larry Anders	Willie Barnes
Joseph Grantham	Boyce Blackmon
Ricky Helton	Estelle W. Brooks
David Hoey	Annie Brown
Dorothy C. Jenkins	Frank Morris
James Loftin	Jesse Parker
James Stewart	Princess Pegues

Fifth Episcopal District

Desi Echols	Alyce Brown
Sidney Hill, Sr.	Emogene W. Crittenden
W. Clyde Jones	Sarah Farris
Albert J. H. Sloan	Steven Hoyt
C. A. Smith	Fred Hughes
Johnny Wilson	Yvonne Kennedy
Roderick Zak	Roscoe Webb

Sixth Episcopal District

Anthony M. Alford	Evelyn Brown
L. K. Allen	Mary Clark
Maurice Cherry	Lucy Dunn
Fay Greer Cook	Michael Ellison
Lindsey Napier	Bryant Magwood
Earnest Pettigrew	Leo Pinkett
Jerry Woodfork	Glendora P. Ryce
Frederick Zak	Robert Turner

Seventh Episcopal District

Clergy	Lay
William Austin	Laura Anderson- Halloway
Bobby Best	Bryan Champion
Wardell Bonner	Faye Crowder
James A. Jones	R. Michael Dixon
Roderick D. Lewis	Nellie B. King
Willie Sturgess	Carole E. Richardson
Robert Williams	Annie Scarboro
	William Simmons

Eighth Episcopal District

Kenneth W. Carter	Helen Crowder
Jerry L. Christian	Fay Griffin
H. Q. Dickerson	Dorothy Phea-Norville
Reginald Garrett	Gladys Stern
Jerome E. McNeil, Jr.	Ozell Ward
W. Edward Lockett	Rhonda Wiley-Keith
Donald R. Madlock	Lizzie Willis
C. E. Mitchell	
David Robinson	

Ninth Episcopal District

Charles Belcher	Theresa Duhart
Nicholas Betts	I. Carlton Faulk
Daryll Coleman	Clifford Harris
Joseph Gardner	P. Grace Jones
Leroy Johnson	Leroy Lindsey
Emmanuel Luther	Truitt Lowery
Robert L. Peoples	Harold McCoy

William D. Smart   Esther Parks

Tenth Episcopal District
Clergy   **Lay**

Clergy	Lay
Monday P. Akpan	Felix Akpan
Sonny Ekpo	Joseph Akpan
Cosmo Grant	Amos Blair
William Pennoh	Windy Ekpono
B. R. Udosen	Eme Ekpo
Godwin Umoette	Edmond Estime'
Suffrant Vincent	Emmanuel Isong
Jackson Yenn—Batah	Nkese Okopedeghe

¶1304. 2 Connectional Commissions

§1. Commission on Faith and Order
Bishop Thomas L. Hoyt, Jr., Chair

First District — Rev. Carmichael Crutchfield
Second District — Rev. Franklin Easterly
Third District — Rev. Dr. O'Neal Shyne, Jr.
Fourth District — Rev. Larry D. Anders
Fifth District — Rev. Gary Collins
Sixth District — Dr. L. H. Whelchel
Seventh District — Rev. Raymond Graves
Eighth District — Dr. Evelyn Parker
Ninth District — Rev. Dr. Cheryl Kirk-Duggan
Tenth District — Rev. Jackson Yenn-Batah

§2. Commission on Life and Witness
Bishop Charles L. Helton, Chair

First District — Rev. Leroy Payne, Sr.
Second District — Rev. John Walker
Third District — Rev. Clarence C. Buchanan

Fourth District — Rev. Edward E. Thomas
Fifth District — Rev. Roderick Zak
Sixth District — Rev. Donald R. Jordan
Seventh District — Dr. William Austin
Eighth District — Rev. W. E. Lockett
Ninth District — Dr. Leroy Haynes
Tenth District — Dr. Godwin Umoette

§3. Commission on Social Justice & Human Concerns
Bishop E. Lynn Brown, Chair

First District — Rev. John M. Gilmore
Second District — Rev. James Washington
Third District — Rev. Larry Batie
Fourth District — Rev. Phillip Bryant
Fifth District — Dr. Willie Clyde Jones
Sixth District — Rev. Percy D. Johnson
Seventh District — Rev. Willie Sturgess
Eighth District — Dr.. Jerry L. Christian
Ninth District — Mr. James Faulk
Tenth District — Rev. Edet Okopedeghe

§4. Commission on Ecumenicity
Bishop Paul A. G. Stewart, Sr., Chair

First District — Rev. Edgar L. Wade
Second District — Rev. Oliver D. Walker
Third District — Dr. Essie D. Clark
Fourth District — Rev. James A. Loftin
Fifth District — Mr. William Henry
Sixth District — Mrs. Alna Porter
Seventh District — Dr. Lloyd Watkins
Eighth District — Rev. Michael DeVaughn
Ninth District — Rev. Jarvis Johnson
Tenth District — Rev. Suffrant S. Vincent

§5. Commission on Ritual & Worship
Bishop Lawrence L. Reddick III, Chair

First District — Rev. Marilyn Lightner
Second District — Rev. Raymond Williams
Third District — Rev. Zachary E. Easterly
Fourth District — Mrs. Mathilda Martin
Fifth District — Rev. Harlan Jones
Sixth District — Rev. Kenneth McMillian
Seventh District — Rev. Weldon Thomas
Eighth District — Rev. H. Q. Dickerson
Ninth District — Rev. Stacey Cole
Tenth District — Dr. Sonny Ekpo

§6. Commission on Women in Ministry
Bishop Thomas L. Hoyt, Jr., Chair

First District — Mr. Earnest Taylor
Second District — Rev. Hallie Black
Third District — Dr. Dixie L. West
Fourth District — Rev. Myrtle Clark
Fifth District — Rev. Uylee Waugh
Sixth District — Dr. Thomas L. Brown, Sr.
Seventh District — Dr. Delores Richardson
Eighth District — Ms. Helen Crowder
Ninth District — Dr. Allidees Beckham

Tenth District — Rev. Philaberta Anderson

§7. Commission on Merger
(African Methodist Episcopal Zion Church)

Bishop Nathaniel L. Linsey
Bishop Thomas L. Hoyt, Jr.
Bishop Othal Hawthorne Lakey
Bishop Paul A. G. Stewart, Sr.
Bishop E. Lynn Brown

§8. Commission on Pan Methodist Cooperation

Bishop Paul A. G. Stewart, Sr.
Bishop Charles L. Helton
Dr. Luther Smith
Mr. Steven Hoyt
Mr. Matthew Davis
Attorney Juanita Bryant

§9. Representatives to the
Consultation on Church Union

Mrs. Esther L. Isom
Dr. W. Clyde Williams
Dr. Vivian Robinson
Rev. Manuel Henderson
Rev. Dr. Robert L. Peoples
Dr. Bassey Ekpono

§10. Commission on Celebration of the New Millennium
Bishop Paul A. G. Stewart, Sr., Chair
Bishop Lawrence L. Reddick III, Co - Chair

First District — Rev. Kenneth Thomas
Second District — Rev. L. L. Napier
Third District — Rev. Henry M. Williamson, Sr.
Fourth District — Dr. Ricky Helton
Fifth District — Dr. Alyce D. Brown
Sixth District — Rev. John W. Honeysucker
Seventh District — Rev. Wendell Oldham
Eighth District — Mr. Artis Barrett
Ninth District — Rev. William Smart
Tenth District — Rev. Astley Sommerville

§11. Committee to Study the Feasibility of an Indigenous
Bishop for Africa

Bishop Lawrence L. Reddick III, Chair

Senior Bishop Nathaniel L. Linsey

Mr. Victor Taylor

Mrs. G. Bernice Richardson

Reverend J. A. A. Solomon (Ghana)

Mr. Richard Davis (Liberia)

Mr. James A. Utuk (Lagos)

Mr. Umana Akpan (Eastern Zone)

Rev. B. R. Udosen (Western Zone)

Rev. A. B. Eshiet (Southern Zone)

Dr. Godwin Umoette (Consultant)

Dr. Sonny Ekpo (Consultant)

Dr. Bassey Ekpono (Consultant)

Dr. I. Carlton Faulk (Consultant)

§12. Board of Directors Connectional Headquarters
Bishop William H. Graves, Sr., Chair

First District	Ms. Linda Watson
Second District	Rev. Oliver DeWayne Walker
Third District	Rev. Henry Williamson
Fourth District	Dr. E. L. McLemore
Fifth District	Dr. Albert Sloan
Sixth District	Rev. Jesse A. Averett
Seventh District	Dr. Jimmy Gilbert
Eighth District	Mrs. Xavier Hill
Ninth District	Mr. Willie Robinson
Tenth District	Dr. Bassey Ekpono

§ 13. Advisory Board of the CME Foundation

First District	Rev. Louis T. Purham
Second District	Rev. Arthur S. Green
Third District	Rev. Jerome B. Price
Fourth District	Rev. Charles Young
Fifth District	Dr. Yvonne Kennedy
Sixth District	Mrs. Rudine Phelps
Seventh District	Mrs. Marvelle Willoughby
Eighth District	Rev. Reginald Garrett
Ninth District	Rev. Leroy Haynes
Tenth District	Dr. Godwin Umoette

Chapter 64
General Conference Standing
Committee on Episcopacy 1998 — 2002

¶1305. Members of the Standing Committee on Episcopacy of the 1998 General Conference serving for the Quadrennium are:

Annual Conference	Clergy	Lay
Western Zone Nigeria	B. R. Udosen	F. T. Akpan
West Tennessee	Q. H. Whitlock	Leonard Mitchel
West Georgia	Jesse A. Averett, Jr.	Earlene Woodson
Southern Zone Nigeria	M. P. Akpan	Akpan P. Atta
Southern California	A. Victor Brown	Esther Parks
Southeast Texas	W. E. Lockett	Ozell Ward
S. E. Mo-IL-Wisconsin	Carrell K. Cargle, Sr.	Zelda Q. Birdsong
Southeast Alabama	Johnny Wilson	Yvonne Kennedy
South Louisiana	A. B. Caesar	Willie Barnes
South Georgia	Maurice Cherry	Lucy Hazel Dunn
South Arkansas	Monteal Rhynes	Laura Bursey
Oklahoma-Muskogee	W. B. Harris	John Green
Ohio-Central Indiana	C. K. Henry	Robert Williamson
Northwest Texas	V. L. Brown	L. J. Hammond
Northern California	Harry Redds	Harold McCoy
North-East Mississippi	Hugh Jones	Lawrence Autry
North Central Alabama	J. H. Lowe	Nettie May
North Arkansas	James W. Johnson	J. W. Cooper
New York-Washington	James Arthur Jones	Nellie B. King
Mississippi-South	E. L. McLemore	Jesse Parker
Michigan-Indiana	James T. Morris	Barbara Bouknight
Louisiana	John Jackson	Jessie F. Moore
Liberia	William Pennoh	Victoria Togbah
Lagos	E. T. Udoukpong	Amos Etifah

Kentucky	Don C. Johnson	Aaron Baker
Kansas-Missouri	David L. Bryant, Jr.	Martenis Tyiska
Jamaica	Cosmo Grant	Colmie Simms
Ghana	J. A. A. Solomon	Charles Achemfour
Georgia, North	Jerry D. Woodfork	Deborah Stallworth
Florida	Roderick Zak	William Henry
Eastern Zone Nigeria	Edom Adams	Umana J. Akpan
East Texas	Herbert Scott	Doris King
East Tennesseee	Ronald Powe	Wesley McClure
Dallas-Ft. Worth	Jerry Christian	Helen Crowder
Central Texas	Donald Madlock	Eddie Wynn
Central Georgia	Frederick J. Zak	Barbara Magwood
Carolina	Irene Clodfelter	Laura A. Holloway
Birmingham	Sidney Hill	Sarah Farris
Arizona-New Mexico	D'Anna Gipson	P. Grace Jones
Alaska-Pacific	Leroy Haynes	Minnie Young

CHAPTER 65
COMMISSION ON PAN-METHODIST COOPERATION

¶ **1306.** Given the historic relationships and shared traditions of the delaminations of the Wesleyan tradition called Methodists in America, there shall be established a Commission on Pan-Methodist Cooperation. The General Conference authorizes the appointment of representatives by the College of Bishops to the commission which will include delegations from the African Methodist Episcopal Church, the African Methodist Episcopal Zion Church, the Christian Methodist Episcopal Church and the United Methodist Church. Each delegation shall consist of six members two bishops, a layman and a lay woman, a young adult, and at least one other member of the clergy.

¶ **1306.1.** The Commission on Pan-Methodist Cooperation shall work to define, determine, plan and, in cooperation with established agencies of the several denominations, execute activities to foster meaningful cooperation among the four Methodist denominations in the collaboration. Such cooperation shall include, but not be limited to, evangelism, mission, publications, social concerns and higher education. Each denomination will pay the expenses of its delegation to participate in Commission affairs.

¶**1306.2.** There shall be a Commission on Pan-Methodist Cooperation developed jointly with the African Methodist Episcopal church, African Methodist Episcopal Zion Church, the Christian Methodist Episcopal Church and the United Methodist Church. The representatives of the C.M.E. Church shall be selected by the College of Bishops. Each delegation shall consist of two bishops, a layman, a lay woman, a young adult, and at least one other member of the clergy. Each denomination will pay the expenses of its delegation to participate in commission affairs.

Purpose: The Commission on Pan Methodist Cooperation shall work to define, determine, plan and in cooperation with established agencies of the several denominations, execute activities to foster meaningful cooperation among the four Methodist denominations in the collaboration. Such cooperation shall include, but not be limited to, evangelism, missions, publications, social concerns and higher education. Each denomination will pay the expense of its delegation to participate in commission affairs.

The Commission may develop one or more Pan-Methodist coalitions to further meaningful cooperation on a particular activity or issue. Each quadrennium, the Commission shall plan and convene a Consultation of Methodist Bishops. The Commission on Pan-Methodist Cooperation may be expanded by the inclusion of the denominations of the Wesley tradition called Methodists in America, and the Commission shall establish guidelines to provide for such expansion. Before another Wesleyan/American Methodist denomination may become a part of the Commission on Pan Methodist Cooperation it must have the approval of its General Conference.

CHAPTER 66
THE BISHOPS'COURSE OF STUDY
FOR PREACHERS ON TRIAL

¶ **1307.** *Admission On Trial*

Purpose: To introduce a licientiate who has been recommended to an Annual Conference by a Quarterly Conference for Admission on Trial to the basic disciplines of the Christian Methodist Episcopal Church.

1. *The Holy Bible (New Revised Standard Version).*

2. *The Discipline of the C.M.E. Church* (Revised 1998).

3. *The C.M.E. Primer.* Bishop C. D. Coleman, Memphis, C.M.E. Publishing House, 1974.

4. *A Catechism For Members of the C.M.E. Church.* Bishop Marshall Gilmore, Memphis, C.M.E. Publishing House, 1984.

5. *The Pastor's Pocketbook of Rituals.* C.M.E. Publishing House, 1987.

6. *Introducing the New Testament.* John Drane, Harper and Row, 1986.

¶ **1307.1.** *First Year*

Purpose: To acquaint the probationer who has been Admitted on Trial with a general overview of the Christian Faith and the history and polity of the CME Church.

1. *The History of the C.M.E. Church.* Othal H. Lakey, Memphis: C.M.E. Publishing House, 1985.

2. *A Short History of Christianity.* 2nd Edition, Martin E. Marty, Fortress Press.

3. *Basic Christian Methodist Beliefs.* Bishop Joseph A. Johnson, Jr., Shreveport, 4th Episcopal District Press, 1978.

4. *Black Preaching.* Henry Mitchell, Philadelphia, J. P. Lippincott, 1972.

5. *Soul Theology.* Henry Mitchell and Nicholas Cooper Lewter, Harper and Row, 1986.

6. *Local Church Ministrations.* Bishop Marshall Gilmore, Shreveport, 1985.

7. *The Gift of Administration.* Thomas C. Campbell and Gary B . Reierson, Philadelphia, Westminster, 1981.

8. *Strong's Exhaustive Concordance.* James Strong, Abingdon.

9. *The Dictionary of Bible and Religion.* William H. Gent, Editor, Abingdon, 1986.

10. *Preaching and Leading Worship.* William Willimon, Westminster, 1984.

11. *Planning for Your Church.* Douglas Alan Walrath, Westminster, 1984.

12. *The Creed in the Gospels.* Alfonse Kemmer, Paulist Press, 1986.

¶ **1307.2.** *Second Year*

Purpose: To prepare the ordained Deacon for responsibility as preacher, leader of worship, and administrator of the sacraments.

1. *Preaching.* Fred B. Craddock, Abingdon, 1986.

2. *The Interpreters' Bible.* Abingdon, Nashville.

3. *The Minister as Crisis Counselor.* 2nd Edition, David K. Switzer, Abingdon, 1986.

4. *African American Worship.* Melba Costen.

5. *The Faith We Confess.* Jan Milis Lochman, Translated by David Lewis, Fortress, 1984.

6. *Pastoral Care in the Black Church.* Edward P. Wimberly, Abingdon, 1978.

7. *Introduction to the Bible.* John H. Hayes, Westminster,1984.

¶**1307.3.** *Third Year*

Purpose: To guide the Preacher on Trial, eligible for Admission into Full Connection, into a fundamental understanding of essential Chrisian doctrines and sound biblical interpretation.

1. *Understanding the New Testament.* 4th Edition, Howard Clark Kee and Wm. Goodwin Aurelio, Prentice-Hall

2. *Understanding the Old Testament,*4th Edition, Bernhard W. Anderson, Prentice Hall.

3. *Proclamation Theology.* Bishop Joseph A. Johnson, Jr., 4th Episcopal District Press, 1977.

4. *John Wesley on the Sacraments.* Ole E. Borgen, Francis Asbury Press.

3. *The Church That Cares.* Kenneth R. Miller and Mary Elizabeth Wilson, Judson, 1985.

4. *Worship is a Verb.* Robert Webber, Ministers Personal Library, Division of Word, 1985.

5. *The International Bible Commentary.* F. F. Bruce, Zondervan.

9. *Images of the Church in the New Testament.* Paul S. Minear. Westminster, 1970.

11. *Hope Within History.* Walter Brueggemann, John Knox, 1986.

12. *The Pastor-Evangelist in Worship.* Richard Stoll Armstrong, Westminster.

14. *Baptism.* Martin E. Mary, Fortress Press.

15. *The Lord's Supper.* Martin E. Marty, Fortress Press.

¶**1307.4.** *Fourth Year*

Purpose: To provide a Traveling Preacher, eligible for ordination as an Elder, helpful insights into the work of ministry, especially Christian Education, pastoral care, and church administration.

1. *The Caring Pastor.* Charles F. Kemp, Abingdon, 1985.

2. *Christian Marriage.* Presbyterian Church U.S.A., Westminister, 1986.

3. *The Funeral: A Service of Witness to the Resurrection.* Presbyterian Church, U.S.A., Westminster, 1986.

4. *Stewardship: A Response to the Gift of Creation.* Richard J. Waddell, Jr., The Alban Institute.

5. *From Light to Darkness: Aspects of Conversion in the New Testament.* Beverly Roberts Gaventa, Fortress Press, 1986.

6. *The Small Church and Christian Education.* Rachel Swam Adams.

7. *Premarital Counseling for Ministers.* Theodore K Pitt, Judson, 1985.

8. *The Creative Word: Canon as a Model for Biblical Education.* Walter Brueggemann, Fortress Press.

9. *Interpreting the Bible.* Terence J. Keegan, O.P. Paulist, 1985.

10. *Reading the Old Testament,* Lawrence Boad Paulist Press. 1984.

CHAPTER 67
RULES AND PROCEDURES
OF THE 1998 GENERAL CONFERENCE

¶ **1308.** The Senior Bishop shall announce in the official publications of the church the hour for the opening session of the General Conference at least 90 days before the date set for the Quadrennial Session of the General Conference of the Christian Methodist Episcopal Church.

¶**1308.1.** General Order of Business

§ 1. The following shall be the General Order of Business:

(a) The Quadrennial Sermon

(b) The Sacrament of Holy Communion

(c) Roll Call

(d) Temporary Organization

(e) Appointment of Committee on Credentials

(f) Reading of the Episcopal Address

(g) Report of Committee on Credentials

(h) Permanent Organization of the General Conference

    (1) Secretary and Staff

    (2) Rules and Procedures

    (3) Special Committees

    (4) Confirmation of Standing Committees

(i) Quadrennial Reports of the Bishops

(j) Quadrennial Reports of General Officers

    (1) Secretary of Finance

    (2) Secretary of Publications

    (3) Editor of *The Christian Index*

    (4) Secretary of Evangelism, Missions and Human
       Concerns

    (5) Secretary of Christian Education

    (6) Secretary of Personnel Services

    (7) Secretary of Lay Ministry

    (8) President of Women's Missionary Council

    (9) Executive Secretary

The quadrennial reports listed in "i" and "j" shall be limited to fifteen (15) minutes for bishops and ten (10) minutes for general officers. Following the reports motions, seconds to receive with commendation and to refer to the proper standing committee shall be in order provided that commendatory remarks shall not exceed a total of five (5) minutes, and in no case shall any demonstration, presentation, or gifts be made in conjunction with the reports.

(k) Report of Connectional Commissions

(1) Report of Special Committees

(m) Report of Standing Committees

¶ 1308.2. Organization

§2. After the service in which the Sacrament of Holy Communion is observed, the conference will convene for the roll call and temporary organization. A temporary secretarial staff will be elected and the appointment of the Committee on Credentials consisting of one lay and one clerical delegate from each Annual conference, will be announced by the Senior Bishop.

§3. The Committee on Credentials shall meet as expeditiously as possible to determine the eligibility of all the delegates certified to the General Conference. It will report to the General Conference on the second day, after the reading of the Episcopal Address, or as soon thereafter as possible.

§4. Upon certification by the Committee on Credentials that at least a majority of the elected delegates are duly elected in accordance with the provisions of the *Discipline,* the General Conference shall then perfect a permanent organization by electing a permanent secretary, assistants to the secretary, and other staff and conference personnel as may be deemed necessary; adopt its rules and procedures; and appoint the Standing Committees and special committees.

Beginning in the 1990 General Conference the delegations will be seated in reverse alphabetical order from the 1986 General Conference right to left according to Annual Conferences, from the view of the Chair, reversing the order alternately in succeeding General Conferences; and appoint the Standing Committees and Special Committees.

§5. The General Conference shall establish its time of meeting and adjournment for each daily session in accordance with the recommendations of the Committee on program, and hold special programs and services at its discretion. Time limitations and orders of the day may be changed at the discretion of the General Conference.

¶ 1308.3. Duty of the President

§6. One of the bishops shall preside each day the General Conference is in session, beginning with the Senior Bishop and proceeding in the order of their seniority until all have presided (cf. Discipline, 209).

(a) The President for the Day shall assume the Chair at the appointed hour, and shall take up the business of the conference in the regular order according to these rules and/or other rules and regulations adopted by the conference.

(b) The President shall decide all questions of order and procedure. His decisions shall be subject to an appeal to the General Conference. When an appeal from his decision has been made, such an appeal shall be decided without debate; provided that the President shall be allowed to state the grounds of his decision, and the appellant the grounds of his/her dissent.

(c) The President shall be fair and impartial in his presiding, recognizing at all times the rights and privileges of each member of the conference, but insuring order and decorum throughout the deliberations.

¶ 1308.4. Daily Order of Business

§7. The order of Business for the daily sessions of the General Conference shall be recommended by a Steering Committee.

¶1308.5. Duties and Privileges of Members

§8. Duly elected delegates, clerical and lay, from the several Annual Conferences, and alternate delegates seated by the conference in lieu of regular delegates, constitute the membership of the General Conference. Such members shall have the right to the floor of the General Conference, engage in all the deliberations, and vote on all issues. Delegates shall have the duty of attending all meetings of committees to which they may be assigned.

§9. A member may speak to an issue, make a motion, or raise a question upon proper recognition by the President. When thusly recognized, the member shall at all times be in order and respectful of the President, the rights of other members, and the conference.

§10. A member shall have the right to raise a Question of Privilege if he/she is misrepresented by another speaker or when matters relating to the rights and welfare of the individual member or of the whole body are so imperative as to justify the interruption of the regular order.

§11. No member shall speak more than twice on any question without the consent of two-thirds of the members present; nor shall a member make a second speech on a question until every member has had opportunity to speak. Except in the case of a representative of a committee, no member shall speak more than three minutes on a question without the consent of the conference.

§12. No member shall absent his/her self from the sessions of the General Conference without justifiable cause. The permanent absence of a member from the sessions shall be brought to the attention of the conference, and an alternate delegate shall be seated. All substitutions made in the delegation of an annual conference shall be reported to the presiding bishop of that annual conference. If the substitute delegate has not been reported by the presiding Bishop of the Annual Conference from which the substitute delegate was elected, the said delegate shall not exercise voice nor vote in the General Conference.

§13. All motions and resolutions, when properly introduced and seconded, and all reports presented to the conference, or stated by the President, shall be deemed the property of the conference. The mover of any motion, upon obtaining consent of the body, may withdraw it at any time before amendment or decision.

¶1308.6. Procedures for Voting and Quorum Requirements

§14. Unless otherwise indicated in these rules or Robert's Rules of Order, motions will be carried by a majority vote of delegates present and voting.

§ 15. Balloting. When the General Conference chooses to vote on any proposition by ballot or when an election (bishops, general officers, or other connectional officers) is to be held, such balloting shall be conducted by an Election Committee established for that purpose in the organization of the General Conference.

§16. Voting. The General Conference may vote on propositions by voice, show of hands, standing, or by Yeas and Nays unless one fourth (1/4) of the members request a secret ballot, in which case, such questions must be voted on by secret ballot; provided that upon the call of one-sixth (1 /6) of the members present and voting, any question related to the nature of the Episcopal Office, individual bishops, or in the interest of bishops — including subsidiary motions, referrals, postponement, substitutions, amendments, etc. — shall be by secret ballot.

¶ 1308.7. Matters for Consideration

§17. The General Conference shall give consideration to those matters that come before it by way of reports and recommendations from designated commissions, committees, boards, and elected officials, and other matters that have been presented to the delegates to the General Conference by way of a special committee on resolutions in accordance with the provisions of the Discipline.

§18. The procedure for consideration of other matters shall be for the roll of the Annual Conferences to be called at which time memorials, resolutions, or proposals endorsed by an Annual Conference delegation may be presented without reading or discussion. Upon presentation, such will be referred to the appropriate Standing Committee. Such matters shall not be considered by the General Conference until acted upon and reported by a Standing Committee to the General Conference.

§19. Matters presented for *immediate consideration* by the General Conference (that is, *without* referral to and action by a Standing Committee) will require a two-thirds (2/3) vote for the suspension of the Order of the Day and a two-thirds vote for passage.

§20. All resolutions requiring changes in the wording and/or legal meaning of provisions in the Discipline shall state the paragraph, section, page, and language of the Discipline to be changed and the language to be substituted.

§21. The Resolutions and proposals received at the General Conference shall be referred to the committee suggested by the Committee on Resolutions as indicated in the booklet of reports, resolutions and proposals.

Unless otherwise indicated by the presenter or the General Conference, preamble(s) to resolution(s) shall be considered only as item(s) of information regarding the resolution and not a part of the resolution itself when considered for adoption.

¶ 1308.8. *Standing Committees*

§22. As the legislative body of the Christian Methodist Episcopal Church, the General Conference shall utilize the following *Standing Committees:*

  (a) Episcopacy
  (b) Itinerancy
  (c) Revision & Legal Affairs
  (d) Finance
  (e) Evangelism & Human Needs
  (f) Connectional Ministries
  (g) Connectional Administration
  (h) Annual and General Conferences Boundaries & Operations
  (i) Ecumenical Relations & World Affairs

§23. The delegation of each Annual Conference to the General Conference shall be entitled to one clerical and one lay member on each of the Standing Committees. However, no delegate shall be assigned to no more than two Standing Committees. Said members shall be recommended by the Presiding Bishop of the Annual Conference and confirmed by the delegation; provided that only alternate delegates properly seated in the regular delegation may serve on a Standing Committee.

§24. The General Conference shall provide each Standing Committee a general outline of the areas of concern under its purview. It shall be the duty of the committee to receive, discuss, question, seek additional information, and make proper recommendation to the General Conference on all matters referred to it. Recommendations from a Standing~ Committee will be concur (recommendation for approval), non-concurrence (i.e., disagreement and recommendation of disapproval), or concurrence with changes (i.e., general agreement and recommendation of approval with certain changes).

¶ 1308.9. *Special Committees*

§25. Each Episcopal District shall be entitled to one person, recommended by the Presiding Bishop from among the regular delegates or alternates who have permanently replaced regular delegates from that Episcopal District and confirmed by the delegation from that Episcopal District, to the following Special Committees designed to facilitate the operation of the General Conference:

(a) Rules and Procedures
(b) General Conference Business Operations
(c) Steering Committee
(d) Committee of Tellers
(e) Committee on Minutes
(f) General Conference Location and Operations
(g) Legislative Review
(h) Orderlies

¶ 1308.10. *Rules of Order*

§26. The General Conference shall at all times and in all matters be governed by the rules herein provided and/or the common practices of parliamentary usage found in *Roberts Rules of Order* and by the *Discipline* of the Christian Methodist Episcopal Church. These rules shall not be suspended except by a vote of two-thirds (2/3) of the members present and voting.

Standing Committees of the General Conference

¶ 1309. The following are the definitions and responsibilities of each of the Standing Committees of the General Conference in accordance with the directives of the 1994 General Conference (cf. *Journal 1994 General Conference,* pages 29 and 30).

¶ 1309.1. *Committee on Episcopacy:*

§1. Examine the Quadrennial Reports of the bishops;
§2. Recommend the passing of the character of each bishop;

§3. Consider appropriate portions of the Episcopal Address;

§4. Recommend the number of bishops the CME Church should have; and the number of bishops that should be elected at any given General Conference.

§5. Recommend, in consultation with the College of Bishops, the assignment of bishops to the several Episcopal Districts;

§6. Consider any resolution, memorial, or proposal related to the episcopacy and make appropriate recommendation to the General Conference;

§7. In the interim of General Conferences the members of the Committee on Episcopacy shall constitute a continuing committee charged with the responsibility of making episcopal assignments, in consultation with the College of Bishops, as required due to the death or incapacity of an active bishop(s).

¶ 1309.2. *Committee on Itinerancy*

§ 1. Consider all resolutions, memorials, or proposals related to the itinerancy of the church such as duties of pastors, requirements for ordination, responsibilities of presiding elders, etc.

§2. Make appropriate recommendations to the General Conference ways of improving the effectiveness of the ministry of the church.

¶ 1309.3. Committee on Revision & Legal Affairs

§1. Consider resolutions, memorials, or proposals related to alterations and changes in the *Book of Discipline*.

§2. Consider legislation dealing with the Judicial Administration of the church.

§3. Consider the report of Legal Counsel to the General Conference.

§4. Recommend revisions in the *Discipline* necessary to remove obvious contradictions, ambiguities, out-dated statements, etc.

¶ 1309.4 Committee on Finance

§1. Consider the report of the General Secretary of Finance;

§2. Consider *all* resolutions, memorials, or proposals submitted to the General Conference related to connectional finances of the church;

§3. Recommend the Connectional Budget for the ensuing quadrennium to the General Conference.

¶ 1309.5. *Committee on Evangelism, Missions & Human Needs*

§1. Consider resolutions, memorials, or proposals submitted to the General Conference related to the program of evangelism, mission, and social ministries of the church.

§2. Consider the report of the General Secretary of Evangelism, Missions and Human Needs.

§3. Recommend to the General Conference legislation related to the church's program of evangelism, missions, and social concerns.

¶ 1309.6. *Committee on Connectional Ministries*

§1. Consider the report of the General Secretary of Christian Education.

§2. Consider the report of the General Secretary of Lay Ministry.

§3. Consider the report of the President of the Women's Missionary Council.

§4. Consider resolutions, memorials, or proposals submitted to the General Conference pertaining to the church's ministry of Christian nurture, the ministry of the laity, and the work of the Women's Missionary Council.

§5. Recommend to the General Conference appropriate legislation related to these phases of the connectional ministries of the church.

¶ 1309.7. *Committee on Connectional Administration*

§1. Consider the report of the General Secretary of Publications.

§2. Consider the report of the Editor of *The Christian Index.*

§3. Consider the report of the General Secretary of Personnel Services.

§4. Consider Collins Chapel Hospital.

§5. Consider resolutions, memorials, or proposals submitted to the General Conference that pertain to the departments of the church responsible for publications, pensions, and insurance.

§6. Recommend to the General Conference appropriate legislation pertaining to the administration of the connectional program in these areas.

¶ 1309.8. *Committee on Annual and General Conferences Boundaries & Operations*

§1. Consider resolutions, memorials, or proposals submitted to the General Conference related to the authority, procedure, or operation of the Annual Conference.

§2. Consider matters related to the boundaries of the Annual Conferences.

§3. Recommend to the General Conference legislation or action pertaining to the Annual Conferences.

§4. Consider matters related to the procedures and operation of the General Conference.

¶ 1309.9. *Committee on Ecumenical Relations & World Affairs*

§5. Prepare and present to the General Conference resolutions on world issues and affairs.

§6. Consider all matters related to the union of the C.M.E. Church with other Christian churches.

§7. Consider the relation the C.M.E. Church has or should have with other ecumenical bodies in the U.S. and other parts of the world.

§8. Recommend to the General Conference appropriate actions the C.M.E. Church should take regarding its role in helping to enhance the oneness of the Body of Christ.

¶ 1310. *Committee Procedures*

§1. Initially, each Standing Committee will meet at the time and place announced in the open session of the General Conference. After being organized, a committee will meet in accordance with its own decisions and announcement within the committee.

§2. Any member of the committee may convene the committee and ask for a temporary secretary. A permanent chairperson, vice-chair person, secretary, and assistant secretary will then be elected.

§3. Each committee will consider all items referred to it and make a recommendation — concurrence, non-concurrence, or concurrence with changes — to the General Conference regarding the same.

§4. Unless otherwise ordered by the General Conference or the committee, any member of the C.M.E. Church may sit in on the committee meeting but only duly appointed members may vote.

¶ 1311. *Accounting of General Conference Funds*

The Special Committee on General Conference Business Operations appointed under ¶ 1307.9 §25 shall perform the following duties:

§1. Make a full and complete report of the source (s) and amounts of all funds collected or caused to be collected by or during a General Conference;

§2. Such report (s) shall be made not later than two months (60 days) after the close of the General Conference;

§3. Such report (s) shall include but not limited to: (a) rebates for housing accommodations, (b) number of complimentary rooms made available, (c) how such rooms were assigned, and (d) person (s) or entity who made the decisions regarding allocation of complimentary rooms and usage of rebates;

§4. Such report (s) shall include the names of persons receiving funds and the amounts paid to each named person, including salaries, honoraria, refunds, and other compensations or considerations;

§5. Such report (s) shall list each expenditure over fifty dollars ($50) as a separate line item disbursement, and no item that exceeds fifty dollars ($50) shall be listed as miscellaneous; and

§6. Such report (s) shall be audited by an outside auditor, selected by the bid process. (cf. ¶ 437.9)

¶ 1312. *Legislative Intent*

It is the intent of the General Conference that any and all legislation and/or actions passed in accordance with these rules shall supersede and replace any legislation and actions, or parts of legislation and actions, passed by previous General Conferences which conflict with legislation enacted by or any action of this General Conference shall be null and void.

¶ 1313. *Video-Taping*

The video-taping or recording of non-deliberative sessions shall be in accordance with contractual agreements approved by the General Conference Business Committee: but, the deliberative (i.e. business) sessions of the General Conference shall not be video-taped or recorded for public sale or consumption.

 **INDEX**

INDEX

A

Abandonment, Property, ¶ 602.6
Accusation, Notice of, ¶ 803
Addresses of
>Bishops, ¶ 1302
>General Officers, ¶ 1304
Administration of
>Board of Christian Education, ¶ 516
>Christian Youth Fellowship, ¶ 518
>Judicial proceedings, ¶ 801
>Local Church, ¶ 422, §2
>Preachers, ¶ 226, §13
>Schools and colleges, ¶ 1130.1
>Sunday Church School, ¶ 517, 517.1
Admission
>Bishops' Course of Study for, ¶ 413, §4; ¶ 415, §3
>Committee on Ministerial Examination, ¶ 223.5
>Duty of Quarterly Conference, ¶ 253, §6
>Local Church membership requirement, ¶ 506
>On Trial, ¶ 413
Admitting
>Into Full Connection, ¶ 420.1; ¶ 420.2; ¶ 420.3; ¶1307
>Missionaries into Full Connection, ¶ 420.2, §6
>Non-members to Love Feast, ¶ 312
>Preachers from other churches, ¶ 421
>Preachers on Trial, ¶ 413
>Restrictions on preachers, ¶ 421, §1
Adult
>Division of Christian Education, ¶1106ff.
>Young, ¶ 1125
Affiliate Member, ¶ 508.2, § 4
African
>Budget allocation, ¶ 1010; §1017, Schedule "G"
Age
>Annual Conference delegates, of, ¶ 213, §3(e)
>Annual Conference Trustees, ¶ 223.6§1
>General Conference delegates,¶ 201.4; ¶201.5
>Retirement, ¶ 436, ¶432.6; ¶439,§2
>Requirement for voting, see Articles of Incorporation
Agent, Corporate (Charter of Incorporation, page 41)
Agent, Chaplain endorsing, ¶423, §2, §3; ¶423.1, §1
Allocation of Connectional Budget, ¶1017

Alternates

    General Conference delegates, ¶201.7

    Judicial Council members, ¶804.5

Amendments to

    Constitution of C.M.E. Church, Constitution, Div. 5

    Constitution, Women's Missionary Council, ¶1134, Article 8

    Constitution Connectional Young Adults, ¶1125, Art. 8

American Bible Society, Day, ¶702

Annual Conference

    Attendance at, ¶215

    Bishops and the, ¶224

    Boards of,

        Christian Education, ¶223.2; ¶1111

        Evangelism, ¶ 223.1

        Missions, ¶1164

        Personnel Services, ¶223.3; ¶1036

        Publishing Interests, ¶1024

        Trustees, ¶223.6

    Boundaries of, ¶1201-1235

    Boundaries and number of, ¶220

    Budget of, ¶223.4, §4 (a)

    Commission on Consolidation of, ¶221, §2

    Committees of

        Deeds, Titles and Abstracts, ¶608

        Ministerial Examination, ¶223.5

    Constitutional provision for, Const., Div.2, Art. 2)

    Creating new conferences, ¶221

    Disciplinary Questions, ¶226

    Duties and responsibilities of, ¶218; ¶ 219

    Duties of members, ¶215

    Dissolution of, ¶221.1

    Elections

        ballot requirement, ¶201.6

        clergy delegates to General Conference, ¶201.4

        lay delegates to General Conference, ¶201.5

        alternate delegates to General Conference, ¶201.7

        number, ¶213, §3 (d)

    Finances of,

        audit requirement, ¶222.2, §7

        bank selection, ¶218, §9

        Bishop's role, ¶224

        Joint Board of Finance, ¶223.4

        operating budget, ¶218, § 5; ¶ 223.4, §4 (a)

        remitting General Funds, ¶223.4, §4 (i)

Treasurer, ¶222.2

Judicial Authority of, ¶ 803.6, § 2; ¶ 225, §3

Lay Council, ¶226, § 46 (c), § 55 (d)

Lay delegates to,

    attendance, ¶215

    authority, ¶218; ¶214, §4

    certification, ¶213, §3c, 1-3

    election of, ¶213, §3 (c)

    eligibility, ¶213, §3e

    description of, ¶213, §3c

Meaning of, ¶213, §1-3

Membership and Personnel

    membership, ¶213

    presiding officer, ¶217

    probationary members, ¶214, §3

    records clerk, ¶222.4

    retired preachers, ¶439; ¶213, §3(a)

    schools, ¶218, §6

    secretary, ¶222.1

    statistician, ¶222.3

    treasurer, ¶222.2

    trustees, ¶223.6

    voting, ¶214

    ratio, ¶213, §3d

Place and time of meeting, ¶216

Appeal

Process of, ¶803.6

Right to, ¶211.5; ¶803.6

Of Bishops' decisions, ¶ 428, §10

To Judicial Council, ¶805.2, §6 (e), (1 - 4)

Appellate Jurisdiction, ¶805

Arbitration

Duty of Joint Board in, ¶223.4, §4 (k)

Arguments before Tribunal, ¶803.4

Articles of Religion, ¶101- ¶125

Assessment of Penalty

Judicial, ¶803.5, § 2

    Late pension payments, ¶1041.2

Assignments of Bishops, ¶432

Associate members, ¶ 508.2, § 3

Associate ministers, ¶ 422.1

Atonement, ¶120

Authority to

Bring suit, ¶602.4

Obligate the CME Church, ¶602.5
Automation, ¶130. 3 (d)

B

Ballot for
  Electing delegates to General Conference, ¶201.6
  Voting in General Conference, ¶1308.6, §15
Baptism
  A Sacrament, ¶116
  Children, ¶ 313
  Duty of Preacher in charge, ¶422, § 1
  Meaning of, ¶117
  Ritual (See Book of Ritual)
Bequests, ¶ ¶1104.1; ¶607.1, §2
Bible
  Articles of Religion on, ¶105
  Duty to study, ¶128
Bibliographies for Courses of Study, ¶1307ff
Bishops
  Addresses of, ¶1302
  Appeal of, ¶803.6, § 2
  Assignment of, ¶432
  Character of, ¶432.7
  Children of deceased, ¶444.5
  College of, ¶437ff
  Constituting, ¶426
  Constitutional provision (see *Constitution*, Division 3)
  Course of Study, ¶1307ff
  Death of, ¶444.4; ¶ 432.8
  Duties of, ¶428
  Early retirement of, ¶436
  Election of, ¶426, §1
  Encouraging pastors' salary, ¶441.1
  Episcopal supervision, ¶1301
  Historical listing, page 16
  Incapacitation and replacement, ¶432.8
  Investigation of complaints on, ¶803.1, § 2
  Proof of birth requirement, ¶426, §2
  Protection of Episcopal office, 211, §3
  Provision for election if none remain, ¶427
  Restrictions on interference in election process, ¶201.6
  Restrictions on receiving extra funds, ¶433.1; ¶ 433.2
  Retired, ¶436
  Retirement, ¶436.1
  Salary, ¶444

Seniority, ¶436.2, §2

Spiritual and temporal supervision, ¶ 437.1

Support of, ¶444ff

Tribunal for, ¶ 803.4, § 2

Treasurer or custodian of funds prohibition, ¶433

Trustees of schools and colleges, ¶434

Widows of, ¶444.4; ¶444.5

Bishops, College of

Authority to appoint commissions, ¶437.3

Constitutional authority (See *Constitution*, Division 3)

Debt making authority, ¶602.5

Directors of CME Corporation, (See Arts. of Inc., §5)

Disciplinary Provisions for, ¶437

Executive body, ¶437.2

Making Legal Decisions, ¶437.5

Management Authority (Articles of Incorporation, §5)

Boards of Annual Conferences

Christian Education, ¶223.2; 1111

Evangelism, ¶223.1; ¶115.4

Finance (See also Joint Bd. of Finance), ¶223.4

Missions, ¶1164

Personnel Services, ¶223.3 ; ¶1036

Publication Services, ¶1024

Trustees, ¶223.6

Board of Directors

Headquarters of C.M.E. Church, ¶ 606, § 1; ¶1304.2, § 12

Boards of District Conferences

Christian Education, ¶1114

Evangelism, ¶1155

Lay Activities, ¶1135.6

Missions, ¶1165

Stewardesses, ¶231

Board, General Connectional, ¶1000

Board, Local Church

Christian Education, ¶ 516

Directors of the local corporation, ¶ 601, §3

Missions, ¶ 1166

Official, ¶ 263

Stewards, ¶ 511

Stewardesses, ¶ 513

Trustees, ¶ 515

Ushers, ¶ 524

Books

Bishops' Course of Study, ¶1307ff

Encouraging reading of, ¶422, §16

General Rule on, ¶126

Borrowing money

Authority, ¶602.5

General Rule on, ¶126

Mortgages, ¶602.3

Boundaries

Annual Conference, ¶1201-1235

General Conference Authority, ¶220

Budget

Annual Conference, ¶223.4, §4 (a)

Connectional, ¶1017

Building churches and parsonages, ¶602.3

Business

Buying and selling church property, ¶602.3

Stewards, ¶511.2, §3

C

Call to Preach, ¶405

Candidates For,

Admission on Trial, ¶413

Church membership, ¶ 506

Full Connection, ¶420

Local Preacher's license, ¶407

Ordination as local preachers, ¶409-410

Ordination as Traveling Preachers, ¶ 415, ¶ 417

Canonical books of the Bible, ¶105

Catechism, ¶313.3

Certification of

Birth for bishops-elect, ¶426, §2

Full Connection, ¶901

Ordination, ¶901

Proof for preachers from other churches, ¶421

Transfer of Church Membership, ¶422, §20

Certified Public Accountant

Annual Conference funds, ¶222.2, §7; ¶224

General Secretary of Finance, ¶1008

General Secretaries, ¶1000.5, §5

Certify

Authority of Committee on Credentials, ¶1308.2, §4

Authority of Quarterly Conference, ¶213, §3c; ¶253, §12, ¶253, §13

Chairman

General Connectional Board, ¶1000.4

Standing Committees, ¶1000.7, §3

Chaplains board, ¶423

Chaplains, military, ¶423.1

Character, ministerial, ¶225

Character, passing of

    Conference evangelists, ¶412, §4

    Supply pastors, ¶412, §2

    Traveling Preachers, ¶225; ¶226, §13

    Charge, Preacher in, ¶422

Charges,

    Pastoral, ¶ 503

    Bill(s) of, ¶803.3

Charitable Institutions, ¶607

Charter, C.M.E. Church, page 41

Chief

    Administrator, ¶422, §2

    Executives, ¶1001

Children

    Baptism of, ¶313

    Bible Classes for, ¶313.4

    Children's Day, ¶700

    Division of Christian Education, ¶1106

    Minister's Attention to, ¶313.1

    Recognized as Members, ¶313.2

    Use of Catechism with, ¶313.3

Choirs

    Presidents of, ¶523, §3

    Provisions for, ¶523, §2

Choristers, ¶523, §6-8

Christian Education (See General Department of)

Christian Index, The

    Agent, ¶1031

    Correspondent, ¶1030

    Department of, ¶ 1003.3

    Editor of, ¶1001.8

    Income, surplus, ¶1029

    Official publication, ¶1026

    Preachers subscibe to, ¶1032

    Publishing of, ¶1026.1; ¶1026.3

    Responsibility for, ¶1026.3

    Reporter, ¶1030, § 2

    Retired Preachers-Widows, ¶1033

    Standing Committee, ¶1000.7, §1

Christian Man, Oath of, ¶125

Christian Men's Goods, ¶124

Christian Methodist Men's Fellowship, ¶1135.2

Christian Military Service, ¶130.4 (2)

Christian Vocation, ¶130.3 (g)

Christian Vocation Day, ¶706
Christian Youth Fellowship
    Age Groups, ¶516.1, §4
    Day to observe, ¶703
    Mandate for, ¶518
    Officers, ¶518, §2
    President, ¶518, §2
    Program Emphasis, ¶518, §1
    Purpose, ¶518, §1
    Youth Week, ¶516.1, §10

Church
    Article of Religion on, ¶113
    Local, ¶500
    Meaning of, Preamble to *Constitution*, page 34
    Organizing a new one, ¶525
Church (C.M.E.)
    Charter of, page 41
    Conferences of, ¶201 - ¶ 262
    Constitution of, pages 34 - 40
    Directors of, Articles of Incorporation, see Note, page 41
    Official name of, *Constitution*, page 34
    Property and insurance, ¶604
Church Conference
    Business of , ¶260
    Disciplinary regulation of, ¶257
    Duties of, ¶260
    Meetings of, ¶257
    President of ¶257
    Secrectary of, ¶258
Church membership
    Affiliate, ¶508.2, §4
    Associate, ¶508.2, §3
    Baptismal requirement, ¶508.2 (b)(c)
    Candidates for, ¶506, ¶ 508.1, ¶1
    Definition, ¶ 505
    Full, ¶508.2, §2
    Instruction for, ¶507, § 3, §4
    Members from other churches, ¶508.2, §2 (b)
    Membership in ¶ 505
    Preparatory, ¶508.2, §1
    Ritual For Reception, (See *Book of Ritual*)
Church School, ¶1107, ¶517
Church School, Vacation, ¶1107.2, ¶516.1, §6
Classes

Bible, ¶313.4
Leaders of, ¶510
Meetings of, ¶308
Membership, ¶508.2, §1
Organization of, ¶308
Pastor's duties, ¶309
Clergy Vestments, restrictions on wearing, ¶409,§4; ¶415,§7
Clerk of the Judicial Council, ¶ 806.1, §3; ¶1303;
Clerk, Pension and Record, ¶222.4

C.M.E. Foundation, 607.1

College of Bishops, ¶437
Commissions
     Concerns of Women in the Ministry, ¶1003.10
     Consolidation of Annual Conferences, ¶ 221, §1
     Ecumenicity, ¶ 1003.9
     Educational Standards, ¶ 1128.2
     Faith and Order, ¶ 1003.6
     Life and Witness, ¶ 1003.7
     Membership and Evangelism, ¶ 520
     Pan-Methodist Cooperation, ¶ 1306
     Social Justice and Human Concerns, ¶ 1003.8
Commissions, Connectional, ¶ 1003.5
Committees
     Communication and Information Technology, ¶ 1111.2, §9
     Connectional Budget ¶ 1016.1
     Credentials, ¶ 1308.2, §3, §4
     Episcopacy, ¶ 430; 432; ¶432.8; ¶1309.1
     Examination on Courses of Study, ¶ 223.5
     General Conference Resolutions, ¶ 206ff, ¶ 1308.7,§21
     General Conference, Special, ¶ 1308.9
     General Conference, Standing, ¶ 1308.8
     General Connectional Board, Standing, ¶ 1000.7
     Of Investigation, ¶ 803.1
     Regional, ¶ 1110
     Resolutions, ¶ 1308.7, §20, §21
     Scouting, ¶ 1107.5; ¶ 1107.6; ¶ 1111.2, §8
     Stewards, ¶ 511.2, §15
Committees, Executive
     Christian Education, ¶ 1101
     Women's Missionary Council, ¶ 1134, Art. 5, §3
Communion, Article of Religon on, ¶ 116
Complaints
     Preacher advised of, ¶ 225, §3
     Question regarding, Quarterly Conference, ¶256, §6
Conferring, Episcopal Committee with College of Bishops, ¶ 433

Conferences (See also particular conferences)

       Annual, ¶ 213

       Church, ¶ 257

       District, ¶ 230

       General, ¶ 201

       Quarterly, ¶ 252

       Relations to, ¶ 226

       Youth and Young Adult, ¶ 237

Connectional Board, General, ¶ 1000

Connectional Board, Members, ¶ 1304.1

Connectional Headquarters, ¶ 606, ¶ 1001.4; ¶ 1013

Connectional Laymen's Day, ¶ 708

Connectional Youth and Young Adult Week, ¶ 516.1, §10

Connectional

       Commissions, ¶ 1003.5 to ¶ 1003.10

       Divisions, ¶ 1002 and ¶ 1003.4

       Headquarters, ¶ 606

       Lay Council, ¶ 1135.3

       Lay Institute, ¶ 1135.10, §1

Consecration of Bishops, $ 426, §1

Constitutions

       C.M.E. Church, See *Constitution*, Chapter 4

       Connectional Young Adult Conference, ¶ 1125

       Women's Missionary Council, ¶ 1134

Consult, ¶ 428.2; ¶ 430; ¶ 432.3

Constituting a tribunal, ¶ 803.4, §2

Contemplated, Where Move is, ¶ 428.2 (b)

Convocation, Annual C.M.E.

       Financial reports on, ¶ 437.9

       Lay Institute incorporated into, ¶ 1135.10, §1

Conventions

       District Sunday School and C.Y.F., ¶ 237 - ¶ 242

Corporation

       of Annual Conferences, ¶ 223.6

       of General Church (See Charter. page 41, and Articles of Incorporation)

       of Local Churches, ¶ 601

       President and CEO (See Articles of Incorporation)

Council

       Judicial, ¶ 804ff

       Women's Missionary, ¶ 1134

       Young Adult, ¶ 519, §3

       Youth, ¶ 1111.1

Counsel,

       Before judicial tribunal, ¶ 803.4, §5

       Legal, ¶ 1014

Stewards role in, ¶ 511.2 ¶ 10
Course of Study, ¶ 1307ff
Credentials
    Deprivation of, ¶ 905
    Issuing of, ¶ 901
    Lost, ¶ 902
    Necessity of, ¶ 422, §1
    Restoration of, ¶ 905.1; 906.1
    Withdrawal or expulsion, ¶ 903
Crime, *Social Creed*, ¶ 130.4(c)
Cross-bearing, ¶ 127
Cup of the Lord, ¶ 119

D

Day of the Lord, ¶ 126
Days Connectional,
    American Bible Society, ¶ 702
    Children's, ¶ 700
    Christian Ministry, ¶ 704
    Christian Vocation, ¶ 706
    Christian Youth Fellowship, ¶ 703
    Connectional Laymen's, ¶ 708
    Graham, W. L., ¶ 710
    Mentorship, ¶ 701
    Missions Beyond the USA, ¶ 712
    NAACP, ¶ 709
    Pitts, L. H., ¶ 701
    Scout, ¶ 711
    Social Concerns, ¶ 707
    Student Recognition, ¶ 705
Deacon, Local
    Eligibility for ordination, ¶ 409, §2
    Meaning of, ¶ 409, §1
    Member of District Conference, ¶ 231
    Member of Quarterly Conference, ¶ 252.2
    Moving to new church, ¶ 411, §2
    Probation for local elder's orders, ¶ 410, §2
    Registration with Quarterly Conference, ¶ 411, §1
    Requirement for ordination, ¶ 409, §3
    Wearing clerical vestments, ¶ 409, §4
Deacon, Traveling
    Duties, ¶ 416
    Election of, ¶ 415, §2
    When elected but not ordained, ¶ 418

Meaning of, ¶ 415

On trial requirement, ¶ 415, §1

Ordination of, ¶ 415, §6

Probation for Elder's orders, ¶ 417, §1

Right of women, ¶ 405, §5

Ritual for ordination (See *Book of Ritual*)

Dead, Ritual for burial of, (See *Book of Ritual*)

Decisions,

Declaratory, ¶ 805.2

In writing, ¶ 806.7

Deeds (Titles)

Committee on, ¶ 608

Educational property, ¶ 1132.4, ¶ 602.3, §4

No restrictions on clergy, ¶ 515.1, §6

Role of pastor regarding, ¶ 608.1

Trust Clause, ¶ 602.2, §4; ¶ 515.1, §13

Trustees, of local church, ¶ 515.1, §13

Delegates, Annual Conference

Constitutional provisions, *Constitution*, Div. 2, §4, Art. 2 - 6

Lay delegates to, ¶ 213, §3 (c), (d), (e), (f)

Delegates, District Conference, ¶ 231

Delegates, General Conference

Alternates, ¶ 201.7

Ballots for electing, ¶ 201.6

Certification, ¶ 222.1, §3

Constitutonal provisions, Constitution, Div. 2, §2, Art. 1

Credentials, 201.9

Determining Number, ¶201.3

Electing More Than Permitted, 201.10

Election of Clergy, ¶201.4

Election of Lay, ¶201.5

Method of Deliberation, ¶201.12

Proportion of Clergy and Lay, ¶201.3

Requirements, ¶201.4, ¶201.5

Restrictive Rule, ¶201.11

Young Adult, ¶201.5

Department of

Christian Education, ¶1002.1; ¶1100ff

Christian Index, ¶ 1001.8; ¶1026ff

Evangelism and Missions, ¶1002.3; ¶1150ff

Finance, ¶1003.1; ¶1004ff

Lay Ministry, ¶1002.2; ¶1135ff

Personnel Services (Board), ¶1003.4; ¶1034ff

Publications, ¶1003.2; ¶1018ff

Deprivation of Credentials, ¶905 - ¶ 906.1

Desire For Salvation, ¶126
Discipline and Doctrine
    Receiving preachers from other churches, ¶421, §1- §5
    Stewards, ¶511.1, § 2
District Conference
    Board of Evangelism, ¶1155
    Composition, ¶231
    Discussion Papers, ¶235
    Duties, ¶234
    Election of Delegates, ¶231
    Permissive Regulation, ¶230
    Presiding Officers, ¶232
    Prominence To Spiritual Exercises, ¶236
    Secretary, ¶233
District Parsonages, ¶605
Division of
    Adult Ministries, ¶ 516.1, §4
    Ministries, Connectional, ¶1002
    Operations, Connectional, ¶1003
    Young Adult Ministries, ¶516.1, §4
Docket, Judicial Council, ¶806.1, §3
Documents, Judicial, ¶806.1, §3

E

Economic Life, ¶130.3
Ecumenicity, Commission On, ¶1003.9
Editor, *The Chrisitian Index*
    A General Officer, ¶1001.1
    Duties of, ¶1001.8
    Election of, ¶1001.8, §1
    Responsible to, ¶1000.7
    Salary of, ¶1001.2
Editor, *The Missionary Messenger,* ¶1134, Art. 5, §2- §4
Education, Christian, Board of, ¶ 516
Education, Higher, ¶1126
Education for
    Admission on Trial, ¶413
    Full Connection, ¶420.2
    Minister's and Lay Persons, ¶1104.2
Educational Institutions
    Annual Conference and, ¶218, §6
    Establishing, ¶1129.1
    Funding, ¶1017, Schedule "D"
    Trustees of, ¶1130.1-1132.3
Educational Senate, ¶1128

Elder, Local
    Eligibility of Local Deacon, ¶410, §2
    Exception, ¶410, §6
    Meaning of, ¶410, §1
    Passing of character, ¶412, §2
    Registered with Quarterly Cionference, ¶411, §1
    Relocating membership, ¶411, §2
    Requirements for, ¶410, §2-6
    Women's rights, ¶405, §5
Elder, Presiding
    Appointment of, ¶428, §7
    Duties of, ¶424; ¶240; ¶509.2
    Restriction of authority, ¶425
    Support of, ¶443
    Tenure, ¶428, §7
Elder, Traveling
    Authority of, ¶419
    Constituted by, ¶417, §3
    Meaning of ¶417
    Probationary Period, ¶417, §1
    Receiving from other churches, ¶421, §3-4
    Requirements for, ¶418
    Special case, ¶418, §1
Election of
    Bishops, ¶426.1
    Choir Presidents, ¶513, ¶523, §3
    Chorister, ¶523, §6-8
    Church School officers and teachers, ¶ 516.2
    Deacons, ¶415
    Delegates to Annual Conference, ¶213
    Delegates to District Conference, ¶231
    Delegates to General Conference, ¶201.3, ¶201.4, ¶201.5
    Elders, ¶417
    General Connectional Board Members, ¶1000.2
    General Officers, ¶210, ¶1000.5
    Judicial Council Members, ¶804.2
    Organist, ¶523, §4
    President of C.Y.F., ¶518
    President of Women's Missionary Society, ¶521
    Recording Steward, ¶512
    Stewards, ¶511, §1
    Superintendent Of Sunday Church School, ¶517.1
    Treasurer (Annual Conference), ¶222.2
    Treasurer (Local), ¶514
    Trustees (Colleges), ¶1130.1

Trustees, (Local), ¶515
Usher President, ¶524
Endowment Fund, ¶1037
Episcopacy
Committee on, ¶ 432-432.7
Constitutionality, See *Constitution*
Restrictive Rule on, ¶211, §3
Episcopal
District Board of Evangelism, ¶1153
Districts, ¶1301
Greetings, page 13
Part of church name (See *Constitution*)
Residences, ¶605
Supervision, ¶1301
Evangelism
Aims and Definition, ¶1152
Annual Conference Board, ¶1154
Commission on Membership and, ¶520
District Board, ¶1155
Episcopal District Board, ¶1153
Local church structure, ¶520
Evangelists, Conference, ¶412
Evasion of
Paying for Goods, ¶126
Tribunal of a church member, ¶803.4, §4
Tribunal of a Traveling Preacher, ¶803.4, §4
Evidence of
Age of Bishop-Elect, ¶426, §2
Age of Judicial Council Nominees, ¶804.2, §2
Birthdate For Admission On Trial, ¶413, §4
Call to Preach, ¶405
Desire of Salvation, ¶126
Education for Admission On Trial, ¶413, §4
Education for Full Connection, ¶420.2, §2
Recommendation for Admission On Trial, ¶413
Examination
Before Admission Trial, ¶413, §4
Committee on, ¶223.5
Of Class Leaders, ¶502
Of those called to preach, ¶405
Required before licensing, ¶407, §4
Required before ordination, ¶420.2, §3
Standard of, ¶223.5, §6
Examine
Church conference records, ¶256, §4

Class Leaders, ¶510.1
Preachers Before Recommending, ¶413, §2
Quarterly Conference journals, ¶234
Executive Secretary, The, ¶1001.1; ¶1000.7, §6; ¶606, §3
Exhorter
    Authority to License, ¶401, §1
    Duties, ¶402
    Member of Quarterly Conference, ¶403
    Not a preacher, ¶402, §2
    Recommendation for license, ¶401, §2
    Signing License of, ¶401, §2
Expulsion
    General Conference Authority to, ¶803.5, §2
    Ministerial Member of Annual Conference, ¶803.5, §2

F

Faith and Order Commission, ¶1003.6
Faith In Christ, ¶420.3, §1 (a)
Family and Private Prayer, ¶128
Families, Support of Retired Ministers of, ¶445
Fighting, ¶126
Finance
    Annual Conference and, ¶218, §5, §8, §9
    Bishops and, ¶428, §16, §17; ¶433
    Disciplinary Questions On, ¶226, c, §47-53
    General Department of, ¶1003.1; ¶1004-1017
    General Secretary of, ¶1001.1; ¶1004.1
    Joint Board of, ¶223.4
    Quarterly Conference and, ¶253, §4 - §5; ¶255, §8
    Recording Steward and, ¶512
    Stewards and, ¶511.2
    Stewardesses and, ¶513.1, §4- §6
Finance, General Department of
    Allocations for General Departments, ¶1009
    Allocations Non-U.S.A. Areas, ¶1010
    Authority, ¶1004
    Authority to Invest, ¶1016
    C.M.E. Colleges, Allocation, ¶1015
    Executive Officer, ¶1004.1
    Expenses, ¶1011; ¶1012
    Fiscal Year of, ¶1005
    General Secretary of, ¶1007, ¶1008
    Handling Connectional Funds, ¶1006
    Investment authority of, ¶1016-1016.2
    Management Allocation for National Headquarters, ¶1013

Finance, Joint Board of
> Duties, ¶223.4, §4
> How constituted, ¶223.4, §1
> Membership, ¶223.4, §1
> Organization of, ¶223.4, §2
> Vacancies, ¶223.4, §3

Free Will, ¶108
Full Connection
> Meaning, ¶420
> Ministers from other churches, ¶421
> Missionary, ¶420.2, §6
> Procedure, ¶420.1
> Requirements For, ¶420; ¶420.2

Full Time Minister, ¶441.2

G

Gambling, ¶130.4 (d)
General Board of Personnel Services
> Annual Conference Board, ¶1036
> Authority, ¶1034.2
> Committee on, ¶1000.7, §1
> Endowment Fund, ¶1037
> Executive Officer, ¶1001; ¶1001.1
> Division of Connectional Operations, ¶1003
> Function, ¶1003.4
> Gift Fund, ¶1035.3
> Objectives, ¶1034.1
> Retirement Plan, ¶1039
> Trust Agreement, ¶1051

General Conference
> Alternate Delegates, ¶201.7
> Called, ¶204
> Committee On Resolutions, ¶206
> Composition of, ¶201
> Constitutionality (See *Constitution*, Div. 2, §2)
> Credentials, ¶201.9
> Delegates, Clerical, ¶201.4
> Delegates, Excess Number, ¶201.10
> Delegates, Lay, ¶201.5
> Delegating Authority, ¶208
> Deliberations, ¶201.11
> Elections of Delegates by ballot, ¶201.6
> Ex-officio members, ¶201.2
> Meeting Dates, ¶202
> Powers of, ¶211

Presiding Officers of, ¶209
Quorum, ¶207
Session, Quadrennial, ¶202
General Connectional Board
    Authority, ¶1000.5
    Committee on Connectional Budget, ¶1000.7, §4-5
    Composition, ¶1000.1
    Connectional Commissions, ¶1003.5- ¶1103.10
    Constitutional Authority (See Constitution)
    General Department of Christian Education, ¶1002.1
    General Department of Evangelism and Missions, ¶1002.3
    General Department of Finance, ¶1003.1
    General Department of *The Christian Index*, ¶1003.3
    General Department of Lay Ministry, ¶1002.2
    General Board of Personnel Services, ¶1003.4
    General Department of Publications, ¶1003.2
    Division of Connectional Ministries, ¶1002
    Division of Connectional Operations, ¶1003
    Election of Members, ¶1000.2
    Meetings, ¶1000.6
    Officers, ¶1000.4
    Standing Committees, ¶1000.7
    The General Officers, ¶1001.1
    Vacancies on, ¶1000.3
General Connectional Days, ¶700- ¶714
General Department of Christian Education
    Adult Division, ¶516.1, §4
    Annual Conference Board, ¶1111
    Annual Conference Director, ¶1113
    Authority, ¶1104.1
    Children's Division, ¶516.1, §4
    Church School Administration, ¶517
    Committee on, ¶1000.7, ¶1100-¶1108.6
    Director, Local Church, ¶516.3
    District Board, ¶1114
    Division of Connectional Ministries, ¶1002
    Division of General Christian Education, ¶1106
    Editorial Department, ¶1108
    Executive Committee, ¶1101
    Executive Officer of, ¶1001; ¶1001.1
    Fellowship, Christian Youth, ¶518
    Function, ¶1002.1, §2
    Groups, Age, ¶516.1, §4
    Leadership Training Department, ¶1109
    Local Church Board, ¶516

Connectional Youth and Young Adult Week, ¶516.1, §10
Purpose, ¶1002.1, §1
Regional Committees, ¶1110
Superintendent, ¶517.1
Young Adult Constitution, ¶1125
Young Adult Division, ¶516.1, §4
Youth Council, ¶ 519, §3
General Department of Evangelism and Missions
Committee on, ¶1000.7
Executive Officer of, ¶1001, ¶1001.1
Function, ¶1002.3, §2
Purpose, ¶1002.3, §1; ¶1150
See Ministry of Evangelism, ¶1153-1155.2
See Ministry of Missions, ¶1156-1166.1
General Department of Finance (See Finance, General Dept. of)
General Dept. of *The Christian Index*, (See Index, The)
General Department of Lay Ministry
Annual Conference Lay Council, ¶1135.4
Authority, ¶1135.1, §2
Committee, ¶1000.7; ¶1135.1
Connectional Lay Council, ¶1135.3
District Board, ¶1135.6
Division of Connectional Ministries, ¶1002
Executive Officer, ¶1001; ¶1001.1
Fellowship, Christian Methodist Men's, ¶1135.2
Function, ¶1135, §4; ¶1002.2, §2
Lay Leader, Annual Conference, ¶1135.4, §1-3
Local Church Board, ¶1135.7, ¶ 522
Objetives, ¶1135, §4 (a) - (k)
Purpose, ¶1002.2, §1
General Deparment of Publications
Annual Conference Board, ¶1024
Church agencies, printing for, ¶1022
Church School Publications, ¶1021
Commision On Records and Blanks, ¶1023
Committee, ¶1000.7; ¶1017.2; ¶1018
Division Of Connetional Operations, ¶1003
Executive Officer, ¶1001-1001.1; ¶1020
Function, ¶1003.2
Historical Library and Society, ¶1025-1025.2
Historical Society, Annual Conference, ¶1025-1025.2
Name, ¶1018
Net Proceeds, use of, ¶1018.3
Objective, ¶1018.1
General Education Development (GED), ¶421.1, §1

General Funds, ¶223.4 §4 (a)
General Officers
       Funds for, ¶1001.2- 1001.4
       Offices of, ¶1001.1
       Responsible to, ¶1001.5
God
       And Country Award, ¶1107.5
       Article of Religion, ¶101
       Questions about in Call to Preach, ¶405
       Stewardship under, ¶130.1
Good Works, ¶110
Government
       Duty to, ¶123
       General Connectional Board (See Constitution)
       Support of, ¶123
Grace
       Call to Preach, ¶405
       Means of, ¶300ff

H

Headquarters, Connectional, 606
Health Services (Social Creed), ¶130.3 (b)
Health Services, Professional, ¶ 438.1
History of C.M.E. Church (See Bishops' Course of Study), ¶1307.1
Historical Library, ¶1019
Historical Society, ¶1019, ¶1025
Historical Statement (Episcopal Greetings, page 13)
Holy Ghost
       Article of Religion, ¶104
       Call To Preach, ¶405
Holy Scriptures, Sufficiency of, ¶105
Holy Trinity, ¶101
Hospital, Collins Chapel, Allocation, ¶1017, Schedule "C"
Human Rights, ¶130.4 (e)

I

Image Worship, ¶114
Incorporation
       Annual conference, ¶223.6 §1
       Local Church, ¶601
Index, The Christian, Department of
       Agent, Local Church, ¶1031
       Correspondents to, ¶1030
       Editor of, ¶1001.8

Official Publication, ¶1026
Preachers must subscribe to, ¶1032
Publication schedule of, ¶1026.1
Reporters to, ¶1030.2
Retired Preachers and Widow(er)s, ¶1033
Infant Baptism, ¶117
Inflation, ¶130.3 (a)
Institutions of Highter Learning
Board of Trustees of, ¶1130.1-1132.3
Connectional support of, ¶1126
Institutions, Charitable, ¶607
Insurance
Disciplinary Question On, ¶226, §54
Group Fire and Casualty, ¶1046-1046.2
Group Life, ¶1034.7 , §4
Property, ¶604
Quarterly Conference Business, ¶255, §9
Trustees (Local) and, ¶515.1, §12(g)
Invest, ¶1016
Investigation Committee, ¶803.1

J

Joint Board of Finance (See Finance, Joint Board of)
Journals of the
Annual Conference, ¶222.1, §1-2; ¶224
Church Conference, ¶258
District Conference, ¶233
Quarterly Conference, ¶234; ¶411, §1
Judicial Administration, ¶801ff
Appeal Process, ¶ 803.6
Appellate Court, ¶ 803.6, §2
Charges, Bill of, ¶ 803.3
Investigation, Committee of, ¶803.1
Notice of Accusation, ¶ 803
Penalty, ¶ 803.5, §2
Practices subject to action, ¶ 802
Representation for the accused, ¶ 803.4, §5
Tribunal, ¶ 803.4
Tribunal Official, ¶ 803.4, §1
Tribunal Secretary, ¶803.4, §1
Witnesses, ¶ 803.4, §1
Judicial Council, ¶804
Alternate members, ¶ 804.5
Appellate jurisdiction, ¶ 805, §4
Arguments before, ¶ 805.2, §4

Decisions, ¶ 806.7
Declaratory Decisions, & 805.2
Docket, ¶ 806.1, §3
Duties, ¶ 805.1
Jurisdiction, ¶ 805
Members, ¶ 804.1
Name of, ¶ 804
Organization, ¶ 806
Quorum, ¶ 806.2
Removal, ¶ 804.6
Vacancies, ¶ 804.6
Justification by Faith, ¶ 109

L

Law
Bishop as interpreter of, ¶ 428, §10, §11 ¶ 805.2 §6 (e)
Going to, ¶ 126
Judicial Council as interpreter of, ¶ 805, ¶ 805.2 §6 (e)
Preacher in charge as interpreter of ¶ 805.2, §6 (e)
Presiding Elder as Interpreter of, ¶ 424, §3(c)l ¶ 805.2, §6 (e)
Laws
Corporation, ¶ 601.2
Election of church trustees, ¶ 515, §1
Local, ¶ 601.5
Lay
Board, ¶ 1135.6
Council, ¶ 1135.4
Delegates, ¶ 201.5 - 201.7; ¶ 213, §3(d); ¶ 214, §4
Ministry, department of, ¶ 1135, ¶ 522
Leaders, Class, ¶ 510 - ¶ 510.2
Leadership Training, ¶ 1109, ¶ 1110.1
Legal Counsel ¶ 437.5, ¶ 806.7, §3, ¶ 1014
License To Preach
Authority, ¶ 407, §1, §3
Procedure for,¶ 407, §4
Time of license, ¶ 407, §5
Valid for, ¶ 407, §1
Licentiate, ¶ 407, ¶ 411
Liquor Problem, ¶ 130.4 (b)
Literature, ¶ 1108
Local Board of Christian Education, ¶ 516
Local Church Officers
Class Leaders, ¶ 510
Director of Christian Education, ¶ 516.3
Lay Leader, ¶ 522, §3

Music Personnel, regulations, ¶ 523

Presidents of Choirs, ¶ 523, § 2-3

President of C.Y.F., ¶ 518, §2; ¶ 1117.3

President of Ushers, ¶ 524

President of Young Adults, ¶ 519, §3 (b)

President of WMS, ¶ 521.4

President of Young Adult Fellowship, ¶ 519, ¶3(b)

Recording Steward, ¶ 512

Stewards, ¶ 511

Stewardesses, ¶ 513

Superintendents of Sunday School, ¶ 517.1

Treasurer, ¶ 514

Trustees, ¶ 515

Incorporation of, ¶ 601.3

Local Church Organizations (See Individual Organization Names)

Local Deacon, ¶ 409

Local Elder, ¶ 410

Local Preacher

Authority to License, ¶ 407, §3

Definition, ¶ 407,§1

Duties of, ¶ 408

Eligibility for Deacon's Order, ¶409,§2

Lay status of, ¶ 407.§2

License of a, ¶ 407,§5

Member of District and Quarterly Conferences, ¶ 231; ¶ 252.2

Moving Membership, ¶ 411, §2

Procedure for being Admitted On Trial, ¶ 413

Procedure for licensing a, ¶ 407

Registered with Quarterly Conference, ¶ 411,§1

Renewing License of, ¶ 407,§5

Restriction on admission recommendation, ¶ 413

Signature on license, ¶ 407,§4

Located Preacher, ¶ 226,§9; ¶ 411, §3

Lord's Day, ¶ 126

Lord's Prayer, ¶ 302

Lord's Supper

Article of Religion on, ¶ 118

Duty to administer, ¶ 422,§1

Monthly administration, ¶ 301

Love Feast

Admitting strangers to, ¶ 312

Mandate for, ¶ 311

Order of Service for, ¶ 311

M

Magistrates and Ministers, ¶ 126
Marriage
   Of ministers, ¶ 121
Means of Grace
   Class Meeting, ¶ 308
   General Rule and, ¶ 128
   Love Feast, ¶ 311
   Prayer Meeting, ¶ 306
   Public Worship, ¶ 301
Meditation and prayer, ¶ 420.3
Meeting, class, ¶ 308
Member of local church
   Actionable offenses, ¶ 802
   Acceptance of, ¶ 506, ¶ 507; ¶ 508.2
   Appeal, ¶ 803.6
   Delinquent, ¶ 508.3, §4
   Investigation of a, ¶ 803.1
   Responsibility of, ¶ 509
   Training classes, ¶ 508.1; ¶ 509.2; ¶ 509.4
   Tribunal for, ¶ 803.4
   Types of, ¶ 508.2
Membership of
   Annual Conference, ¶ 213, §3
   Annual Conference Board of Trustees, ¶ 223.6,§1
   Church Conference, ¶ 257
   C.M.E. Church, ¶ 505, ¶ 506
   Commissions Connectional, ¶ 1304.2
   Connection, ¶ 508
   District Conference, ¶ 231
   General Conference, ¶ 201ff
   General Connectional Board, ¶ 1000.1
   Inclusiveness (*Constitution*, Art. 4)
   Judicial Council, ¶ 804
   Local Church, ¶ 505
   Official Board, ¶ 264
   Quarterly Conference, ¶ 252.2
   Special Committee, of General Board, ¶ 1000.7, §2
   Standing Committees, ¶ 1000.7
   Steward Board, ¶ 511,§2
   Stewardess Board, ¶ 513.§2
   Trustee Board, ¶ 515.1, §1 - §3
Membership rolls, ¶ 508.3
Membership, receiving into, ¶ 505, ¶ 506, ¶ 507;¶ 508.1
Ministerial Members
   Annual Conference, ¶ 213, §3a

Ministers
    Rights to use of assigned churches, ¶ 515.1,§6,¶ 602.2
    Prohibition from speaking evil of, ¶ 126
Ministry, Department of Lay, ¶ 522, ¶ 1135
Ministry, enlistment and recruitment, ¶ 406
Ministry, support of
    Bishops, and their widows, ¶ 444;¶ 444.4;¶ 444.5
    Bishops, incapacitated, ¶ 444.2
    Bishops, retired, ¶ 444.3
    Endowment fund, pension, ¶ 1037-1037.4
    General Officers, ¶ 1017, ¶ 1001.2
    General Officers, retired, ¶ 1039.4
    Preachers In Charge, ¶ 441; ¶ 511.2, §1; ¶513.1, §6
    Preachers, retired and families of, ¶ 445
    Presiding Elders, ¶ 443, ¶ 223.4, §4 (e), ¶ 424, §5
    Retirement Plan, ¶ 1039
Ministry, Table of, ¶ 513.1
Mission Conference, ¶ 1162.5
Missionary Rule
    Local Elder, ¶ 410, §6
    Traveling Deacon, ¶415, §2
    Traveling Elder, ¶ 417, §1
Morning Worship, directions on, ¶ 301
Mortgages, ¶ 602.3; ¶ 602.5
Moving Expenses, pastors, ¶ 441.3; ¶ 442

N

Name of Church (See *Constitution*, Division 1, Art. 2)
Names of
    Bishops, ¶ 1302
    General Officers, ¶ 1304
    Members of Judicial Council, ¶ 1303
    Members of Committee on Episcopacy, ¶ 1305
National Council of Churches, ¶ 1017
National Mission's Director, ¶ 1159
Needy, ¶ 265.1; ¶ 511.2, §4
Neglect of Means of Grace, ¶ 129
Notice of accusation, ¶ 803
Notified, ¶ 428, §2 (b)(c)(d)

O

Oaths, ¶ 125
Obedience to civil authority, ¶ 123

Oblation of Christ, ¶ 120
Offenses, actionable, ¶ 802
Offices, clergy
　Bishop, ¶ 426
　Pastor, ¶ 422
　Presiding Elder, ¶ 424
Official Board
　Business of, ¶ 265
　Constitutionality, Constitution, Division 2, §9
　Meeting of, ¶ 265 1
　Members of, ¶ 264
　Presiding officer of, ¶ 263.1
Order, Defined Judicially, ¶ 801
Order of Service for Love Feast, ¶ 311
Orders
　Deacon, ¶ 409,¶ 415
　Elder's, ¶ 410,¶ 417
　Election To Local Deacon, ¶ 409
　Election To Local Elder, ¶ 410
　Election To Traveling Deacon, ¶ 415
　Election To Traveling Elder, ¶ 417
Organizing a Local Church, ¶ 525
Organist, Church, ¶ 523, §4 - 5
Original jurisdiction, ¶ 805, §1
Original or Birth Sin, ¶ 107
Orphanage, ¶ 607

P

Parliamentary Practice
　General Conference, ¶ 1308.10
　Women's Missionary Council, ¶ 1134, Art. 9
Parsonage, district, ¶ 605.2
Parsonage, local church
　Reporting number of, ¶ 515.1, §12
　Stewards and Stewardesses, ¶ 511.2, §15
　Title to, ¶ 602.2
Pastor (See Preacher In Charge)
Pastoral appointments, ¶ 428, §2
Pastoral visitations, ¶ 422, §1
Pastors, supply, ¶ 412
Penalty, assessment of,
　Judicial, ¶ 803.5, §2
　Pension payments, ¶ 1041.2
Penance, ¶ 116

Pension, ¶ 1040.2

Peace and world order, ¶ 130.4 (a)

Personnel Services, General Board of, ¶ 1034

Poor, table of the, ¶ 513, §2

Poverty and unemployment, ¶ 130.3(a)

Prayer

        Family, ¶ 128

        In worship, ¶ 301

        Meeting, ¶ 402, §1; ¶ 306

        Silent, ¶ 301, §2

Preacher in Charge, Duties

        Administer Sacraments, ¶ 422, §1

        Attend District and Annual Conferences, ¶ 422, §21 and 22

        Bury the dead, ¶ 422, §1

        Collect the General Funds, ¶ 422, §23

        Direct Services, ¶ 422.§5

        Encourage Members to buy and read books, ¶ 422, §16

        Execute officers' training ¶ 509.3

        Furnish appropriate certificates, ¶ 422, §20

        Give reports, ¶ 422, §11

        Hold class leaders' and stewards' meetings, ¶ 422, §10

        Hold Quarterly Conferences, ¶ 422, §9

        Instruct Children, ¶ 313, ¶313.1

        Instruct New Members, ¶ 507

        Keep Directory, ¶ 422, §13

        Keep Permanent Record of Baptism and Marriages, ¶ 422, §15

        Leave account of charge when moved, ¶ 422, §17

        Organize Board of Christian Education, ¶ 422, §19

        Preach, ¶ 422, §1

        Preside, ¶ 257; ¶ 422, §2; ¶ 263.1

        Promote Church Interests, ¶ 422, §18

        Receive, try, expel members, ¶ 422, §7

        See that all funds are reported, ¶ 422, §24

        See that reports are made, ¶ 422, §12

        Serve as administrator, ¶ 422, §2

        Serve as president of corporation, ¶ 422, §3

        Solemnize Marriages, ¶ 422, §1

        Subscribe to *The Christian Index*, ¶ 422, §8

Preacher, local, ¶ 407

Preparatory members, ¶ 508.2, §1

Presiding Elders' Conference, ¶ 425.1

Presiding Elder,

    Appointment of, ¶ 424, §1; ¶ 428, §7

    Duties of, ¶ 424, § 2ff

        advise and approve, ¶ 424, §3d

confirm officers and delegates, ¶ 424, §3e
license Persons to preach, ¶ 424, §3b
receive Connectional funds, ¶ 424, §3 (f)
report official data, ¶ 424, §3 (g)
serve as liaison, ¶ 424, §3
supervise, ¶ 424, §1-2
Limitations on, ¶ 425

Forming districts for, ¶ 428, §12
Preachers, moving expenses of, ¶ 441.3
Probation time for
Admission on Trial, ¶ 413, §1; ¶ 413, §4
Election to Local Deacon, ¶ 409, §2
Election to Local Elder, ¶ 410, §2
Election to Traveling Deacon, ¶ 415, §2
Election to Travel Elder, ¶ 417, §1
Full Connection, ¶ 420 - ¶ 420.2
Preacher from another church, ¶ 421.1
Retirement eligibility, ¶ 439
Property
Acquisition and sales, ¶ 601; ¶ 602.3
Annual Conference, ¶ 223.6, §2-3
Corporation which ceases to exist, ¶ 601.4
Deeds, ¶ 601.1; ¶ 602.2
Discontinuation of local property, ¶ 602.6
District parsonage, ¶ 605.2
Episcopal residence, ¶ 605; ¶ 602.1
Insurance, ¶ 604. §2
Local church, ¶ 515.1, §12-13
Making available to preachers, ¶ 515.1, §6
Rental of parsonages, ¶ 603, §1
Rental property, ¶ 603, §2
Report on, ¶ 515.1, §12
Statistician, ¶ 222.3, §1
Title, ¶ 602
Trust, ¶ 602.2
Publication of decisions, ¶ 806.7, §3
Publications, Department of, ¶ 1018
(See Also General Department of Publications)

Q

Quadrennial Meetings
Assembly, Women's Missionary Council, ¶ 1134, Art. 6
General Conference, ¶ 202

Connectional Lay Institute, ¶ 1135.10
Connectional Young Adult Conference, ¶ 1125, Art. 4
Quadrennial reports of Bishops, ¶ 428, §18; ¶ 435
Quadrennial sermon, ¶ 429
Quadrennial Session, Election At Each, ¶ 804.2
Quarterly Conferences
    Constitutional provision, See Constitution, Division 2, Sec. 7
    Meetings, ¶ 252.3
    Members, ¶ 252.2
    Nature of, ¶ 252
    Presiding Officer, ¶ 252.1
    Regular Business, ¶ 254
    The Order Of Business, ¶ 255
Orders, lost or deprived,
    Local Preachers, ¶ 906
    Traveling Preachers, ¶ 905
Quorum
    General Conference, ¶ 207
    Judicial Council, ¶ 806.2

R

Ratio General Conference Delegates, ¶ 201.3
Real Property, Articles of Incorporation, Art.3; ¶ 602.3
Reception of.
    Members into the church, ¶ 422, §7; ¶ 507
    Ministers from other churches, ¶ 421
    Ministers into Full Connection, ¶ 420.3
Recommendation for
    Admission on Trial, ¶ 413
    License to Exhort, ¶ 401
    License to Preach, ¶ 407
    Local Deacon's Order, ¶ 409
    Local Elder's Order, ¶ 410
    Traveling Deacon's Order, ¶ 415
    Traveling Elder's Order, ¶ 417
Record(s)
    Annual Conference, ¶ 222.1, §1
    Church Conference, ¶ 258
    Clerk, ¶ 222.4
    District Conference, ¶ 233
    Duty of Preacher In Charge, ¶ 422, §11, §15
    Duty of The Recording Steward, ¶ 512, § 2
    Quarterly Conference, ¶ 254; ¶ 422, §11
Records, inspection of,

Annual Conference, ¶ 224
Church Conference, ¶ 256, §4
Quarterly Conference, ¶234
Records and Deeds Committee, ¶608
Relations to Annual Conference, ¶ 226
Religion, Articles of, ¶ 101-125
Rent from parsonages, ¶ 603, §1
Resolutions, General Conference Committee on, ¶ 206
Restoration
Delinquent church member, ¶ 508.3, §4, ¶259
Orders of Local Preachers, ¶ 906
Orders of Traveling Preachers, ¶ 905
Restrictive Rules, ¶ 201.11
Resurrection of Christ, ¶ 103
Retirement of
Bishops, ¶ 436
General Officer, ¶ 439, §2
Judicial Council Members, ¶ 439, §2
Preachers, ¶ 439
Rites and ceremonies, ¶ 122
Ritual, use of, ¶ 300, §6; ¶ 304
Rules, The General, ¶ 126-129
Rules, C.M.E., ¶ 420.3, §1 (h)

S

Sabbath, breaking of, ¶126
Sacraments, The
Article of Religion on, ¶ 116
Authority to Administer, ¶ 419
Lord's Supper, ¶ 302
Ordination Requirement, ¶ 422, §1
Salary of
Bishops, active, ¶ 444
Bishops, disabled, ¶ 444.2
Bishops, retired, ¶ 444.3
General Officers, active, ¶ 1001.2
General Officer, retired, ¶ 439, §2
Preachers In Charge, ¶ 441.1
Presiding Elders, ¶ 443
Sale of property, ¶ 602.3
Scholarship, W. L. Graham, ¶ 710
School, Church, ¶ 517
School, Vacation, ¶ 516.1, §6
Scouting

Boys, ¶ 1107.5; ¶ 1107.6
Girls, ¶ 1107.5; ¶ 1107.6
Scout Sunday, ¶ 711
Scripture, ¶ 105
Securing property for
District parsonage, ¶ 605.2
Episcopal residence, ¶ 605
Local Church, ¶ 602.3, §1
Self Denial, ¶ 127
Self Indulgence, ¶ 126
Sex and Christian life, ¶ 130.4 (f)
Sick Persons
Class Leaders and, ¶ 510.2, §2 (a)
Official Board and, ¶ 265, §1
Pastoral visits to. ¶ 422, §1
Stewards And, ¶ 511, §5
Sin, Original, ¶ 107
Singing, Directions On, ¶ 300, §5
Slander, ¶ 126
Societies, General Rules of United, ¶ 126-129
Society, Women's Missionary, ¶ 1134
Softness, Forbidden, ¶ 126
Song, improper, ¶ 126
Speaking in strange tongues, ¶ 115
Spirituous liquor, ¶ 126
Statistics, Annual Conference questions, ¶ 226, §24 ff
Statistician, ¶ 222.3
Steward, Recording, ¶ 512
Stewards
Accountability, ¶ 511
Duties, ¶ 511.2
Election, ¶ 511, §2
Number, ¶ 511, §2
Qualifications, ¶ 511.1
Stewardess Annual Conference, ¶ 223.7
Stewardess, District, ¶ 231
Stewardess, Local Church
Duties, ¶ 513.1
Election, ¶ 513
Number, ¶ 513
Study, Bishops' Course of, ¶ 1307
Sunday
Christian Ministry, ¶ 704
C.M.E. Founders Day, ¶ 714
Mentorship, ¶ 701

NAACP, ¶ 709

Missions Beyond USA, ¶ 712

Scout, ¶ 711
Social Concerns, ¶ 707
Sunday Church School
    Administration Of, ¶ 517.1
    Board of Christian Education and the, ¶ 1107.2
Sunday Church School And C.Y.F. Convention, ¶ 237
Supererogation, works of, ¶ 111
Superintendents, Sunday Church School
    Administrative Officer, ¶ 517.1
    Election Of Departmental, ¶ 517.1, §6
    Election Of General, ¶ 517.1, §1
    Report To Quarterly Conference, ¶ 517.1, §4
Supernumerary Preachers, ¶ 438
Supervision, Episcopal, ¶ 1301
Supply Pastors, ¶ 412
Suspension of,
    Bishop, ¶ 803.5
    General Officers, ¶ 1000.5, §2
    Lay Member, ¶ 803.5
    Ministerial Member, ¶ 803.5

T

Task Forces, Special, ¶ 1000.7,§7
Temperance, ¶ 127
Tongues, Speaking In, ¶ 115
Transfer
    Members, Certificate of, ¶ 422, §20
    Of General Connectional Board Members, ¶ 1000.3
    Of Licentiates, ¶ 411, §2
    Of Traveling Preachers, ¶ 429, ¶ 428, §2 (c)(d)
Transubstantiation, ¶ 118
Travel
    Bishops, ¶ 428, §14
    Definition of, ¶ 1011
    Expense of Bishops, ¶ 433.2
    Expenses of General Officers, ¶ 1001.3

Expense of Pastors, ¶ 441.1; ¶ 441.3
Expenses of Presiding Elder, ¶ 443
Preacher In Charge, ¶ 422
Traveling Connection, ¶ 413
Traveling Deacon, ¶ 415
Traveling Elder, ¶ 417
Traveling Preachers
   Admission on Trial, ¶ 413
   Admitting into Full Connection, ¶ 420
   Amenable to, ¶ 420
   Full Connection of, ¶ 420
   Judicial Procedures, ¶ 801
   Location of, ¶ 411, §3
   Member of District Conference, ¶ 231
   Member of Quarterly Conference, ¶ 252.2
   Military Chaplains, ¶ 423
   Preachers in Charge, ¶ 422
   Presiding Elders, ¶ 424
   Retired, ¶ 439
   Retirement of, ¶ 439, §2
   Supernumerary, ¶ 438
   Support of, Active, ¶ 441, ¶ 443
   Support of, Retired, ¶ 445
   Tribunal, see Judicial Administration, ¶ 803
Treasurer, Annual Conference
   Audit of funds, ¶ 222.2, §7
   Bond of, ¶ 218, §8
   Duties of, ¶ 222.2
   Election of, ¶ 222.2
Treasurer, Local Church, ¶ 514
Treasurer, WMC, ¶ 1134, Art. 5, §2
Treasures on earth, ¶ 126
Trial
   Admission on, ¶ 413
   Meaning of, ¶ 413, §1
   Remaining on, ¶ 414
Tribunal
Meaning of, ¶ 803.4
   Presiding Official, ¶ 803.4, §1
   Decisions of, ¶ 803.5
   Appeal from, ¶ 803.6
Trinity, Holy, ¶ 101
Trustees, Annual Conference
   Authority of, ¶ 223.6, §2

Incorporation of, ¶ 223.6, §1
Parsonages, district, ¶ 605; ¶ 605.1; ¶ 605.3
Ratio, ¶ 223.6, §1
Trustees, Local Church
    Accountability, ¶ 515.1, §7
    Automatic dismissal, ¶ 515.1, §10
    Automatic removal, ¶ 515.1, §11
    Directors, ¶ 601, §3
    Election, ¶ 515, §1, §2
    Minimum age for, ¶ 515.1, §1
    Number, ¶ 515.1, §3
    Report of, ¶ 515.1, §12
    Restriction on Authority, ¶ 515.1, §8
    Vacancies, ¶ 515.1, §4
Trustees, Schools And Colleges
    Authority, ¶ 1130.1 - ¶ 1133
    Bishops as members of, ¶ 434

U

Unction, extreme, ¶ 116
Undermines, Behavior Which, ¶ 802
Unemployment, ¶ 130.3 (d)
United Nations, ¶ 130.4(a)(1)
United Societies, General Rules Of, ¶ 126
Unknown tongues, ¶ 115
Urban life, ¶ 130.3 (f)
Use of C.M.E Name and Logo, ¶ 602.1
Ushers, Local Church Boards of
    Disciplinary provision, ¶ 524, §1
    Duties, ¶ 524, §3
    Election of officers, ¶ 524, §2
    Presidents, ¶ 524, §2
    Report of, ¶ 255, §7 (d)
Usury, ¶ 126
Vacancies, Filling
    General Connectional Board, ¶ 1000.3
    Joint Board of Finance, ¶ 223.4, §3
    Judicial Council, ¶ 804
    Local Church Board of Trustees, ¶ 515.1, §4
    Preachers in Charge, ¶ 428, §8
Vacation Bible Schools, ¶ 516.1, §2; ¶ 1107.3
Visiting

From house to house, ¶ 420.3, §1, (3)(c)

Pastoral, ¶ 313.1

The Sick, ¶ 422, §1

Visitors, General Conference, ¶ 201.8

Voluntarily Located, ¶ 226, §9 (a)

Voting

On Readmission, ¶ 214, §2

To Recommend for Admission on Trial, ¶ 214, §2

To Recommend for Local Deacon Orders, ¶ 409, §1

Voting By Ballot

For General Conference Delegates, ¶ 201.6

To License To Preach, ¶ 407, §4

Voting Electronically, ¶201.13

Voting by Class, ¶ 201.12

W

Wages and working Conditions, ¶ 130.3 (c)

Week, Youth and Young Adult, ¶ 516.1, §10

Welfare, General, ¶ 130.4

Widows and Orphans of Bishops, ¶ 444.4 - ¶ 444.5

Will, Free, ¶ 108

Witness, ¶ 803.4, §1

Women's Missionary Council

Amendments to constitution, ¶ 1134, Art. 8

Authority, ¶ 1134, Art. 3

Constitution, ¶ 1134

Funds, ¶ 1134, Art. 7

Government, ¶ 1134, Art. 9

Meetings, ¶ 1134, Art. 6

Membership, ¶ 1134, Art. 4

Name, ¶ 1134, Art. 1

Organization, ¶ 1134, Art. 4

Purpose, ¶ 1134, Art. 2

Women's Missionary Society

Annual Conference

members, ¶ 226, §46 (b)

officers, ¶ 226, § 55 (c)

Church Conference, reports to, ¶260, §1 (k)

District Conference, President, Member of, ¶ 231

Local Church, ¶ 521

Official Board, ¶ 264

Quarterly Conference

confirmation of president, ¶ 253, §3

reports made to, ¶ 255, §7 (a)

Women, Clergy Rights, ¶ 405, §5
Word, The, or Son of God, ¶ 102
Works, Good, ¶ 110
Works of Supererogation, ¶ 111
Workshops, ¶ 509.3
Worship, Public,
    Attending, ¶ 128
    Conduct of, ¶ 300
    Divine, ¶ 602.2
    Lord's Prayer in, ¶ 302
    Order of, ¶ 305
    Participation in, ¶ 509
    Ritual, ¶ 304, ¶ 300, §6
    Singing in, ¶ 300, §5

Y

Young Adult Constitution, ¶ 1125
Young Adult Council, ¶ 519, §3
Young Adult Division, ¶ 516.1, §4
Young Adult Week, ¶ 516.1, §10
Youth, Age Groupings, ¶ 516.1, ¶4
Youth Conference, ¶ 237
Youth Division, ¶ 516.1, §4
Youth Fellowship, Christian, ¶ 518
Youth Fellowship Convention, District. ¶239
Youth Week, ¶ 516.1, §10